*Pelican Library of Business and Management*
*Advisory Editor: T. Kempner*

# CASE STUDIES IN MANAGEMENT ACCOUNTING

Professor John Sizer was born in Grimsby, Lincolnshire, in 1938. After leaving school in 1954 he worked for companies in the trawling, frozen food and dairy industries. During this period he studied for the examinations of the Institute of Cost and Management Accountants, of which he is now a Fellow, and in 1961 he was awarded their Leverhulme Prize. He read Industrial Economics at Nottingham University from 1961 to 1964. After graduating he spent a year as a financial adviser in the Group Controller's Department at Guest, Keen & Nettlefolds Ltd. In 1965 he became Teaching Fellow and subsequently lecturer in management accountancy in the Department of Business Studies at Edinburgh University. He moved to the London Graduate School of Business Studies as Senior Lecturer in Accounting in 1968, and became Assistant Academic Dean (Postgraduate Studies) in July 1969. Since 1970 he has been Professor of Financial Management at Loughborough University of Technology, where he is now Head of the Department of Management Studies, and Dean of the School of Human and Environmental Studies. John Sizer is a member of the American Accounting Association and the British Institute of Management, and a Director of Loughborough Consultants Ltd. He wrote *An Insight into Management Accounting* (Penguin, 1969), and frequently contributes to the leading British accounting and management journals. He also undertakes consulting work and conducts seminars for a number of leading international companies and the National Economic Development Office.

GW00600981

# CASE STUDIES IN
# MANAGEMENT ACCOUNTING

## JOHN SIZER

PENGUIN BOOKS

Penguin Books Ltd, Harmondsworth, Middlesex, England
Penguin Books Inc., 7110 Ambassador Road, Baltimore, Maryland 21207, U.S.A.
Penguin Books Australia Ltd, Ringwood, Victoria, Australia
Penguin Books Canada Ltd, 41 Steelcase Road West, Markham, Ontario, Canada
Penguin Books (N.Z.) Ltd, 182–190 Wairau Road, Auckland 10, New Zealand

First published by the Longman Group Ltd 1974
Published in Pelican Books 1975

—

Copyright © John Sizer, 1974

—

Made and printed in Great Britain
by Richard Clay (The Chaucer Press) Ltd,
Bungay, Suffolk
Set in Monotype Times

This book is sold subject to the condition
that it shall not, by way of trade or otherwise,
be lent, re-sold, hired out, or otherwise circulated
without the publisher's prior consent in any form of
binding or cover other than that in which it is
published and without a similar condition
including this condition being imposed
on the subsequent purchaser

*To Valerie, Richard, Stuart and Jonathan*

# Contents

*Preface*                                                                9

MOORCROFT HALL POULTRY FARM                                              15
Should a partnership experiencing serious financial difficulties
be wound up?

BIGTOWN PRINTERS LTD                                                     33
What interpretation should be made of interfirm comparison
data?

PRINTED CARTONS LTD                                                      46
Has correct interpretation been made of interfirm comparison
data?

FISHNET DRESSES LTD                                                      60
When, how much and in what form should expanding company
raise permanent capital?

KNITTED GARMENTS COMPANY                                                 68
How realistic are the future plans of a company that has been
trading at a loss for a number of years?

HARDWOOD, SOFTWOOD & PLYWOOD COMPANY                                     85
How should the managing director secure a more effective
allocation of capital to units and encourage managers to
improve the return on the capital his unit employs?

WESSEX KNITTING                                                         98
Should a subsidiary's freehold land and buildings be transferred to parent company's property owning subsidiary?

BLOGGS & CLOGGS                                                        100
Should Bloggs & Cloggs raise a loan from a finance company or
lease essential fixed assets?

DOORMOUSE LTD                                                          107
Should financial director have recommended leasing of
machinery?

# CONTENTS

JAMES WILSON & SON (A)  114
Is the monthly management accounting report for the board of directors satisfactory?

KEEPDRY LTD  141
Should the company install sprinkling equipment to obtain reduction in fire insurance premiums?

JOHN JONES LTD  143
Should the company move into new premises?

MOONSHINE LTD  148
What assessment should the financial director make of the capital application from the operating division?

PORTOBELLO KNITWEAR COMPANY  164
Should the company utilize spare capacity to produce cashmere garments?

URBAN UNDERWEAR COMPANY  178
Should the managing director accept proposed set of financial guidelines for selecting lines for its range of products?

KETTLE KNITWEAR LTD  183
Does the costing procedure lead to incorrect selection of garments in limiting capacity situation?

JAMES WILSON & SON (B)  193
What are strengths and weaknesses of the management accountant's method of arriving at the recommended selling prices?

JAMES WILSON & SON (C)  197
What pricing strategy should be adopted for negotiations with a multiple retail stores group?

MILKY DAIRIES LTD  200
Are applications of marginal costing by a dairy firm satisfactory?

DIVERSIFIED ENGINEERING LTD  220
What recommendations should the consultant make concerning the profitability of company's activities and its future prospects?

# Preface

But misery still delights to trace
Its semblance in another's case.

*The Castaway*, William Cowper (1731–1800)

*Case Studies in Management Accounting* is a follow-up to *An Insight into Management Accounting* (Penguin Books, 1969). The latter provides executives in general management and in other management specialisms with an insight into the financial aspects of management and the techniques available to the management accountant. It may be used as an introductory text for postgraduate management students, and could also form the basis for a course in management accounting for science and engineering students. The case book complements *An Insight into Management Accounting*, providing the reader with an opportunity to relate the insights he was gained to real-life situations.

Case studies are being used increasingly by business schools, by management-studies departments in polytechnics and universities, and by independent management-training centres. Students are required to analyse a situation, decide upon a course of action, and present and defend their decisions in syndicate discussions and in plenary session. As in the real world, there is rarely a finite solution to a case study, but a number of alternative courses of action each with its advantages and disadvantages. These alternatives have to be evaluated against a background of uncertainty as to the possible outcome if a particular course of action is adopted. Frequently the information available in the case study is imperfect and inadequate. Case studies thus expose students to real-life situations, and also provide a vehicle for developing a cross-fertilization of experience between students with differing backgrounds.

It is widely known that the case-study method of teaching was developed by the Harvard Graduate School of Business Administration in the United States, and many Harvard case studies are used by British educational establishments. While numerous excellent case studies have emanated, and continue to emanate, from Harvard, not surprisingly a large proportion of the case studies describe real-life events that took place in the United States. Therefore some of the case studies are not relevant to conditions in Britain, and there is sometimes resentment by British executives and postgraduate students of excessive use of Harvard case studies. A typical comment appears in the report on *Business School Programmes: the requirements of British manufacturing industry* (The Owen Committee Report):

'There he is', observed one of our respondents of a certain lecturer, 'with a pile of old Harvard case studies at his elbow. Why doesn't he come and find out what my problems are?'

There is no excuse for using old, out-of-date Harvard case studies; there is a constant flow of new ones. However, one important reason why Harvard case studies are extensively used, apart from their quality, is the serious shortage of British case studies. This case book is offered as a small, but I hope useful, contribution towards meeting this shortage.

All the case studies describe events that actually took place in Britain. In order to preserve confidentiality it has been necessary to change the names of companies, executives, locations of premises within Britain, brand and product names, and, in some instances, the financial data. The majority of the case studies are concerned with the examination of systems and procedures, and the evaluation and interpretation of control and decision information presented to management. However, some case studies require computation work prior to the evaluation and interpretation stage. The reader is required to reach conclusions and make recommendations based upon his study of the case, and his consideration of the situation described.

Arranging the case studies into a logical sequence was not an easy task. Unlike the chapters of a book, the case studies are independent of each other. There is no requirement that they should be studied in a particular sequence. After an introduction to financial and cost accountancy, *An Insight into Management Accounting* considers the various stages of the company profit-planning control cycle:

> analysing historical performance;
> examining the future environment in which the company will be operating;
> developing long-term objectives, including financial objectives;
> formulating a strategy to achieve the objectives;
> translating this strategy into operating plans for the next three to five years, and more detailed budgets for the next year;
> motivating people to achieve the plans and budgets; and
> continually comparing actual with planned performance and reporting to responsible management, as a basis for improving managerial efficiency and the effectiveness of the planning process.

Within this framework of long- and short-term planning, companies must seek out and appraise investment opportunities, and make various tactical (short-term) decisions such as pricing and product-mix decisions.

The case studies are presented in the same sequence, with the exception of a general introductory case (Moorcroft Hall Poultry Farm) for the reader to cut his teeth on, and a final comprehensive case study (Diversified Engineering Ltd). The reader should find the sequence logical, but it may well be that lecturers and tutors using the book to complement a course in management accounting would prefer to consider the case studies in a different sequence.

Discussion questions are suggested at the end of each case. These questions are not intended to be exhaustive but are provided as a lead into some of the issues raised in the case. The suggested background reading at the end of each case provides a cross reference with the relevant chapter(s) of *An Insight into Management Accounting*. A limited number of additional readings is suggested, but they are not intended to be comprehensive. Lecturers and tutors may wish to pose additional or alternative questions and recommend other readings.

It is often argued by fellow academics that one important reason for the dearth of British case studies is the unwillingness of senior executives of British companies to allow case writers access to suitable material. It is pleasing to report that in the preparation of these case studies a high level of cooperation and support was received. Very rarely did companies refuse access to material, or requests for permission to publish. Because of the need to preserve confidentiality, it is not possible to fully acknowledge the help received from cooperating companies and their senior executives in the preparation of the case studies. However, I would like to acknowledge support received from a number of other sources. At the time the Economic Development Committee for the Hosiery and Knitwear Industry was dissolved, a series of case studies, illustrating both sound and unsound practices within the industry was in the course of preparation. After the E.D.C. was dissolved, the National Economic Development Office agreed to the work proceeding independently, which resulted in the production of ten case studies. The material for the cases was collected by David Riddle, a postgraduate student at the London Graduate School of Business Studies employed by N.E.D.O. David Barker and George Gater of N.E.D.O. provided considerable assistance and guidance to David Riddle. Associated Industrial Consultants Ltd, Cooper Brothers, P.A. Management Consultants Ltd, and Robson Morrow & Company kindly provided introductions to clients operating in the hosiery and knitwear industry. Two further cases are based on material collected by Associated Industrial Consultants Ltd as part of an Investment Appraisal Study for the Economic Development Committee for the Clothing Industry.

Undergraduate students in the Department of Management Studies at Loughborough University of Technology undertake a substantial field investigation of a 'management' topic, and three cases were derived from these investigations. They would not have been possible without the assistance provided to the undergraduates by a large number of individuals and companies. The editors of *Accounting and Business Research*, *Accountancy*, *Hosiery Trade Journal*, and *Management Accounting* willingly gave permission to reproduce case studies that were first published in their journals. In preparing the manuscript I was extremely fortunate throughout to receive first-class assistance from my secretary, Mrs Barbara Brewer. My wife and sons were, as always, a constant source of encouragement.

*Loughborough, March 1973*                    JOHN SIZER

## Moorcroft Hall Poultry Farm

MOORCROFT HALL FARM was a nine-acre plot of land set back about 300 yards from the main A16 Grimsby to Louth road, near North Thoresby in North Lincolnshire. The farm was owned jointly by Bill Thompson and his son-in-law James Swift. The two men and their wives lived in what was Moorcroft Hall, which they converted into a house and an attached cottage. Bill Thompson and his wife lived in the house, and James Swift and his wife with their baby daughter in the cottage.

Before moving to Moorcroft Hall Farm, Bill Thompson was for several years the poultry manager at the North Lindsey School of Agriculture, Market Rasen. He felt that he would like to capitalize on the knowledge and experience of poultry farming acquired in his job by establishing and running his own business. On first hearing that Moorcroft Hall was for sale, Thompson was not over-keen on the idea of purchasing it. He and his wife considered it to be too large and expensive.

Mr and Mrs Swift, who had not been married very long, were living in a small bungalow in Louth, which they had acquired by means of a mortgage. Mrs Swift suggested that, though Moorcroft Hall was a little large and expensive for her father on his own, it would not be too much for the two families to purchase and run together. She argued that they would have eventually to move from the bungalow into a house, and that they might as well buy somewhere that possibly could provide them with an additional source of income as well as a home.

Everyone, with the exception of Mrs Swift, was a little sceptical about the idea at first, because of the magnitude of the venture and the financial risk involved. They realized that it would be quite a time before the farm would have sufficient income to support anyone working on it full time. Thompson and Swift would have to maintain full-time jobs, working on the farm in the

15

evenings and at weekends. James Swift, a surveyor by profession, did not want to work on the farm full time. However, he said that he would enjoy working in his spare time, treating it more as an interesting, yet profitable hobby and also a means of keeping fit and active. Bill Thompson would have to leave the North Lindsey School of Agriculture, and look for a job a little nearer Moorcroft Hall. After long discussions they decided to proceed with the venture, possibly because of Mrs Swift's enthusiasm and personality.

On 30 June 1965 Thompson and Swift formed a business partnership and opened a joint bank account with Westland Bank Ltd, Louth. They made initial payments of £100 each into this account, and £20 per month for three months, subsequently increased to £25 per month. When Swift sold his bungalow at Louth, the net proceeds of sale, £769, were paid into the joint account. Mr and Mrs Thompson also made additional payments of £245 into the joint account from their Post Office savings accounts and from the sale of premium savings bonds. In July 1965 Moorcroft Hall was valued at £7,100, and a mortgage for £5,065 was obtained from the Brigsly Life Assurance Company, on condition that Bill Thompson took out a life-insurance policy on himself as collateral security. Additional capital in the form of a mortgage loan was obtained in February 1967 from Westland Bank Ltd, Louth. The loan was for £3,000, and was to be repaid at the rate of £25 per month.

The two families moved into Moorcroft Hall in March 1966. There were no henhouses on the site and, in order to commence the business of poultry farming, they bought 250 hens and put these in deep litter in a cow shed at the back of the house. There was an old stable at the back of the house, subsequently deemed insanitary and demolished, and 450 cockerels were put in this stable to raise and sell as broilers. In Spring 1966 materials were purchased to erect a henhouse (No. 1). Work started on constructing this henhouse in the evenings and at weekends, and it was completed in November 1966. It was contracted to the North Lindsey Contract Egg Production Scheme (see Appendix A for further details), because of a shortage of working capital. Bill Thompson finished full-time work at the North Lindsey School of Agriculture and took up a part-time post with a local egg-packing station, so that he could look after the hens. As explained in Appendix A, considerable difficulty was encountered with the henhouse, and a loss of over £1,500 was incurred during the life of the first flock of hens. On leaving the North Lindsey School of Agriculture, Thompson was given two pigs which he kept in some pig sties on the farm. A few weeks later two more pigs were purchased, which, with those from the School of Agriculture, were fattened up and later sold for a small profit.

In 1967 two secondhand prefabricated buildings were purchased and converted into another henhouse (No. 2). Five hundred hens were reared in this house on deep litter in May of that year. Mr Thompson started working full time on the farm in November. During 1968 two further secondhand prefabricated buildings were purchased and one was converted into a henhouse (No. 3) by October. The house was partitioned and stocked. Two hundred hens with six cockerels were kept in one half of the house, for the production of fertile eggs to sell to the North Lindsey School of Agriculture at a premium price of 40–45p per dozen. In the other half 250 hens of a special breed were kept in deep litter for the production of brown-shelled eggs. The other prefabricated building, plus some secondhand battery cages and electric fans purchased at the same time, were not utilized, because of lack of sufficient working capital to purchase hens and feed. One of the electric fans and most of the battery cages were used in Autumn 1969, when the old cowshed was converted into a battery unit.

It was at this time that the farm started experiencing serious financial difficulties, due mainly to a shortage of working capital. All the cash available had been spent in expanding the business by the purchase of henhouses, battery cages, etc., until there was no cash left for new hens or feed. The Westland Bank refused to cash any more cheques though the bills for feed kept coming in. In November 1969 Thompson & Swift's accountants, having completed recently the accounts for the year ending 31 March 1969 (see Tables 1, 2 and 3), advised that the business should be

*Table 1*
Trading and Profit and Loss Accounts

| | Year ending 31 March 1968 £ | Year ending 31 March 1969 £ |
|---|---|---|
| Sale of eggs | 5,751 | 6,971 |
| *less* Opening stock | 4 | — |
| | 5,747 | 6,971 |
| | | |
| Opening value of poultry | 1,968 | 1,105 |
| *plus* Purchases | 508 | 1,786 |
| | 2,476 | 2,891 |
| *less* Closing value of poultry | 1,105 | 1,550 |
| | 1,371 | 1,341 |
| *less* Poultry sales | 557 | 310 |
| Loss in value of poultry | 814 | 1,031 |
| Feed consumed | 4,365 | 5,347 |
| Cleaning paper | 68 | 50 |
| Light and heat | 211 | 167 |
| Repairs and renewals | 47 | 15 |
| Motor expenses | 6 | 54 |
| Rates and water | 92 | 98 |
| Insurance | 26 | 43 |
| Telephone | 37 | 29 |
| Bank charges and interest | 243 | 268 |
| Professional charges | 83 | — |
| Accountancy | 42 | 42 |
| Depreciation | | |
| Houses | 163 | 221 |
| Equipment | 169 | 172 |
| Veterinary supplies | 51 | 38 |
| Sundries | 29 | 4 |
| | 6,446 | 7,579 |
| *less* Salvage | 15 | 29 |
| Sale of pigs | — | 203 |
| Grazing rights | 30 | 24 |
| | £6,401 | £7,323 |
| | | |
| *Net loss* | £654 | £352 |

## Table 2
### Balance Sheet as at 31 March 1968

| | £ | £ | £ | £ |
|---|---|---|---|---|
| *Capital accounts* | | | | |
| Mr Bill Thompson: | | | | |
| Balance 1 April 1967 | | 227 | | |
| Cash paid in | | 300 | | |
| | | 527 | | |
| *less* Half share of loss | 327 | | | |
| Drawings | 695 | | | |
| | | 1,022 | | |
| | | | (495) | |
| Mr James Swift: | | | | |
| Balance 1 April 1967 | | 620 | | |
| Cash paid in | | 503 | | |
| | | 1,123 | | |
| *less* Half share of loss | 327 | | | |
| Drawings | 560 | | | |
| | | 887 | | |
| | | | 236 | |
| | | | (259) | |
| *Liabilities* | | | | |
| Mortgage | | 5,065 | | |
| Bank loan | | 2,852 | | |
| Creditors | | 2,975 | | |
| Bank overdraft | | 592 | | |
| | | | 11,484 | |
| | | | £11,225 | |

| | £ | £ | £ |
|---|---|---|---|
| *Property at cost* | | | 7,558 |
| *Poultry houses (at cost)* | | | |
| House 1 | | 622 | |
| House 2 | | 513 | |
| House 3 | | 499 | |
| Site hut | | 107 | |
| | | 1,741 | |
| Depreciation | | 226 | |
| | | | 1,515 |
| *Poultry equipment at cost* | | 1,127 | |
| Depreciation | | 292 | |
| | | | 835 |
| *Current assets* | | | |
| Stocks – poultry feed | | 1,105 | |
| | | 108 | |
| Debtors and prepayments | | 101 | |
| Cash | | 3 | |
| | | | 1,317 |
| | | | £11,225 |

*Table 3*

Balance Sheet as at 31 March 1969

| | £ | £ | £ |
|---|---:|---:|---:|
| **Capital accounts** | | | |
| Mr Bill Thompson: | | | |
| Balance 1 April 1968 | | (495) | |
| Cash paid in | | 486 | |
| | | (9) | |
| less Half share in loss | 176 | | |
| Drawings | 495 | | |
| | | 671 | |
| | | | (680) |
| Mr James Swift: | | | |
| Balance 1 April 1968 | 236 | | |
| Cash paid in | 36 | | |
| | | 272 | |
| less Half share in loss | 176 | | |
| Drawings | 406 | | |
| | | 582 | |
| | | | (310) |
| | | | (990) |
| | | | |
| **Liabilities** | | | |
| Mortgage | 5,065 | | |
| Bank loan | 2,744 | | |
| Creditors | 4,329 | | |
| Bank overdraft | 658 | | |
| | | | 12,796 |
| | | | £11,806 |

| | £ | £ |
|---|---:|---:|
| **Property at cost** | | 7,558 |
| *Poultry houses (at cost)* | | |
| House 1 | 977 | |
| House 2 | 627 | |
| House 3 | 513 | |
| Site hut | 107 | |
| | 2,224 | |
| Depreciation | 447 | |
| | | 1,777 |
| *Poultry equipment at cost* | 1,150 | |
| Depreciation | 464 | |
| | | 686 |
| *Current assets* | | |
| Stocks – poultry feed | 1,550 | |
| Debtors and prepayments | 131 | |
| Cash | 101 | |
| | 3 | |
| | | 1,785 |
| | | £11,806 |

declared bankrupt and wound up. Thompson & Swift discussed the situation and agreed that they had better 'call it a day'. Mrs Swift suggested they should seek the advice of her cousin, Jim Banks, before making the decision. Banks had completed recently a course in farm management at the North Lindsey School of Agriculture. He agreed to the idea, and spent a long weekend at the farm studying the situation and collecting information. He analysed the data during the following week, and was able to produce a written report (see Appendix B) when he visited the farm at the weekend. Bill Thompson and James Swift agreed that they would read the report over the weekend, have dinner together on Sunday evening, and afterwards discuss the report and make a decision on the future of their partnership.

QUESTIONS

1. What mistakes did Thompson & Swift make?
2. Critically examine Jim Banks's report. Has he given adequate consideration to the situation facing Thompson & Swift?
3. Should Thompson & Swift wind up their partnership?

SUGGESTED BACKGROUND READING

*An Insight into Management Accounting*, Chapter 8.

# APPENDIX A

*Henhouse 1: The North Lindsey*
*Contract Egg Production Scheme*

N.L.C.E.P.S., which is organized by the North Lindsey Chicken Company, enables farmers who have the necessary henhouse(s), equipment, etc. to commence egg production without any further outlay for the birds and feed. The North Lindsey Chicken Company supply the birds at a relatively high price, but are never directly paid for them. The company supply feed for the birds through a local feed store, and they settle the account with the store. As the birds come on to lay, the eggs are sent to the local packing station, and the packing station settle with the company. When the birds have finished laying and are sold as scrap, the farmer receives as a lump-sum payment the difference between the revenue the company receive from the sale of the eggs and the cost of the hens and feed. In addition the company pays the farmer each month for his labour. The N.L.C.E.P.S. contract lasts for the life of the birds, about twelve to fifteen months.

If Thompson & Swift had not contracted henhouse 1 on the N.L.C.E.P.S., they estimated that the cost of the 2,000 eighteen-week-old birds for henhouse 1 would have been between £1,500–1,600 (approximately £0·75 to £0·80 per bird), the cost of the feed for the birds until they come on to lay between £100 and £200, and the total cost of a bird and its feed until the end of its life approximately £2·50. Allowing for trade credit and possible delay in receiving payment for eggs, to keep 2,000 birds for egg production they estimated they would require working capital of approximately £2,000. Provided everything went satisfactorily, they estimated that under the N.L.C.E.P.S. each bird would make about £0·50 profit throughout its life, and they would receive at the end of contract a lump-sum payment of approximately £1,000, plus payments of £32 per month during the life of the birds.

The first flock of birds were housed in November 1966, as soon as the henhouse was completed. All went well with the henhouse for the first month, then the pullets started laying a high proportion of seconds* and eggs with bloodspots,† and there was a drop in the rate of egg production. Bill Thompson attributed this to variations in the intensity of the electric artificial lighting given to the birds to stimulate egg production. Over Christmas 1966 the voltage of the electricity fell from 220–240 volts by 25 per cent to 180 volts at times. As a result Thompson & Swift received no lump-sum payment from the North Lindsey Chicken Company. In fact the loss in income was so great that at the end of the life of this first flock of birds in henhouse 1, Thompson & Swift owed the North Lindsey Chicken Company £1,500.

## APPENDIX B

### Report on Moorcroft Hall Farm

Your main problem at Moorcroft Hall Farm is the under-utilization of your plant and equipment. You will see from Schedule A that you are utilizing only 78 per cent of your laying facilities. This under-utilization has resulted from

1. your failure to plan the capital expenditure of the business;
2. your failure to realize that all plant and equipment represents money tied up which could be more profitably employed in, say, a deposit account at the Westland Bank.

Furthermore the utilization of 78 per cent makes no allowance for the fact that often there has been a three-week delay in taking delivery of a new flock of poultry.

---

*Seconds are eggs with deformed, damaged or weak shells, and are unsuitable for sale with the other eggs – even though inside the yolk and white may be perfect.

†Eggs with blood and meat spots are caused by the rupture of small blood vessels in the ovary of the pullet and are in general unfit for marketing with perfect eggs.

I have prepared an estimate of your income and expenditure for the year ending 31 March 1970, and, as you can see from Schedule B, I estimate that there will be £326 remaining to pay Bill Thompson's salary. Though you are earning £40 per month for labour costs under North Lindsey Contract Egg Production Scheme, I have not included this in your estimated income. I have assumed this will be used to pay off the debt you incurred with your first batch of hens. My detailed calculations and assumptions are shown in a schedule at the end of this report.

I suggest that you should consider two alternatives to winding up the business:

## ALTERNATIVE A

You could acquire 750 hens to use the present facilities available on the farm to the full. I estimate this would result in an additional annual income of £1,000, and, after allowing Bill Thompson to draw his full salary of £1,200 per year, leave a profit before tax of £26. This proposal would require capital of £713 to pay for the birds, including an allowance for feed, until the income for egg sales is sufficient to offset the expenditure.

## ALTERNATIVE B

You could, in addition to Alternative A, erect a new henhouse. The foundations for a new house were prepared in 1968, when you purchased prefabricated sections similar to henhouse 3 together with electric fans and battery cages, but due to a lack of further capital they were never erected. The battery cages and one of the fans were used in your recent conversion of the cowshed into a battery unit. The extra eggs produced in the new henhouse could be sold through your existing wholesale and retail outlets at an average selling price of 20p per dozen. I understand that the demand from these sources is increasing, and, until recently, in order to retain the business and goodwill, you supplied these outlets with some eggs purchased from other producers. It is estimated, on the basis of a detailed analysis of

24

the cost of your existing houses, that the erection of a new house could be carried out for approximately £400. The house would take 600 hens on deep litter, and this would require £570 for the hens including an allowance for feed. Thus the total capital requirement for the new house would be £970. The total capital requirement for Alternative B, including 750 hens to fully utilize your existing capacity, would be £1,683, say £1,700.

As you will see from Schedule B, if you adopted Alternative B, it would be possible for Bill Thompson to draw a reasonable income of £1,200 per year, leaving a profit before tax of £726.

FUTURE DEVELOPMENTS

If you proceeded with Alternative B, the £726 could be used to pay off any remaining creditors from the troubles in 1967–8. At a later date cost-reducing equipment could be purchased, such as manure-disposal and food-milling and -mixing equipment. Eventually it would be possible for Messrs Thompson & Swift to consider making personal drawings from the business, and/or for Mr Thompson to receive an increase in salary. Alternatively any profit from the business could be ploughed back into the business and used for the purchase of new henhouses and equipment. Battery cages could be installed in all the henhouses with resulting benefits of higher efficiency and output from each henhouse. However, care must be taken not to expand too quickly and repeat the mistakes of the past.

After implementing Alternative B, and obtaining full utilization of equipment, it would be advisable for you to concentrate on increasing the percentage of egg sales through the wholesale/retail outlets at the expense of the Packing Station sales. The profit contribution you obtain is highest for the deep-litter units, because eggs are sold for an average of £0·20 per dozen through wholesale/retail outlets. (£0·40 per dozen to the North Lindsey School of Agriculture.) The battery units produce the lowest contribution per bird of all the henhouses, simply because the price obtained for the eggs sold to the Packing Station is so low. The 33⅓ per cent increase in price obtained for the sales of eggs from the battery units through the wholesale/retail outlets would increase the profit contribution per bird by £1 to £1·66. This would result in additional profit of £2,650 per annum for no further capita l outlay. Thus, in order that the business thrives, it is essential that sales through the wholesale/retail outlets be continued, and even increased to include the production of the battery units. Any further possible increase in the sales of fertile eggs to the North Lindsey School of Agriculture will be very welcome. The hens employed in this aspect of the business are by far the most profitable.

The low income obtained when the birds have finished laying could be greatly improved by an increase in the average price of 11p per bird obtained at present. 100 to 200 of the best birds could be prepared for the table and sold at premium prices through some of the wholesale/retail outlets. However, it must be remembered that, when an old flock of birds has finished laying and is replaced, it is most important, from the equipment utilization point of view, to get the henhouse cleaned out, disinfected and the new birds installed as quickly as possible. Thus, should the processing of birds distract Mr Thompson in any way from this important task, then this proposal should be ignored.

FINDING THE CAPITAL

In May 1969 Moorcroft Hall Farm was valued at £12,000, an increase of £4,900 upon the valuation of £7,100 in 1965. A mortgage of £10,000 could be obtained on this new value. Since your current mortgage on the house stands at £5,065, this would provide additional capital of about £5,000. £2,500 of this additional capital could be used to pay off the bank loan at Westland Bank, £700 to pay off the bank overdraft at the same bank, and a further £500 to reduce the level of trade creditors, leaving £1,300 to finance expansion. I estimate that the capital you require to finance Alternative B is £1,700. It is possible to purchase hens on a form of hire purchase, 50 per cent of the cost to be paid as a deposit and the remainder to be paid during the next six months. Since over £1,000 of the additional capital is required for the purchase of hens, only £500 need be found immediately, the remaining £500 being paid off from the income from the sale of the additional eggs, which after six months would be over £700.

CONCLUSION

My calculations show that it is not necessary for the partnership to be wound up, and that, if the recommendations outlined in this report are implemented, the partnership could prosper.

JIM BANKS

### Schedule A
#### The Utilization of Henhouses at Moorcroft Hall Farm

|  | Capacity | Utilization |
|---|---|---|
| Henhouse 1 | 2,000 battery | 2,000 battery |
| Henhouse 2 | 500 deep litter | empty |
| Henhouse 3 | 500 deep litter | 250 deep litter (brown shell) |
| Cowshed | 650 battery | 650 battery |
| Building-site hut | 200 deep litter | 80 deep litter (fertile) |
| Total capacity | 3,850 | 2,980 |
| Total percentage utilization | 77·5 | |

### Schedule B
#### Profit Estimates

|  | Year ending 31 March 1970 | Alternative A operating at full capacity | Alternative B operating with new house 5 |
|---|---|---|---|
|  | £ | £ | £ |
| Contribution from 2,650 birds in battery units contracted to N.L.C.E.P.S. | 1,405 | 1,405 | 1,405 |
| Contribution from deep-litter units. Henhouse 3 | 332 | 332 | 332 |
| Contribution from 80 birds and 6 cockerels in building-site hut for production of fertile eggs | 189 | 189 | 189 |

*Schedule B (Cont.)*

| | Year ending 31 March 1970 | Alternative A operating at full capacity | Alternative B operating with new house 5 |
|---|---|---|---|
| | £ | £ | £ |
| Contribution from additional 750 birds when working at full capacity | — | 1,000 | 1,000 |
| Contribution from proposed new henhouse (5) with 600 hens on deep litter | — | — | 800 |
| | 1,926 | 2,926 | 3,726 |
| *less* Fixed costs | 1,600 | 1,700 | 1,800 |
| Margin before labour costs | 326 | 1,226 | 1,926 |
| *less* Salary for Mr Thompson of £1,200 | 1,200 | 1,200 | 1,200 |
| Profit before taxation | (£874) | £26 | £726 |
| *Total estimated capital requirements* | — | £713 | £1,683 |

## Schedule of Detailed Calculations and Assumptions

### A *Estimated Profit for Year Ending 31 March 1970*

1. Contribution from 2,650 birds contracted to N.L.C.E.P.S. (in henhouse 1 and cowshed)

| Income | £ |
|---|---|
| *Sale of eggs* | |
| 20 dozen per bird at an average price of 15p per dozen to packing station | 3·00 |
| *Sale of hens* | |
| Scrap value per bird | 0·11 |
| | 3·11 |

| Variable costs | |
|---|---|
| *Cost of bird* | |
| Point-of-lay pullet (18 weeks old) | 0·80 |
| *Cost of feed* | |
| 18-week-old to the end of lay | 1·65 |
| | 2·45 |

Schedule of Detailed Calculations and Assumptions (*Cont.*)

|  | £ |
|---|---|
| Thus contribution per bird over 15 months is | 0·66 |
| Contribution per bird per year | 0·53 |
| *Total contribution from 2,650 birds per year* | **£1,405** |

2. Contribution from 250 birds on deep litter (henhouse 3)

Income

*Sale of eggs* £

20 dozen per bird at an average price of 20p per dozen through
retail and wholesale outlets      4·00

*Sale of hens*

Scrap value per bird      0·11

     4·11

Variable costs

*Cost of bird*

Point-of-lay pullet (18 weeks old)      **0·80**

*Cost of feed*

18-week-old to end of lay      1·65

     2·45

| Thus contribution per bird over 15 months is | 1·66 |
|---|---|
| Contribution per bird per year | 1·33 |
| *Total contribution from 250 birds per year* | **£332** |

3. Contribution from 80 birds and 6 cockerels for production of fertile eggs
for sale to North Lindsey School of Agriculture in the converted building-
site hut

Income

*Sale of eggs* £

8 dozen per bird to School of Agriculture at price of 40p per
dozen      3·20

12 dozen per bird at price of 20p per dozen through wholesale
and retail outlets      2·40

*Sale of hens including allowance for cockerels*

Scrap value per bird      0·13

     5·73

Schedule of Detailed Calculations and Assumptions (*Cont.*)

| | £ |
|---|---|
| Variable costs | |
| *Cost of birds* | |
| 18-week-old White Leghorn hybrid bird | 0·90 |
| Allowance of 8p per hen to pay for cost of cockerels | 0·08 |
| *Cost of feed* | |
| For hens from 8 weeks to end of lay per bird | 1·65 |
| Allowance for cockerels' share per bird | 0·15 |
| | 2·78 |
| Contribution per hen over 15 months | 2·95 |
| Contribution per hen over 12 months | 2·36 |
| *Total contribution from unit over 12 months* | £189 |

## B *Additional Contribution and Capital Requirement when Working at Full Capacity, i.e. an additional 750 hens on deep litter (Alternative A)*

| | |
|---|---|
| *Total contribution from 750 birds* at £1·33 per bird (see A2 above) | £1,000 |

Fixed capital
   There would be no fixed capital requirement, since all the necessary equipment has been purchased and is available for use — 

| | £ |
|---|---|
| Working capital | |
| 750 18-week-old pullets at £0·80 each | 600 |
| Feed costs, until the egg sales income is sufficient to cover them, at 15p per bird | 113 |
| | £713 |

## C *Additional Contribution from and Capital Requirement for Expansion (Alternative B)*

1. Profit contribution from new 600-hen deep-litter unit
*Total contribution from 600 birds* on deep litter at £1·33 per bird (see A2 above)      £800

Schedule of Detailed Calculations and Assumptions (*Cont.*)

## 2. Capital requirements for expansion plans

| Fixed capital | £ |
|---|---:|
| The prefabricated building was paid for in 1968 and merely awaits erection | — |
| Insulation of house | 250 |
| Electrical fittings | 30 |
| Water supply | 30 |
| Additional building materials | 50 |
| Sundry items | 40 |
| | £400 |

| Working capital | £ |
|---|---:|
| 600 18-week-old pullets at £0·80 each | 480 |
| Feed costs, until the egg sales are sufficiently high to meet them, at 15p per bird | 90 |
| | £570 |

| *Total capital requirement* | £970 |
|---|---:|

## 3. Estimation of Fixed Costs

Fixed costs are those that tend to remain the same, irrespective of output. From the Profit and Loss Accounts these were calculated for the two years ending March 1968 and March 1969 by the additions of the following items.

| | 1968 £ | 1969 £ |
|---|---:|---:|
| Cleaning paper | 68 | 50 |
| Light and heat | 211 | 167 |
| Repairs and renewals | 47 | 15 |
| Motor expenses | 6 | 54 |
| Rates and water | 92 | 98 |
| Insurance | 26 | 43 |
| Telephone | 37 | 29 |
| Bank charges and interest | 243 | 268 |
| Professional charges | 83 | — |
| Accountancy | 42 | 42 |
| Depreciation | | |
|     Houses | 163 | 221 |
|     Equipment | 169 | 172 |
| Veterinary supplies | 51 | 38 |
| Sundries | 29 | 4 |
| Mortgage payments | 300 | 300 |
| *Total fixed costs* | £1,567 | £1,501 |

The above costs will all tend to remain the same (or only change marginally) even if more birds are purchased. In estimating fixed costs for the year ending March 1970, allowance has been made for inflation, and it is assumed that these costs will be £1,600 for the year. It is also assumed that the adoption of Alternative A and B will each in turn increase the fixed costs by about £100, most of this being in motor expenses for the delivery of the additional eggs produced.

### 4. Assumptions

(a) The figure of 20 dozen eggs per bird is an average figure, and a very realistic one. Considering Bill Thompson's skill with poultry, it is quite possible that this figure could be bettered.

(b) The figure of 11p scrap value for a hen is an average price, depending upon the weight of the birds sold, the price varying from 10 to 12½p.

(c) The cost of a bird 18 weeks old will vary depending upon market conditions and the breed of the bird. Price can vary between £0·75 and £0·90, but the hens used on Moorcroft Hall Farm work out at an estimated cost of £0·80 each. The hens in the fertile deep-litter unit are a better breed and their cost has been taken at £0·90.

(d) The feed costs used are again an average, the cost varying from about £1·60 to £1·70 per bird. The feed costs used take into account the fact that Bill Thompson mixes his own mash and can feed his birds at a slightly lower cost.

(e) A reasonable living salary for Mr and Mrs Thompson is £1,200 per annum.

(f) Since the North Lindsey School of Agriculture only require about 10 dozen eggs per week, of the 20 dozen eggs that a bird will lay, 8 dozen per bird will be sufficient to meet this demand. The remaining 12 dozen eggs will be sold through wholesale/retail outlets at the usual average price of 20p per dozen.

(g) All the estimates, by virtue of their conservativeness, include an allowance for the fact that the facilities can never be fully utilized because of delays incurred when one flock is moved out and another moved in, which is usually caused by

 (i) time taken to clean out and disinfect laying quarters;
 (ii) possible delay in the delivery of new birds.

(h) There is no allowance in any of the estimates for marketing costs. However, this is not too important since it is understood that most of the eggs are collected from the farm. Deliveries are made each week to the North Lindsey School of Agriculture but the school pays a delivery charge each journey of 35p to cover this.

# Bigtown Printers Ltd

BIGTOWN PRINTERS LTD was a medium-sized firm of general letterpress printers with an annual turnover in excess of £300,000 and 117 employees. The company occupied valuable freehold premises in the centre of a provincial city in Ruritania.

James Cameron, the managing director, emphasized that the company prided itself in providing a reliable service to customers. He described his business as follows:

We have been solving print problems for customers since 1775. Solutions are hard to come by, but we still succeed. We print by letterpress or litho, our main interest being the production of catalogues, brochures, calendars, company reports, technical literature, periodicals and fine colour print. We design, plan and print to suit all requirements.

It was Cameron's policy to purchase the most up-to-date machinery and, after his annual visit to the Leipzig Trade Fair, he purchased two Condor machines during 1965. These machines produced three times the amount of work and used one third of the space of the existing machines. During 1965 a firm of management consultants installed an incentive payment scheme in the finishing department.

Bigtown Printers was a member of the Ruritanian Federation of Master Printers, and participated in the Federation's Management Ratio Scheme. Summaries of the ratios received from the Federation in 1964 and 1965 appear in Tables 1 and 2. Summaries of the basic information used in the calculation of Bigtown Printers' ratios appear in Tables 3 and 4.

The Ruritanian Federation of Master Printers did not supply an interpretation of the ratios. Bigtown Printers did not employ a qualified accountant and the ratios were interpreted for Cameron by the company secretary, William Biggs. Biggs's comments on the 1964 and 1965 ratios appear in Tables 5 and 6.

QUESTIONS

1. Using a pyramid of ratios, examine the 1965 ratios to determine any significant changes that have taken place during the year, and prepare a report for James Cameron.

2. Critically examine the ratios calculated by the Ruritanian Federation of Master Printers.

*Hint:* From the information provided below, calculate for each company the following information:

> Profit/Sales
> Production cost/Cost of output
> Other costs/Cost of output
> Production cost/Sales
> Other costs/Sales

|  | Company A £ | Company B £ | Company C £ |
|---|---|---|---|
| Sales | 100 | 100 | 100 |
| Production costs | 78 | 76 | 69 |
| Other costs | 17 | 14 | 16 |
| Cost of output | 95 | 90 | 85 |
| Profit | £5 | £10 | £15 |

SUGGESTED BACKGROUND READING

1. *An Insight into Management Accounting*, Chapter 4. An interpretation of the 1964 ratios appears in Appendix B of Chapter 4.
2. H. W. G. Kendell, 'The use of ratios in the printing industry', *Business Ratios*, summer 1967.

## Table 1
### Ruritanian Federation of Master Printers
### General Printing Letterpress – 101 and over employees
### 35 firms (5,707 employees)

| | | Ratios 1964 | | | |
|---|---|---|---|---|---|
| | Unit | 1st quartile | Median | 3rd quartile | Bigtown Printers |
| **PRIMARY RATIOS** | | | | | |
| 1. $\dfrac{\text{operating profit}}{\text{operating capital}}$ | % | 2·5 | 6·9 | 12·5 | 11·4 |
| *Operating-cost ratios* | | | | | |
| 2. $\dfrac{\text{operating profit}}{\text{net sales}}$ | % | 2·2 | 6·5 | 9·3 | 7·5 |
| 3. $\dfrac{\text{value of output}}{\text{net sales}}$ | % | 99·5 | 100·6 | 101·8 | 105·8 |
| 4. $\dfrac{\text{production cost (gross)}}{\text{cost of output}}$ | % | 82·9 | 84·9 | 85·6 | 85·5 |
| 5. $\dfrac{\text{distribution cost}}{\text{cost of output}}$ | % | 1·1 | 1·4 | 2·0 | 1·6 |
| 6. $\dfrac{\text{selling cost}}{\text{cost of output}}$ | % | 3·3 | 4·0 | 5·4 | 5·2 |
| 7. $\dfrac{\text{administration cost}}{\text{cost of output}}$ | % | 8·4 | 9·9 | 11·1 | 7·7 |
| *Use-of-capital ratios* | | | | | |
| 8. $\dfrac{\text{net sales}}{\text{operating capital}}$ | % | 113·8 | 133·8 | 153·9 | 152·5 |
| 9. $\dfrac{\text{fixed assets}}{\text{operating capital}}$ | % | 52·2 | 58·7 | 66·9 | 53·9 |
| 10. $\dfrac{\text{plant}}{\text{fixed assets}}$ | % | 78·6 | 83.9 | 93·2 | 92·6 |
| 11. $\dfrac{\text{value added}}{\text{plant}}$ | % | 148·6 | 204·8 | 242·9 | 189·0 |
| 12. $\dfrac{\text{materials}}{\text{stock}}$ | Times per year | 2·5 | 3·9 | 5·2 | 6·0 |
| 13. $\dfrac{\text{debtors}}{\text{sales per day}}$ | Days' credit | 51·2 | 59·7 | 68·3 | 58·5 |
| **SECONDARY RATIOS** | | | | | |
| *Production costs* | | | | | |
| 14. $\dfrac{\text{value added}}{\text{factory employees}}$ | £ per employee | 1,669·1 | 1,835·0 | 2,043·1 | 2,032·2 |
| 15. $\dfrac{\text{value added}}{\text{factory wages}}$ | Per £ | 1·8 | 2·0 | 2·2 | 2·2 |

## Table 1 (Cont.)

| | | | Ratios 1964 | | |
|---|---|---|---|---|---|
| | Unit | 1st quartile | Median | 3rd quartile | Bigtown Printers |
| 16. $\dfrac{\text{production cost (net)}}{\text{cost of output}}$ | % | 46·0 | 54·4 | 59·7 | 40·8 |
| 17. $\dfrac{\text{factory wages}}{\text{production cost (net)}}$ | % | 68·6 | 71·0 | 76·1 | 70·0 |
| 18. $\dfrac{\text{factory-management salaries}}{\text{production cost (net)}}$ | % | 4·4 | 6·4 | 7·8 | 8·0 |
| 19. $\dfrac{\text{depreciation}}{\text{production cost (net)}}$ | % | 7·3 | 8·7 | 10·0 | 8·5 |
| 20. $\dfrac{\text{other factory expenses}}{\text{production cost (net)}}$ | % | 10·2 | 12·0 | 15·3 | 13·4 |
| 21. $\dfrac{\text{factory wages}}{\text{factory employees}}$ | £ per capita | 820·1 | 946·5 | 1,046·9 | 923·1 |
| 22. $\dfrac{\text{male factory employees}}{\text{factory employees}}$ | % | 67·8 | 78·7 | 83·5 | 74·2 |
| 23. $\dfrac{\text{factory-management salaries}}{\text{factory-management staff}}$ | £ per capita | 1,408·0 | 1,651·1 | 1,939·9 | 1,429·7 |
| 24. $\dfrac{\text{plant}}{\text{factory employees}}$ | £ per employee | 732·7 | 940·1 | 1,126·1 | 1,075·3 |
| *Selling costs* | | | | | |
| 25. $\dfrac{\text{sales-staff remuneration}}{\text{sales staff}}$ | £ per capita | 1,318·7 | 1,794·9 | 2,203·5 | 1,847·8 |
| *Administrative costs* | | | | | |
| 26. $\dfrac{\text{administration expenses}}{\text{administration cost}}$ | % | 34·8 | 43·6 | 50·2 | 50·2 |
| 27. $\dfrac{\text{general-management salaries}}{\text{administration cost}}$ | % | 6·8 | 10·7 | 14·6 | 17·9 |
| 28. $\dfrac{\text{administrative-staff salaries}}{\text{administration cost}}$ | % | 36·0 | 46·5 | 53·1 | 31·9 |
| 29. $\dfrac{\text{administration cost}}{\text{printing jobs}}$ | £ per job | 4·6 | 7·5 | 16·9 | N.A. |
| 30. $\dfrac{\text{general-management salaries}}{\text{general-management staff}}$ | £ per capita | 2,189·7 | 2,996·7 | 3,838·0 | 2,764·0 |

## Table 1 (Cont.)

| | | | Ratios 1964 | | |
|---|---|---|---|---|---|
| | Unit | 1st quartile | Median | 3rd quartile | Bigtown Printers |
| 31. administrative-staff salaries / administrative staff | £ per capita | 698·1 | 855·6 | 931·8 | 738·7 |
| 32. male-administrative staff / administrative staff | % | 36·1 | 49·3 | 61·1 | 30·0 |

The three comparison ratios given provide an indication of the middle performance and range of results. For each ratio the figures are listed in order of size from the lowest to the highest. The median is the figure which comes half-way down the list. The first and third quartiles are the figures a quarter and three quarters down the list. The median and quartiles are therefore figures from actual firms, but it is very probable that they will be different firms for each ratio.

## Table 2
### Ruritanian Federation of Master Printers
General Printing Letterpress – 101 and over employees
33 firms (5,620 employees)

| | | | Ratios 1965 | | |
|---|---|---|---|---|---|
| | Unit | 1st quartile | Median | 3rd quartile | Bigtown Printers |
| PRIMARY RATIOS | | | | | |
| 1. operating profit / operating capital | % | 3·4 | 6·8 | 12·3 | 9·8 |
| *Operating-cost ratios* | | | | | |
| 2. operating profit / net sales | % | 3·0 | 5·9 | 9·5 | 7·6 |
| 3. value of output / net sales | % | 99·3 | 100·0 | 101·8 | 103·7 |
| 4. production cost (gross) / cost of output | % | 81·4 | 82·9 | 84·5 | 83·3 |
| 5. distribution cost / cost of output | % | 1·2 | 1·5 | 2·2 | 1·5 |
| 6. selling cost / cost of output | % | 3·0 | 4·3 | 5·7 | 5·8 |
| 7. administration cost / cost of output | % | 9·6 | 11·2 | 12·4 | 9·4 |
| *Use-of-capital ratios* | | | | | |
| 8. net sales / operating capital | % | 111·7 | 130·5 | 152·4 | 128·9 |

*Table 2 (Cont.)*

|  | | | Ratios 1965 | | | |
|---|---|---|---|---|---|---|
|  | | Unit | 1st quartile | Median | 3rd quartile | Bigtown Printers |
| 9. | fixed assets / operating capital | % | 55·2 | 61·8 | 66·5 | 55·4 |
| 10. | plant / fixed assets | % | 80·8 | 88·4 | 94·9 | 93·7 |
| 11. | value added / plant | % | 129·7 | 175·2 | 233·1 | 156·2 |
| 12. | materials / stock | Times per year | 2·7 | 3·6 | 6·5 | 6·7 |
| 13. | debtors / sales per day | Days' credit | 49·7 | 63·5 | 67·8 | 67·3 |

SECONDARY RATIOS

*Production costs*

|  | | | | | | |
|---|---|---|---|---|---|---|
| 14. | value added / factory employees | £ per employee | 1,761·6 | 1,991·0 | 2,183·3 | 2,129·7 |
| 15. | value added / factory wages | per £ | 1·9 | 2·1 | 2·3 | 2·3 |
| 16. | production cost (net) / cost of output | % | 48·4 | 53·1 | 59·1 | 40·8 |
| 17. | factory wages / production cost (net) | % | 67·6 | 70·1 | 74·0 | 68·5 |
| 18. | factory-management salaries / production cost (net) | % | 4·3 | 6·2 | 7·7 | 8·0 |
| 19. | depreciation / production cost (net) | % | 7·6 | 8·7 | 11·5 | 10·6 |
| 20. | other factory expenses / production cost (net) | % | 11·3 | 13·4 | 15·5 | 12·9 |
| 21. | factory wages / factory employees | £ per capita | 786·1 | 974·7 | 1,054·4 | 910·1 |
| 22. | male factory employees / factory employees | % | 63·0 | 79·0 | 82·5 | 76·6 |
| 23. | factory-management salaries / factory-management staff | £ per capita | 1,497·2 | 1,633·8 | 2,033·5 | 1,442·8 |
| 24. | plant / factory employees | £ per employee | 814·4 | 954·0 | 1,389·0 | 1,363·3 |

*Selling costs*

|  | | | | | | |
|---|---|---|---|---|---|---|
| 25. | sales-staff remuneration / sales staff | £ per capita | 1,568·8 | 1,854·8 | 2,141·1 | 1,953·1 |

### Table 2 (Cont.)

|  |  | Ratios 1965 | | | |
| --- | --- | --- | --- | --- | --- |
| Administration costs | Unit | 1st quartile | Median | 3rd quartile | Bigtown Printers |
| 26. administration-expenses / administration cost | % | 34·8 | 41·7 | 49·8 | 58·8 |
| 27. general-management salaries / administration cost | % | 6·8 | 9·9 | 17·4 | 13·5 |
| 28. administrative-staff salaries / administration cost | % | 34·7 | 44·1 | 52·0 | 27·7 |
| 29. administration cost / printing jobs | £ per job | 5·9 | 9·7 | 16·9 | N.A. |
| 30. general-management salaries / general-management staff | £ per capita | 2,210·8 | 3,140·8 | 4,402·8 | 2,976·2 |
| 31. administrative-staff salaries / administrative staff | £ per capita | 775·1 | 928·0 | 1,053·4 | 795·1 |
| 32. male administrative staff / administrative staff | % | 41·1 | 47·3 | 55·6 | 40·0 |

For interpretation see Table 1.

### Table 3

Basic Interfirm Comparison Information 1964

| OPERATING CAPITAL | £ | £ |
| --- | --- | --- |
| Fixed assets at current values | | |
| Plant, machinery, fixtures and fittings | 100,000 | |
| Metal and type | 4,500 | |
| Cars | 3,358 | |
| Vans | 133 | |
| | | 107,991 |
| Current assets | | |
| Loans to employees, sports clubs, employees' housing associations, etc. | — | |
| Stock of materials/goods (average holding) | 12,300 | |
| Work in progress (average holding) | 30,000 | |
| Trade debtors (average holding) | 50,000 | |
| Cash (at bank, in hand) (average holding) | 80 | |
| | | 92,380 |
| | | £200,371 |

*Table 3 (Cont.)*

## OPERATING PROFIT

|  | £ | £ |
|---|---|---|
| *Gross sales* | 312,272 | |
| *less* Purchase tax | 6,688 | |
| | | |
| Net sales | 305,584 | |
| *add* Closing work in progress | 41,069 | |
| | | 346,653 |
| *less* Opening work in progress | | 23,343 |
| | | |
| *Value of output* | | £323,310 |
| | | |
| Cost of output | | |
| Production cost | | |
| Factory wages | 85,848 | |
| Factory-management salaries | 9,865 | |
| Depreciation | 10,450 | |
| Other factory expenses | 16,468 | |
| | | |
| Production cost (net) | 122,631 | |
| Materials | 73,527 | |
| Outwork | 60,792 | |
| Production cost (gross) | | 256,950 |
| Selling cost | | |
| Sales-staff remuneration | 8,500 | |
| Selling expenses | 7,019 | |
| | | 15,519 |
| Distribution cost | | 4,765 |
| Administration cost | | |
| General-management salaries | 4,146 | |
| Administrative-staff salaries | 7,387 | |
| Administration expenses (including consultants' fees) | 11,612 | |
| | | 23,145 |
| | | |
| *Cost of output* | | £300,379 |
| | | |
| OPERATING PROFIT | | £22,931 |

## OTHER INFORMATION

| *Average no. of employees* | *Directors apportioned* | *Male* | *Female* | *Total* |
|---|---|---|---|---|
| Factory | — | 69 | 24 | 93·0 |
| Factory management | 0·9 | 6 | — | 6·9 |

### Table 3 (Cont.)

| Average no. of employees | Directors apportioned | Male | Female | Total |
|---|---|---|---|---|
| Selling | 1·6 | 3 | — | 4·6 |
| Distribution | — | 1 | — | 1·0 |
| General management | 1·5 | — | — | 1·5 |
| Administration | — | 3 | 7 | 10·0 |
| Total | 4·0 | 82 | 31 | 117·0 |

Shift working is operated in certain departments.

### Table 4
#### Basic Interfirm Comparison Information 1965

| OPERATING CAPITAL | £ | £ |
|---|---|---|
| Fixed assets at current values | | |
| Plant, machinery, fixtures and fittings | 128,150 | |
| Metal and type | 4,500 | |
| Cars | 4,084 | |
| Vans | — | |
| | | 136,734 |
| Current assets | | |
| Loans to employees, sports clubs, employees' housing associations, etc. | — | |
| Stock of materials/goods (average holding) | 10,000 | |
| Work in progress (average holding) | 40,000 | |
| Trade debtors (average holding) | 60,000 | |
| Cash (at bank, in hand) (average holding) | 70 | |
| | | 110,070 |
| | | £246,804 |

| OPERATING PROFIT | | |
|---|---|---|
| *Gross sales* | 325,504 | |
| *less* Purchase tax | 7,374 | |
| Net sales | 318,130 | |
| *add* Closing work in progress | 52,920 | |
| | | 371,050 |
| *less* Opening work in progress | | 41,069 |
| *Value of output* | | £329,981 |

*Table 4 (Cont.)*

Cost of output

| Production cost | £ | £ |
|---|---:|---:|
| Factory wages | 85,553 | |
| Factory-management salaries | 9,955 | |
| Depreciation | 13,265 | |
| Other factory expenses | 16,123 | |
| Production cost (net) | 124,896 | |
| Materials | 66,718 | |
| Outwork | 63,070 | |
| Production cost (gross) | | 254,684 |
| Selling cost | | |
| Sales-staff remuneration | 9,375 | |
| Selling expenses | 8,494 | |
| | | 17,869 |
| Distribution cost | | 4,497 |
| Administration cost | | |
| General-management salaries | 3,869 | |
| Administrative-staff salaries | 7,951 | |
| Administration expenses (including consultants' fees) | 16,901 | |
| | | 28,721 |
| *Cost of output* | | £305,771 |

OPERATING PROFIT | | £24,210

OTHER INFORMATION

| Average no. of employees | Directors apportioned | Male | Female | Total |
|---|---|---|---|---|
| Factory | — | 72 | 22 | 94·0 |
| Factory management | 0·9 | 6 | — | 6·9 |
| Selling | 1·8 | 3 | — | 4·8 |
| Distribution | — | 1 | — | 1·0 |
| General management | 1·3 | — | — | 1·3 |
| Administration | — | 4 | 6 | 10·0 |
| *Total* | 4·0 | 86 | 28 | 118·0 |

Shift working is operated in some departments.

NOTES RELATING TO TABLES 3 AND 4

1. Current values of fixed assets in the comparison are either estimated cost of replacement in present condition or 60 per cent

of new replacement value. For Bigtown Printers they are estimated cost of replacement in present condition.

2. Depreciation is 10 per cent of current values of plant, machinery, fixtures and fittings, and metal and type, and 25 per cent of current values for cars and vans.

3. Rateable value of freehold premises (£3,200) is included in other factory expenses.

*Table 5*

Interfirm Comparison 1964

William Biggs's Comments

| Ratio | Comments |
|---|---|
| 1 | Reasonable but one quarter of firms in group made higher profit |
| 2 | Fair – nearly half firms in group made a greater return on sales |
| 3 | Probably due to work in progress being higher at end of year than at beginning |
| 4 | High? |
| 5 | Middle |
| 6 | High? Selling cost |
| 7 | Good |
| 8 | Turnover of capital satisfactory. High production cost ratio 4 prime cause of only reasonable return on ratio 1 |
| 9 | Lower proportion of capital invested in fixed assets than median firm |
| 10 | Plant and machinery related to metal, cars and vans |
| 11 | Use of plant – below extent to use of median firm. Work done related to value of plant |
| 12 | Materials too high? Production delays – under-utilization of plant |
| 13 | Below median credit |
| 14 | Good use made of personnel available |
| 15 | As for ratio 14 |
| 16 | Reflection of lower than median firm |
| 17 | Good |
| 18 | Higher than median figure should be justified by satisfactory results for ratios 1, 11, 14, 15 |
| 19 | Median depreciation – age of plant |
| 20 | Expenses to production costs slightly above median |
| 21 | Lower than median wages paid but see 22 |
| 22 | Now bearing on ratio 21 |
| 23 | Much lower than median – weakness at this level leads to inefficiency |
| 24 | Above median degree of mechanization |
| 25 | Above median |

## Table 5 (Cont.)

| Ratio | Comments |
|-------|----------|
| 26 | High – examine administration expenses |
| 27 | High |
| 28 | Low |
| 29 | — |
| 30 | Below median |
| 31 | Low but see ratio 32 |
| 32 | Below median |

## Table 6

### Interfirm Comparison 1965
### William Biggs's Comments

| Ratio | Comments |
|-------|----------|
| 1 | Above median but compares unfavourably with profit earned by most profitable firm |
| 2 | 2% below third quartile – reflected in ratio 1. Profit margin earned on sales |
| 3 | Value of output higher than net sales again, indicating high work in progress figures |
| 4 | High ratio – reflected in ratio 2 |
| 5 | Median |
| 6 | High rates reflected in ratio 2 |
| 7 | Again below 1st quartile – administration costs lower than median reflected in ratio 28 |
| 8 | Rate of asset turnover below median |
| 9 | Lower proportion of capital invested in fixed assets than median firm |
| 10 | High ratio and plant to employees also high, yet low value added to plant ratio |
| 11 | Use of plant – below extent of use of median firm |
| 12 | Materials too high |
| 13 | Above median – invoicing? |
| 14 | Good use made of personnel available |
| 15 | As for ratio 14 |
| 16 | Materials and outwork to cost of output again much higher than other firms. Ratio itself good – reflected in ratio 17 |
| 17 | Compares favourably with lowest-cost firms |
| 18 | Higher than median figures should be justified by satisfactory result for ratios 1, 11, 14, 15 |
| 19 | Above median |
| 20 | Expenses to production costs slightly below median |
| 21 | Below median – lower proportion male employees. See ratio 22 |

## Table 6 (Cont.)

| Ratio | Comments |
|---|---|
| 22 | Reflected in ratio 21 |
| 23 | Much lower than median – most staff, but lower paid? |
| 24 | High degree of mechanization |
| 25 | Above median – reflected in high ratio 6 |
| 26 | Again at maximum – examine administration expenses |
| 27 | Above median but see ratio 28 *re* costs |
| 28 | Below 1st quartile – administration costs lower than average |
| 29 | — |
| 30 | Below median |
| 31 | Lower than median. Low but see ratio 22 |
| 32 | Below median |

# Printed Cartons Ltd

PRINTED CARTONS LTD was an independent firm of carton printers with an annual turnover in excess of £2,600,000 and over 800 employees. The company occupied freehold premises on the outskirts of a provincial city in Ruritania.

Printed Cartons' products ranged from soap cartons and biscuit cartons to relatively costly whisky cartons. The company had a reputation for high-quality multi-coloured cartons, and during 1965 installed an additional new four-colour litho machine, which became fully operational during 1966. It was planned to install a six-colour sheet-fed photogravure machine early in 1967. The management of Printed Cartons recognized that the trend was increasing for the carton industry to become a packaging industry, making it necessary for companies such as Printed Cartons to be able to advise on packaging systems, and become responsible for installing suitable systems on their customers' premises.

The company's profit before taxation for the year ending 31 December 1966 showed a slight reduction compared with the previous year after a five-year period of increasing profits. The directors felt the slight reduction in 1966 reflected the continued competition within the carton industry, particularly from the integrated paper groups, and the general trend of reduced profit margins.

Printed Cartons was a member of the Ruritanian Federation of Master Printers and had participated for a number of years in the Federation's Management Ratio Scheme. A summary of the information submitted to the Federation for the year ending 31 December 1966 is shown in Table 1, and a summary of the ratios received from the Federation in Table 2. In earlier years the management of Printed Cartons had made little use of the management ratio information. Their ratio of operating profit to operating capital had been above the 3rd quartile ratio, and the company secretary/chief accountant, David Masters, had not presented a complete analysis of the ratios to the managing director, John Simpkins. In the 1966 comparison Printed Cartons' ratio of operating profit to operating capital fell below that of the third-quartile firm. At the time Simpkins was attending at the local university a series of seminars on management accounting for senior managers.

*Table 1*

Printed Cartons Ltd

Basic Interfirm Comparison Information 1966

| | £ | £ |
|---|---|---|
| OPERATING CAPITAL | | |
| Fixed assets at current values | | |
| Plant, machinery, fixtures and fittings | 954,436 | |
| Vans | 3,829 | |
| | | 958,265 |
| Current assets | | |
| Stock of materials/goods (average holding) | 190,000 | |
| Work in progress (average holding) | 430,000 | |
| Trade debtors (average holding) | 225,000 | |
| Cash (at bank, in hand) (average holding) | — | |
| | | 845,000 |
| | | £1,803,265 |
| | | |
| OPERATING PROFIT | | |
| *Net sales* | 2,650,434 | |
| *add* Closing work in progress | 517,050 | |
| | | 3,167,484 |
| *less* Opening work in progress | | 424,259 |
| *Value of output* | | £2,743,225 |
| | | |
| Cost of output | | |
| Production cost | | |
| Factory wages | 525,491 | |
| Factory-management salaries | 37,163 | |
| Depreciation | 95,444 | |
| Other factory expenses | 85,171 | |
| Production cost (net) | 743,269 | |
| Materials | 1,462,325 | |
| Outwork | 78,035 | |
| Production cost (gross) | | 2,283,629 |

### Table 1 (*Cont.*)

| | £ | £ |
|---|---|---|
| Selling cost | | |
| Sales-staff remuneration | 31,338 | |
| Selling expenses | 50,678 | |
| | | 82,016 |
| Distribution cost | | 69,201 |
| Administration cost | | |
| General-management salaries | 42,743 | |
| Administrative-staff salaries | 55,676 | |
| Administration expenses | 29,731 | |
| | | 128,150 |
| *Cost of output* | | £2,562,996 |
| OPERATING PROFIT | | £180,229 |

OTHER INFORMATION

| *Average no. of employees* | Working directors | Male | Female | Total |
|---|---|---|---|---|
| Factory | — | 385 | 330 | 715 |
| Factory management | 1 | 20 | — | 21 |
| Selling | 1 | 10 | — | 11 |
| Distribution | — | 8 | — | 8 |
| General management | — | — | — | — |
| Administration | — | 41 | 40 | 81 |
| *Total* | 2 | 464 | 370 | 836 |

Jobs completed during year: 2,015
Shift working is operated in certain departments.

NOTES RELATING TO TABLE 1

1. Current values of fixed assets in the comparison are either estimated cost of replacement in present condition or 60 per cent of new replacement value. For Printed Cartons they are 60 per cent of new replacement value.

2. Depreciation is 10 per cent of current values of plant, machinery, fixtures and fittings, and 25 per cent of current values of vans.

3. Rateable value of freehold premises (£14,370) is included in other factory expenses.

4. General-management salaries (£42,743) is a management fee charged by the parent company, Sigma Printers Ltd.

## Table 2
### Ruritanian Federation of Master Printers
### Carton Printing
### 21 firms

| | | Ratios 1966 | | | |
|---|---|---|---|---|---|
| | Unit | 1st quartile | Median | 3rd quartile | Printed Cartons |
| **PRIMARY RATIOS** | | | | | |
| 1. $\dfrac{\text{operating profit}}{\text{operating capital}}$ | % | 4·0 | 8·5 | 13·1 | 10·0 |
| *Operating-cost ratios* | | | | | |
| 2. $\dfrac{\text{operating profit}}{\text{net sales}}$ | % | 1·8 | 6·3 | 9·5 | 6·8 |
| 3. $\dfrac{\text{value of output}}{\text{net sales}}$ | % | 100·0 | 101·7 | 103·4 | 103·5 |
| 4. $\dfrac{\text{production cost (gross)}}{\text{cost of output}}$ | % | 84·4 | 87·0 | 89·8 | 89·1 |
| 5. $\dfrac{\text{distribution cost}}{\text{cost of output}}$ | % | 1·9 | 2·3 | 2·7 | 2·7 |
| 6. $\dfrac{\text{selling cost}}{\text{cost of output}}$ | % | 1·7 | 3·0 | 4·3 | 3·2 |
| 7. $\dfrac{\text{administration cost}}{\text{cost of output}}$ | % | 5·5 | 7·4 | 9·9 | 5·0 |
| *Use-of-capital ratios* | | | | | |
| 8. $\dfrac{\text{net sales}}{\text{operating capital}}$ | % | 118·8 | 135·5 | 155·2 | 147·0 |
| 9. $\dfrac{\text{fixed assets}}{\text{operating capital}}$ | % | 43·3 | 50·0 | 54·2 | 53·1 |
| 10. $\dfrac{\text{plant}}{\text{fixed assets}}$ | % | 94·7 | 97·0 | 99·6 | 99·6 |
| 11. $\dfrac{\text{value added}}{\text{plant}}$ | % | 122·5 | 151·0 | 179·7 | 126·2 |
| 12. $\dfrac{\text{materials}}{\text{stock}}$ | Times per year | 3·2 | 5·2 | 7·1 | 7·7 |
| 13. $\dfrac{\text{debtors}}{\text{sales per day}}$ | Days' credit | 45·1 | 61·0 | 63·5 | 31·0 |
| **SECONDARY RATIOS** | | | | | |
| *Production costs* | | | | | |
| 14. $\dfrac{\text{value added}}{\text{factory employees}}$ | £ per employee | 1,566·7 | 1,815·6 | 2,135·4 | 1,682·5 |
| 15. $\dfrac{\text{value added}}{\text{factory wages}}$ | per £ | 2·3 | 2·5 | 2·8 | 2·3 |

*Table 2 (Cont.)*

| | | Ratios 1966 | | | |
|---|---|---|---|---|---|
| | Unit | 1st quartile | Median | 3rd quartile | Printed Cartons |
| 16. $\dfrac{\text{production cost (net)}}{\text{cost of output}}$ | % | 29·1 | 34·3 | 38·2 | 29·0 |
| 17. $\dfrac{\text{factory wages}}{\text{production cost (net)}}$ | % | 55·8 | 62·3 | 68·2 | 70·7 |
| 18. $\dfrac{\text{factory-management salaries}}{\text{production cost (net)}}$ | % | 3·9 | 5·9 | 7·4 | 5·0 |
| 19. $\dfrac{\text{depreciation}}{\text{production cost (net)}}$ | % | 8·5 | 10·3 | 12·1 | 12·8 |
| 20. $\dfrac{\text{other factory expenses}}{\text{production cost (net)}}$ | % | 15·9 | 20·6 | 26·0 | 11·5 |
| 21. $\dfrac{\text{factory wages}}{\text{factory employees}}$ | £ per capita | 603·3 | 729·4 | 851·8 | 734·9 |
| 22. $\dfrac{\text{male factory employees}}{\text{factory employees}}$ | % | 40·4 | 55·2 | 64·0 | 53·8 |
| 23. $\dfrac{\text{factory-management salaries}}{\text{factory management staff}}$ | £ per capita | 1,350·7 | 1,600·5 | 2,049·2 | 1,769·7 |
| 24. $\dfrac{\text{plant}}{\text{factory employees}}$ | £ per employee | 937·0 | 1,167·2 | 1,520·9 | 1,334·9 |
| *Selling costs* | | | | | |
| 25. $\dfrac{\text{sales-staff remuneration}}{\text{sales staff}}$ | £ per capita | 1,870·2 | 2,206·4 | 2,515·3 | 2,848·9 |
| *Administration costs* | | | | | |
| 26. $\dfrac{\text{administration expenses}}{\text{administration cost}}$ | % | 34·8 | 38·8 | 54·3 | 23·2 |
| 27. $\dfrac{\text{general-management salaries}}{\text{administration cost}}$ | % | 3·6 | 7·3 | 10·9 | 33·4 |
| 28. $\dfrac{\text{administrative-staff salaries}}{\text{administration cost}}$ | % | 35·9 | 52·8 | 57·6 | 43·4 |
| 29. $\dfrac{\text{administration cost}}{\text{printing jobs}}$ | £ per job | 11·5 | 31·9 | 101·7 | 63·6 |
| 30. $\dfrac{\text{general-management salaries}}{\text{general-management staff}}$ | £ per capita | 2,738·2 | 4,553·3 | 5,125·7 | — |
| 31. $\dfrac{\text{administrative-staff salaries}}{\text{administrative staff}}$ | £ per capita | 647·5 | 703·5 | 848·0 | 687·4 |

Table 2 *(Cont.)*

| | | Ratios 1966 | | | |
| | Unit | 1st quartile | Median | 3rd quartile | Printed Cartons |
|---|---|---|---|---|---|
| 32. $\dfrac{\text{male administrative staff}}{\text{administrative staff}}$ | % | 45·9 | 52·3 | 58·0 | 50·6 |
| *Work in progress* | | | | | |
| 33. $\dfrac{\text{average work in progress}}{\text{current assets}}$ | % | 15·0 | 21·0 | 37·0 | 51·0 |
| 34. $\dfrac{\text{average work in progress}}{\text{value of output}}$ | % | 5·1 | 7·7 | 13·0 | 15·7 |

The three comparison ratios given provide an indication of the middle performance and range of results. For each ratio the figures are listed in order of size from the lowest to the highest. The median is the figure which comes half-way down the list. The first and third quartiles are the figures a quarter and three quarters down the list. The median and quartiles are therefore figures of actual firms, but it is very probable that they will be different firms for each ratio.

An interfirm-comparison case study was presented by the tutor, Bernard Knowall, at one of the seminars. As a result, Simpkins invited Knowall to prepare an interpretation of Printed Cartons' management ratios for 1966.

After preparing his interpretation Knowall sent it with the following covering letter to Simpkins.

Dear Mr Simpkins,

I have now had an opportunity to look at the Management Ratio information for Printed Cartons Ltd for 1966. On the basis of my limited knowledge of Printed Cartons Ltd I have prepared an interpretation of the information received from the Ruritanian Federation of Master Printers. I enclose a copy of my interpretation, which I hope will be of some interest to you.

I have also constructed a pyramid of ratios showing the relationship between the various ratios provided in the management ratio scheme. Some additional ratios have been deduced from the ratios provided. Unfortunately the pyramid could not be typed on one sheet so I have had to present the two sides of the pyramid on separate sheets (figures 2 and 3). You will see that I have entered on the pyramid the first-quartile, median and third-quartile ratios together with Printed Cartons' ratios. To interpret the information it is necessary to work systematically down each side of the pyramid in order to reveal the cause(s) of an unsatisfactory ratio in the higher part of the pyramid. If my interpretation of the information is read in conjunction with the pyramid of ratios, you will see how this systematic analysis is undertaken.

You can also incorporate into the interpretation the key information revealed in the previous year's interfirm comparison to show whether your performance in relation to your competitors has improved or not. Similarly you can analyse your own performance over a number of years.

I am enclosing a second copy of the interpretation for Mr Masters. If you have any difficulty in following my thinking I shall be pleased to discuss the matter with you.

Yours sincerely,
BERNARD KNOWALL

# PRINTED CARTONS LTD

*Interfirm Comparison 1966*

On the assumption that your firm is comparable with the other carton-printing firms in the comparison, you would deduce from the table of ratios provided by the Ruritanian Federation of Master Printers:

1. Your *operating profit on operating capital* (ratio 1) (indicating the earning power of the operations of your business) is above the median earned by carton-printing firms taking part in the comparison but well below that earned by the most profitable firms.

2. This is due to the fact that your *operating profit on sales* (ratio 2) and your *turnover of operating capital* (ratio 8) compare unfavourably with those of the third-quartile firms.

Ratio 2 shows what profit margin you have earned on sales, while ratio 8 indicates how often with your operating assets you have been able to earn it in a year.

Ratio 3 shows the relationship between *value of output* and *value of sales* and indicates whether your work in progress has increased or decreased during the year. In your case your value of output is higher than net sales and indicates that your work in progress increased during the year, and increased more than that of three quarters of the firms in the comparison. The increase will become more apparent when ratios 33 and 34 are examined.

3. *Operating profit to sales* (ratio 2) is lower than the most profitable firms because your ratios of *production cost* (*gross*) *to cost of output* (ratio 4) and *distribution cost to cost of output* (ratio 5) are comparatively high.

4. *Production costs* (ratios 4 and 16). Your production costs (gross) are comparatively high because your ratio of *materials cost to cost of output* is considerably higher than your competitors'. This ratio is deduced by comparing the ratio of *production cost* (*gross*) *to cost of output* (ratio 4) with the ratio of *production cost* (*net*) *to cost of output* (ratio 16). Your ratio of *materials cost to cost of output* may be higher because (a) you sub-contract more work than your competitors, (b) your competitors are members of integrated paper groups and can purchase their raw materials at a lower price, or (c) you are manufacturing a higher-quality product than your competitors, e.g. whisky cartons.

Your higher raw-materials costs are also reflected in your ratio of *materials stocks to total stocks* (ratio 12), which is far higher than that of your competitors.

You will see your *ratio of production cost* (*net*) *to cost of output* (ratio 16) compares favourably with that of your competitors. This is because your ratios of *factory management salaries to production cost* (*net*) (ratio 18) and *other factory expenses to production cost* (*net*) (ratio 20) compare favourably with your competitors'. While ratio 18 compares favourably, your *average factory-management salary* (ratio 23) is higher than the median firm's. This would indicate that you have fewer factory-management staff but that they are more highly paid.

While ratios 18 and 20 compare favourably, your ratio of *factory wages to production cost* (*net*) (ratio 17) and *depreciation to production cost* (*net*) (ratio 19) compare unfavourably with the third-quartile figures.

Your ratio 17 is high despite the fact that your *average wage per factory employee* (ratio 21) is close to that of the median firm. This is because you have a lower proportion of *male employees* (ratio 22) than the median firm. However, ratios 21 and 22 contradict ratio 17 and this may indicate that you are not utilizing your factory labour as efficiently as the other firms. This conclusion is supported by the fact that your *value added per factory employee* (ratio 14) is considerably lower than the median figure. Similarly your *value added per £ of factory wages* (ratio 15) is very low compared with the other firms. I understand a high proportion of your hand work is carried out by temporary employees, and this may be a reason why ratios 14 and 15 are low.

These low added-value ratios are particularly alarming because your ratios of *depreciation to production cost* (*net*) (ratio 19), *plant to fixed assets* (ratio 10) and *plant per factory employee* (ratio 24) would indicate that you have more plant than your competitors, and that it is probably more modern. These ratios suggest that you are not utilizing your capacity to the same extent as are your competitors. This conclusion is supported by the fact that your *ratio of value added to plant* (ratio 11) is lower than a large majority of your competitors. Your higher surplus capacity may indicate that you have not appraised past investment decisions satisfactorily, or that your pricing policy is too rigid in relation to your production capacity and requires revision.

A further reason why your added-value ratios and utilization of factory employees compare unfavourably may be because your ratio of *work in progress to value of output* (ratio 34) compares very unfavourably with that of the other firms. It may be that your production planning and control system is not satisfactory.

5. *Other costs*. Ratio 25 indicates that you have fewer sales staff than your competitors, but that they are more highly paid.

Your ratio of *administration costs to costs of output* (ratio 7) indicates that your administration costs compare favourably with other firms. However, ratios 26, 27 and 28 indicate that you may have analysed your management salaries differently from other firms in the comparison.

6. *Turnover of operating capital* (ratio 8). Reverting to this ratio, you will see that your turnover of operating capital compares favourably with the median firm. However, the analysis of this ratio indicates the following important points.

(a) Your ratio of *fixed assets to operating capital* (ratio 9) is comparatively high compared with other firms, and this appears to be because you have a higher ratio of *plant to fixed assets* (ratio 10) and more *plant per factory employee* (ratio 24). However, as we have seen, you do not appear to utilize your plant and employees as effectively as other firms.

(b) It follows from ratio 9 that your ratio of *current assets to operating capital* is lower than your competitors'. However, while your *debtors outstanding* (ratio 13) are very low, your ratios of *materials to stock* (ratio 12), *average work in progress to current assets* (ratio 33) and *average work in progress to value of output* (ratio 34) are very high. These high ratios may be a reflection of the type of cartons you print.

7. *Summary*

The important points to note from this comparison are:

(a) Your materials costs are considerably higher than those of your competitors;

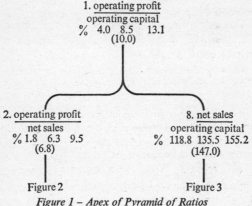

Figure 1 – Apex of Pyramid of Ratios

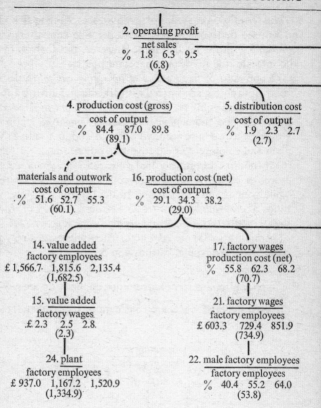

2. operating profit
net sales
% 1.8 6.3 9.5
(6.8)

4. production cost (gross)
cost of output
% 84.4 87.0 89.8
(89.1)

5. distribution cost
cost of output
% 1.9 2.3 2.7
(2.7)

materials and outwork
cost of output
% 51.6 52.7 55.3
(60.1)

16. production cost (net)
cost of output
% 29.1 34.3 38.2
(29.0)

14. value added
factory employees
£ 1,566.7 1,815.6 2,135.4
(1,682.5)

17. factory wages
production cost (net)
% 55.8 62.3 68.2
(70.7)

15. value added
factory wages
£ 2.3 2.5 2.8
(2.3)

21. factory wages
factory employees
£ 603.3 729.4 851.9
(734.9)

24. plant
factory employees
£ 937.0 1,167.2 1,520.9
(1,334.9)

22. male factory employees
factory employees
% 40.4 55.2 64.0
(53.8)

——— 1st quartile, median,
3rd quartile 1966
(——) Carton Printers 1966
– – – Derived ratios

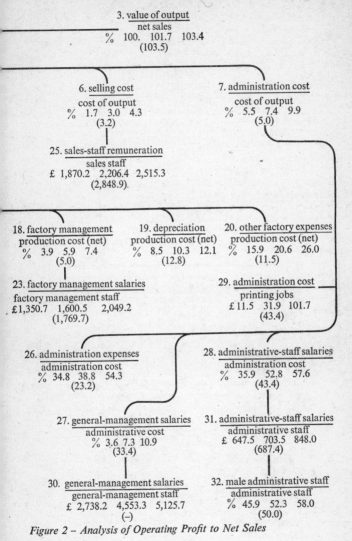

*Figure 2 – Analysis of Operating Profit to Net Sales*

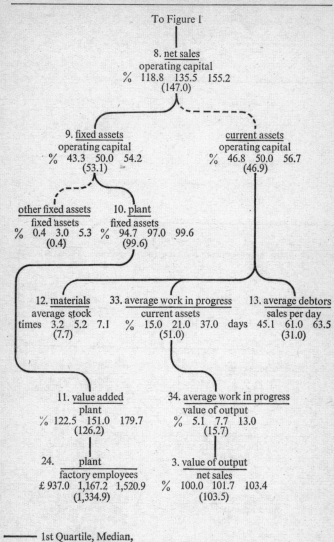

*Figure 3 – Analysis of Turnover of Operating Capital*

(b) Your factory employees' productivity is comparatively low despite the fact that you have more plant and probably more modern plant.

(c) You do not utilize your plant to the same degree as do your competitors. This may be because your work in progress is high.

(d) Your stocks of materials are high.

BERNARD KNOWALL

May 1967

QUESTION

Critically examine Knowall's interpretation of Printed Cartons' management ratio information.

SUGGESTED BACKGROUND READING

1. *An Insight into Management Accounting*, Chapter 4 and Appendix B of Chapter 4.

2. H. W. G. Kendell, 'The use of ratios in the printing industry', *Business Ratios*, summer 1967.

# Fishnet Dresses Ltd*

FRED COTTON and Bill Needle, the joint managing directors of Fishnet Dresses Ltd, were concerned about the financing of future growth of their private company. Fishnet Dresses was established by Cotton and Needle in 1967. The company manufactured and marketed high-quality jersey dresses through appointed retail outlets under the brand name 'Fish'. It also supplied dresses to mail-order stores, and under contract to Russia. The dresses were cut and sewn from double-jersey fabric supplied by United Weft Knitters, a subsidiary of a large synthetic-fibre manufacturer. United Weft Knitters allowed Fishnet Dresses extended credit terms, and assisted with the advertising of the brand name 'Fish'.

Cotton and Needle started the business in freehold premises in Cod Road, Nottingham. A successful marketing policy, combined with an increased share of the total dress market of dresses made from knitted fabric, led to a rapid increase in sales. By the end of 1969 the company was producing the maximum possible output at their Cod Road premises (2,200 garments per week). Cotton and Needle's confidence in the future demand for jersey dresses led them to purchase new leasehold premises in Haddock Road, Grantham, in March 1970. The purchase of the Grantham premises was financed by a secured bank loan of £100,000. Cotton and Needle's confidence was further increased in July 1970 when they received a report of the Economic Development Committee for the Hosiery and Knitwear Industry entitled *Hosiery and Knitwear in the 1970s*. In this report, prepared by Associated Industrial Consultants, they read:

We forecast that the U.K. market for knitted dresses will more than double over the next decade, with an average annual growth rate in excess of 8 per cent per annum. This is almost twice the forecast rate of

*This case first appeared in *Management Accounting*, March 1972, pp. 64–6.

growth of the total dress market, because we expect the share of dresses made from knitted fabrics to rise from 48 per cent in 1968 to 70 per cent in 1978 of total expenditure on all dresses. We expect exports to grow faster than imports. (p.71)

By the end of 1970 output had increased to 4,000 garments per week, and by the end of 1971 the Grantham factory alone was producing 3,100 garments per week. £50,000 of the secured bank loan was repaid in March 1971, and it was planned to repay the balance in December 1971.

Each January Cotton and Needle prepared, with the assistance of their accountant, a budgeted profit and loss account, balance sheet and cash-flow analysis for the following accounting year ending 31 March. They updated the forecasting at the end of October by adding to the six months actual to the end of September their estimates for the six months to the end of March. The updated estimates for year ending 31 March 1972 appear in Tables 1, 2 and 3. Cotton and Needle were concerned about their net-current-liability position. United Weft Knitters allowed Fishnet Dresses four months' credit, but had proposed that this should be reduced by two months by 31 March 1973. They wondered whether they should strengthen their financial position by raising additional permanent finance. They were seeking advice from their financial advisor, Simon Simpson, as to when, how much and in what form they should raise permanent capital. Simpson obtained the following information from Fred Cotton and Bill Needle:

## 1. Production capacity (garments)

| | Average per week | | | Total per |
|---|---|---|---|---|
| | Nottingham | Grantham | Total | annum |
| Maximum achievable in existing premises with full staff | 2,175 | 3,350 | 5,525 | |
| 1971–2 estimated | 2,170 | 3,126 | 5,296 | 242,000 |
| 1972–3 (47·6 weeks) | 2,125 | 3,100 | 5,225 | 248,500 |
| 1973–4 (47·6 weeks) | 2,175 (max) | 3,350 (max) | 5,525 | 263,000 |
| 1974–5 (47 weeks) | 2,175 | 3,518* | 5,693 | 268,000 |
| 1975–6 (47 weeks) | 2,175 | 3,693 | 5,868 | 276,000 |

* Building extension proposed, see 8.

## 2. Sales

|  | 1972–3 | | | 1973–4 | | |
|---|---|---|---|---|---|---|
|  | Garments | S.P. | £'000 | Garments | S.P. | £'000 |
| Fish | 153,000 | £6·30 | 964 | 163,500 | £6·50 | 1,063 |
| Mail order | 60,500 | £5·00 | 302 | 63,500 | £5·25 | 334 |
| Russian contracts | 25,000 | £4·75 | 119 | 23,000 | £4·87½ | 112 |
| Other contracts | 10,000 | £4·50 | 45 | 13,000 | £4·62½ | 60 |
|  | 248,500 | | £1,430 | 263,000 | | £1,569 |

|  | 1974–5 | | | 1975–6 | | |
|---|---|---|---|---|---|---|
| Fish | 176,000 | £7·00 | 1,232 | 189,000 | £7·50 | 1,417 |
| Mail order | 66,500 | £5·62½ | 374 | 70,000 | £5·75 | 403 |
| Russian contracts | 15,000 | £5·12½ | 77 | 6,000 | £5·25 | 31 |
| Other contracts | 10,500 | £5·00 | 52 | 11,000 | £5·00 | 55 |
|  | 268,000 | | £1,735 | 276,000 | | £1,906 |

The forecast sales of Fish, mail order and Russian-contract garments do not balance with expected production. The balance has been included in the sales as 'other contracts' at marginal selling prices which could be even lower than the Russian contracts. For each of the four years the average selling prices have been increased to allow for expected rises in costs.

3. *Cost of sales.* The material content of sales for 1970–71 and 1971–2 was approximately 50 per cent and is expected to remain at this level. Direct and indirect labour, outworkers' costs, etc. are expected to increase substantially in 1972–3 if wage proposals now under consideration are put into effect. It is expected that these costs will increase by 20 per cent in 1972–3 and in the following three years an average increase of 10 per cent per annum will be necessary to cover further increases in number of employees and wage rates.

4. *Factory, administration and selling expenses.* Consumable stores, selling salaries, carriage out, packing, advertising and discounts allowed are expected to increase in proportion to the rise in sales. Additional depreciation is set out in 8 below. The remainder of expenses is expected to increase by 10 per cent per annum.

5. *Trading profit.* The aim is to achieve a trading profit of 9 per cent, which has been the case in 1970–71 and 1971–2.

6. *Miscellaneous income.* Discounts receivable are expected to be at the same level as 1971–2, i.e. 2·57 per cent of material purchase. The balance of miscellaneous income is interest receivable, S.E.T. premium, training grant, etc., which, it is estimated, will total £7,500 per annum.

7. *Corporation tax and dividend policy.* The net effective rate of corporation tax is expected to be the same as for 1971–2. The objective is to increase the dividend (gross) by 10 per cent per annum.

8. *Capital expenditure and depreciation.* The forecast of capital expenditure and additional depreciation for the four years under review is

| | Plant and machinery | | Buildings | | Office equipment | |
| | Cost £ | Depreciation per annum £ | Cost £ | Depreciation per annum £ | Cost £ | Depreciation per annum £ |
|---|---|---|---|---|---|---|
| 1972–3 | 16,500 | 2,000 | | | | |
| 1973–4 | 8,250 | 1,000 | 25,000 | 500 | 5,000 | 500 |
| 1974–5 | 11,000 | 1,500 | | | | |
| 1975–6 | 8,000 | 1,000 | | | | |

9. *Stocks, debtors and creditors.* Sales for the four years are expected to increase by about 10 per cent per annum; volume of stocks and debtors will increase at the same rate. After allowing for the reduction in balance of United Weft Knitters' account, creditors also are expected to increase at 10 per cent per annum.

### Table 1

Estimated profit and loss account, year ending 31 March 1972

| | | £'000 | £'000 | % | % |
|---|---|---|---|---|---|
| Sales | | | | | |
| Fish | 142,500 at £6 | | 855 | | |
| Mail order | 57,500 at £4·50 | | 259 | | |
| Russian contract | 27,500 at £4·50 | | 123 | | |
| Other contracts | 14,500 at £2·70 | | 39 | | |
| | | | £1,276 | | 100 |
| Cost of sales | | | | | |
| Material | | 645 | | 50·57 | |
| Direct labour, overhead, etc. | | 158 | | 12·38 | |
| | | | 803 | | 62·95 |
| *Gross margin* | | | £473 | | 37·05 |
| Factory costs | | | | | |
| Consumable stores | | 14 | | 1·10 | |
| Depreciation | | 15 | | 1·21 | |
| Balance | | 79 | | 6·19 | |
| | | | 108 | | 8·50 |
| Administration | | | | | |
| Depreciation | | 10 | | 0·75 | |
| Balance | | 112 | | 8·77 | |
| | | | 122 | | 9·52 |
| Selling | | | | | |
| Salaries | | 46 | | 3·60 | |
| Carriage | | 8 | | 0·67 | |
| Packing | | 13 | | 0·98 | |
| Advertising | | 15 | | 1·14 | |
| Discounts | | 34 | | 2·70 | |
| Depreciation | | 1 | | 0·08 | |
| Balance | | 3 | | 0·27 | |
| | | | 120 | | 9·44 |
| *Total expenses* | | | £350 | | 27·46 |
| *Trading profit* | | | 123 | | 9·59 |
| Miscellaneous income | | | | | |
| Discounts | | 16 | | | |
| Balance | | 12 | | | |
| | | | 28 | | 2·23 |
| *Net profit* | | | £151 | | 11·82 |
| Corporation tax | | | 52 | | |
| *Net profit after tax* | | | £99 | | |

*Table 1 (Cont.)*

|  | £'000 | £'000 | % | % |
|---|---|---|---|---|
| Appropriation of profit |  |  |  |  |
| Proposed dividend (gross) |  | 50 |  |  |
| Retained in business |  | 49 |  |  |
|  |  | £99 |  |  |

*Table 2*

Estimated balance sheet as at 31 March 1972

|  | £'000 | £'000 | £'000 |
|---|---|---|---|
|  |  | Accumulated |  |
|  | Cost | depreciation |  |
| Fixed assets |  |  |  |
| Freehold premises | 50 | 15 | 35 |
| Leasehold premises | 100 | 10 | 90 |
| Plant and machinery | 110 | 40 | 70 |
| Office equipment | 20 | 9 | 11 |
|  | £280 | £74 | £206 |
| Current assets |  |  |  |
| Stocks |  | 101 |  |
| Debtors |  | 216 |  |
| Cash in hand |  | 12 |  |
|  |  | 329 |  |
| Current liabilities |  |  |  |
| Trade creditors and accrued expenses |  | 272 |  |
| Corporation tax |  | 52 |  |
| Proposed dividend (gross) |  | 50 |  |
|  |  | 374 |  |
| Net current assets |  |  | (45) |
| Net assets employed |  |  | £161 |

### Table 2 (Cont.)

| | £'000 |
|---|---|
| Financed by | |
| Share capital | 80 |
| Capital reserves | 10 |
| Revenue reserves | 71 |
| | £161 |

### Table 3

Estimated cash flow analysis, year ending 31 March 1972

| | £'000 |
|---|---|
| Internal sources of cash | |
| Net profit before taxation | 151 |
| Depreciation | 26 |
| Increase in trade creditors | 58 |
| | £235 |
| Uses of cash | |
| Expenditure on fixed assets | 27 |
| Increase in stocks | 20 |
| Increase in debtors | 14 |
| Corporation tax paid | 40 |
| Dividend paid (gross) | 45 |
| | £146 |
| Surplus of internal sources of cash | 89 |
| Repayment of bank loan | 50 |
| Net cash inflow for year | 39 |
| Bank overdraft at 1 April 1971 | 27 |
| Cash in hand 31 March 1972 | £12 |

QUESTION

What advice should Simpson give Cotton and Needle?

SUGGESTED BACKGROUND READING

1. *An Insight into Management Accounting*, Chapter 5.
2. G. P. E. Clarkson and B. J. Elliott, *Managing Money and Finance*, Gower Press, 1972, Part III.

# Knitted Garments Company*

THE KNITTED Garments Company, a subsidiary of Rochester Knitwear, was a manufacturer and distributor of cut and sewn and fully fashioned outerwear. The company had traded at a loss for a number of years. It produced a net loss before taxation of £165,000 for the year ending 31 December 1965 and this increased to £216,000 in 1966. During 1966 the company moved from its existing premises in Nottingham to a new factory in Peterlee. Expenses of, and resulting directly from, the removal to Peterlee (£13,000) were shown separately in the profit and loss account and not included in the loss of £216,000.

The original expectation of output from the new factory when fully equipped was 2,000–2,250 dozen garments per week. In September 1967 plant capacity, assuming a reasonable output and a full order book, was 1,555 dozen per week. The order book was far from full, however, and the budgeted output for 1967, 1968 and 1969 was:

|                                                      | Dozens per annum | % of 1 |
|------------------------------------------------------|------------------|--------|
| 1. Capacity of factory fully equipped and loaded     | 104,000          | 100    |
| 2. Full capacity of present plant if fully loaded    | 81,000           | 78     |
| 3. Current budgets                                   |                  |        |
| 1967                                                 | 30,000           | 29     |
| 1968                                                 | 40,000           | 38     |
| 1969                                                 | 53,000           | 51     |

1. was based on three-shift knitting and one-shift making-up.
2. was based on some positional rearrangement of plant.
1. and 2. depended on reasonable size of orders.

Expansion envisaged in 1968 and 1969 depended on engagement and training of additional knitting-machine operators.

*This case first appeared in *Management Accounting*, May 1972, pp. 120–26.

68

The management of Knitted Garments had received a statement of the estimated trading results for 1967 (shown in Tables 1 and 2), concluded that it was a long way off achieving its original objective (104,000 dozen per annum), and decided that two bases for future planning must be examined:

(a) Keep to the original objective and prepare a phased programme to achieve this objective;

(b) Abandon original objective and agree a new attainable objective.

It was recognized that the marketing implications of the two alternatives must be considered and that overhead expenditure would have to be brought into line with the expected level of operations. Overhead attributable to the building, including rent, rates, insurance, heat, light and part of power, amounted to £47,000. The cost attributable to the unused part of the building was estimated at £25,000. Overhead relating to administration mainly salaries, was out of line with the current level of output, being based on the full-capacity objective. Management recognized that these were policy-fixed costs and that, if a change in policy was agreed, these overhead costs would have to be adjusted accordingly.

The sales director, Mr Cashmere, was asked to prepare a projection of sales to 1971 and, after consulting distributors and customers, he predicted, 1968: 40,000 dozen, 1969: 53,000, 1970: 63,000, 1971: 73,500. In preparing his forecast Mr Cashmere recognized that because of technological advances in fully fashioned machinery the trend in knitted outerwear had moved away from cut and sewn to fully fashioned garments. Also, he considered that no future growth after 1971 could be predicted with certainty. The sales forecast indicated that present plant capacity would be effectively utilized in 1971. After discussion of the forecast, it was agreed that the original objective of 104,000 dozen garments a year should be abandoned and that a phased programme to achieve sales of 73,500 dozen garments in 1971 should be adopted. It was agreed also that the company should plan to increase the output of fully fashioned garments.

In November 1967 Mr Richards, financial director of Knitted Garments, prepared a budget for 1968, as in Table 3, which was submitted to Rochester Knitwear for approval. On 1 December 1967 Mr Tom Pringle, a financial analyst employed by the parent company, was sent by Mr Hardie, managing director of Rochester Knitwear, to Peterlee with a brief to

1. critically examine the budget for 1968 and report to Mr Hardie by 20 December;

2. prepare a financial plan to 1971 for submission to a meeting of Rochester Knitwear board of directors on 30 January 1968.

Mr Pringle began his examination of the 1968 budget by investigating the various elements. He made the following notes during his investigation:

## Materials

|  | Budget output in dozens | Standard cost per dozen of 1967 output | Budgeted cost 1968 |
|---|---|---|---|
|  |  | £ | £'000 |
| Fully fashioned | 24,151 | 6·625 | 160 |
| Cut and sewn | 9,915 | 8·850 | 87 |
| Jersey dresses | 983 | 28·000 | 28 |
| Standard cost of budgeted output |  |  | 275 |
| Allowance for excess of actual over budget |  |  | 13 |
| Per budget |  |  | 288 |

5 per cent allowance is reasonable, being calculated actual material variances; the materials budget is acceptable.

## Wages

|  | Budget output in dozens | Actual cost per dozen in 1967 |  |
|---|---|---|---|
|  |  | £ | £'000 |
| Fully fashioned | 24,151 | 3·95 | 95 |
| Cut and sewn and jersey dresses | 10,898 | 2·62 | 29 |
| Cost of budgeted output at 1967 costs |  |  | 124 |
| Budgeted labour cost, 1968 |  |  | 106 |
| 1968 budget shows improvement of |  |  | £18 |

The 14·7 per cent improvement is expected to arise from increased productivity and lower piece rates. An analysis of the improvement shows:

|  | Cost at 1967 level* £'000 | Costs in budget £'000 | Difference £'000 |
|---|---|---|---|
| Productive wages | 90 | 79 | 11 |
| Non-productive wages | 18 | 13 | 5 |
| Cost of living | 16 | 14 | 2 |
|  | £124 | £106 | £18 |

* Analysed on the basis of November 1967.

## Table 1
### Profit and Loss Account

|  | 1966 £'000 | Estimate 1967 £'000 |
|---|---|---|
| Sales |  |  |
| Retail | 566 | 339 |
| Contract | 147 | 153 |
| Jobbing and seconds | 95 | 76 |
|  | 808 | 568 |
| Cost of sales |  |  |
| Materials | 271 | 231 |
| Wages | 131 | 105 |
| Fixed overhead | 136 | 139 |
|  | 538 | 475 |
| Increase in finished goods | (45) | (7) |
| Bought in garments | 312 | 140 |
|  | 805 | 608 |
| Margin | 3 | (40) |
| Selling and distribution costs | 124 | 104 |
| General administrative overhead | 95 | 71 |
|  | 219 | 175 |
| Loss before tax | (216) | (215) |
| Output in dozens | 34,586 | 29,388 |

*Table 2*
Estimated Balance Sheet as at 31 December 1967

|  | £'000 | £'000 |
|---|---|---|
| Fixed assets | | |
| Property | | 43 |
| Tenants and improvements | | 6 |
| Plant and machinery | | 268 |
| Motor vehicles | | 16 |
| Fixtures and fittings | | 44 |
| Canteen equipment | | 10 |
| Total cost | | 387 |
| *less* Accumulated depreciation | | 166 |
| *Book value* | | 221 |
| Goodwill | | 50 |
| Current assets | | |
| Stocks and work in progress | 300 | |
| Debtors and payment in advance | 102 | |
| Subvention | 130 | |
| Cash | 2 | |
| | 534 | |
| Current liabilities | | |
| Creditors and accrued expenses | 71 | |
| Due under hire-purchase agreements | 12 | |
| Bank overdraft | 172 | |
| | 255 | |
| *Net current assets* | | 279 |
| *Net assets employed* | | 550 |
| Sources of capital | | |
| Ordinary shares | | 300 |
| Reserves | | 48 |
| Loan from parent company | | 202 |
| | | 550 |

*Table 3*
Budgeted profit and loss account 1968

|  | £'000 |
|---|---|
| Sales | |
|   Retail | 413 |
|   Contract | 294 |
|   Jobbing and seconds | 88 |
|  | 795 |
| Cost of sales | |
|   Materials | 288 |
|   Wages | 106 |
|   Fixed overhead | 150 |
|  | 544 |
| Bought in garments | 175 |
|  | 719 |
| Margin | 76 |
| Selling, distribution costs | 117 |
| General administration | 67 |
|  | 184 |
| Loss before tax | (108) |
| Output in dozens | |
|   Fully fashioned | 24,151 |
|   Cut and sewn | 9,915 |
|   Jersey dresses | 983 |
|  | 35,049 |

The difference in cost of living can represent only a reduced labour force producing an equivalent output. The difference in non-productive wages is compatible with this. The increase in productivity of about 11 per cent and a reduction in the present piece rates of 12 per cent are not unattainable. However, their influence on the budget needs to be noted and, in particular, the conditions attaching to the increase in productivity, including acceptable batch sizes and improved manufacturing times, need to be defined. If an 11 per cent increase in productivity is not achieved, a reduction of output compared to budget would give an increased loss of £25,000 or an increase in wages cost of £4,000–4,500 for budgeted output. If reduction in piece rates is not obtained, the increased cost of wages will be £13,500. The wages budget is acceptable if revised to £112,000. Training costs included in factory overhead of £9,000 are acceptable.

*Factory, selling and distribution, and administration overhead:* compare favourably with expected normal level.

*Product profitability:* Is Mr Cashmere correct in advising an increase in fully fashioned sales? In 1967 50 per cent were contract sales and 50 per cent retail sales. The retail sales consisted of 56⅔ per cent at full price, 28⅓ per cent at reduced price and 15 per cent job sales.

Seconds were 6 per cent of output. Selling prices obtained were:

|  | Fully fashioned £ per dozen | Cut and sewn £ per dozen |
|---|---|---|
| Contract sales | 15·5 | 13·7 |
| Retail sales |  |  |
| Full price | 20·2 | 17·9 |
| Reduced price | 15·5 | 13·7 |
| Job sales | 13·5 | 11·9 |
| Seconds | 12·3 | 10·7 |
| Variable costs per dozen: | Fully fashioned £ per dozen | Cut and sewn £ per dozen |
| Material at standard cost | 6·625 | 8·850 |
| Labour at actual 1967 | 3·950 | 2·620 |
| Variable cost | £10·575 | £11·470 |

The average contribution per dozen of fully fashioned garments sold is £5·84 and for cut and sewn garments £3·04 (see Table 4). Both use similar inputs of machine capacity and, although different machines are used on each line, the purchase of new or replacement machines could just as easily be fully fashioned as cut and sewn. The greatest substitution of fully fashioned for cut and sewn should be made. Mr Cashmere recommends, however, that fully fashioned sales should not exceed more than 75 per cent of total sales; cut and sewn sales do make a positive contribution to overheads. Endorse the decision to increase fully fashioned sales to 75 per cent of total if this does not reduce the total sales volume. Mr Cashmere is preparing a schedule of sales, introducing the new mix, so that the eventual outcome will be 75 per cent fully fashioned and 25 per cent cut and sewn in 1969.

*Table 4*

Product Profitability

| | Selling price per dozen £ | Variable cost per dozen £ | Contribution per dozen £ | % of total sales | Average contribution per dozen £ |
|---|---|---|---|---|---|
| Fully fashioned | | | | | |
| Contract | 15·5 | 10·575 | 4·925 | 47·00 | 2·31 |
| Retail | | | | | |
| Full price | 20·2 | 10·575 | 9·625 | 26·63 | 2·56 |
| Reduced price | 15·5 | 10·575 | 4·925 | 13·32 | 0·66 |
| Job | 13·5 | 10·575 | 2·925 | 7·05 | 0·21 |
| Seconds | 12·3 | 10·575 | 1·725 | 6·00 | 0·10 |
| | | | | 100·00 | £5·84 |
| Cut and sewn | | | | | |
| Contract | 13·7 | 11·470 | 2·23 | 47·00 | 1·05 |
| Retail | | | | | |
| Full price | 17·9 | 11·470 | 6·43 | 26·63 | 1·71 |
| Reduced price | 13·7 | 11·470 | 2·23 | 13·32 | 0·30 |
| Job | 11·9 | 11·470 | 0·43 | 7·05 | 0·03 |
| Seconds | 10·7 | 11·470 | (0·77) | 6·00 | (0·05) |
| | | | | 100·00 | £3·04 |

*Sales.* The original sales budget failed to account for finished goods in the warehouse awaiting dispatch and invoicing at year ends. After consultation with Mr Cashmere the sales budget has been revised:

|  | Original budget £'000 | Revised £'000 | Difference £'000 |
|---|---|---|---|
| Retail | 413 | 480 | +67 |
| Contract | 294 | 201 | −93 |
| Jobbing and seconds | 88 | 97 | +9 |
|  | £795 | £778 | £−17 |

Comparison of 1967 and 1968

|  | 1967 £'000 | 1968 £'000 | Improvement £'000 | % |
|---|---|---|---|---|
| Retail | 339 | 480 | 141 | 42 |
| Contract | 153 | 201 | 48 | 32 |
| Jobbing and seconds | 76 | 97 | 21 | 26 |
|  | £568 | £778 | £210 | 37 |

A large increase in sales is budgeted, but sales in 1966 were £808,000, of which £566,000 were retail. This budget has been based on a detailed quantity forecast by type of garment. However, to achieve the budget, the size of order must be acceptable. Minimum economic size of order on the factory are 100 dozen of one style of classic or neo-classic garment and 25 dozen of one style of fancy garment. The delivery period should be twelve weeks from receipt of a sales order.

*Profit and loss account.* A revised profit and loss account has been prepared (Table 5). A budgeted loss of £125,000 for 1968 appears reasonable, subject to improved productivity and lower piece rates. The contingency allowance of £18,000 is a balancing figure. Part of the allowance may be required to meet cost of management changes.

A budgeted balance sheet as at 31 December 1968 has also been prepared (Table 6). The management is planning to spend £38,500 on fully fashioned machinery during the year in accordance with the policy to increase the production of fully fashioned knitwear. The increase in stocks of £63,000 is made up of yarn and work in progress £36,000, sundry stocks and fittings £3,000 and finished stocks £24,000. These increases appear to be consistent with the rise in output and the higher proportion of fully fashioned knitwear. The company has bank permission to extend its overdraft to £237,500 in 1968; thereafter some reduction is expected.

On the basis of these notes, Mr Pringle prepared his report and sent it to Mr Hardie on 18 December.

*Table 5*

Revised Budgeted Profit and Loss Account 1968

|  | £'000 |
|---|---|
| Sales |  |
| Retail | 480 |
| Contract | 201 |
| Jobbing | 97 |
|  | 778 |
| Cost of sales |  |
| Materials | 288 |
| Wages | 112 |
| Fixed overhead | 150 |
|  | 550 |
| Increase in finished stocks | (24) |
| Bought in garments | 175 |
|  | 701 |
| Margin | 77 |
| Selling and distribution costs | 117 |
| General administration overhead | 67 |
| Contingency allowance | 18 |
|  | 202 |
| *Loss* | (125) |
| *Output in dozens* | 35,049 |

*Table 6*

Budgeted Balance Sheet as at 31 December 1968

|  | £'000 |
|---|---|
| Fixed assets | |
| Property | 43 |
| Tenants and improvements | 6 |
| Plant and machinery | 307 |
| Motor vehicles | 16 |
| Fixtures and fittings | 44 |
| Canteen equipment | 10 |
| Total cost | 426 |
| *less* Accumulated depreciation | 206 |
| Book value | 220 |
| Goodwill | 50 |
| Current assets (net) | |
| Stocks and work in progress | 363 |
| Debtors less creditors | 28 |
| Subvention payments | 125 |
| Bank overdraft | (236) |
| *Net current assets* | 280 |
| *Net assets employed* | 550 |
| Shares | 300 |
| Reserves | 48 |
| Loan | 202 |
| | 550 |

# LONG-TERM FINANCIAL PLAN

After Christmas, Mr Pringle met the directors of Knitted Garments Company to agree the output assumptions on which the financial plan should be based. It was agreed:

1. production and sales should be built up to 1,585 dozen garments a week by October 1970 and that 1971 would be the first full year at this level of production;

2. the proportion of fully fashioned garments would be increased to 75 per cent of output during 1969 and the normal

## Table 7
### Output Forecast 1969–71

Output budget (dozens)

| Year | Periods | No. of working weeks | Fully fashioned | | Cut and sewn | | Jersey dress | |
|---|---|---|---|---|---|---|---|---|
| | | | Average weekly | Total | Average weekly | Total | Average weekly | Total |
| 1969 | 1, 2, 3 | 11 | 695 | 7,640 | 300 | 3,300 | 25 | 275 |
| | 4–10 | 26 | 802·5 | 20,865 | 300 | 7,800 | 37·5 | 975 |
| | 11, 12, 13 | 12 | 910 | 10,920 | 300 | 3,600 | 50 | 600 |
| | | 49 | | 39,425 | | 14,700 | | 1,850 |
| 1970 | 1, 2, 3 | 11 | 910 | 10,010 | 300 | 3,300 | 50 | 550 |
| | 4–10 | 26 | 1,017·5 | 26,455 | 337·5 | 8,775 | 67·5 | 1,625 |
| | 11, 12, 13 | 12 | 1,125 | 13,500 | 375 | 4,500 | 75 | 900 |
| | | 49 | | 49,965 | | 16,575 | | 3,075 |
| 1971 | Normal | 49 | 1,125 | 55,125 | 375 | 18,375 | 87·5 | 4,165 |

production of 1,585 dozen garments a week should be made up of 1,125 dozen fully fashioned garments, 375 dozen cut and sewn and 85 dozen jersey dresses.

On these assumptions Mr Cotton, the production director, prepared an output forecast to 1971 (Table 7). He estimated also that expenditure on new machinery would be necessary, 1969: £42,000, 1970: £45,000, 1971: nil.

Mr Cashmere used Mr Cotton's forecast as the basis for a forecast of normal sales (Table 8). In preparing his quantity forecast, he assumed contract sales and retail sales in dozens would each represent 50 per cent of total sales, and that retail sales would consist of $56\frac{2}{3}$ per cent full-price, $28\frac{1}{3}$ per cent reduced-price and 15 per cent job sales. He allowed for 6 per cent of output as seconds.

*Table 8*

Forecast Normal Sales

| Quantity (dozens) | Total | Own production | | | Bought in | |
|---|---|---|---|---|---|---|
| | | Fully fashioned | Cut and sewn | Jersey dress | Jersey dress | Hosiery |
| Contract sales | 37,235 | 25,909 | 8,636 | 2,690 | — | |
| Retail sales (full price) | 23,378 | 14,682 | 4,894 | 1,041 | 2,761 | |
| (reduced price) | 9,788 | 7,341 | 2,447 | — | — | |
| Job sales | 5,853 | 3,886 | 1,295 | 184 | 488 | |
| | 76,254 | 51,818 | 17,272 | 3,915 | 3,249 | |
| Seconds (6%) | 4,660 | 3,307 | 1,103 | 250 | — | |
| Total sales | 80,914 | 55,125 | 18,375 | 4,165 | 3,249 | |
| *Value (£)* | | | | | | |
| Contract sales | 627,270 | 401,841 | 118,313 | 107,116 | — | |
| Retail sales (full price) | | 296,126 | 87,309 | 53,914 | 143,018 | 30,000 |
| (reduced price) | 757,750 | 113,859 | 33,524 | — | — | |
| Job sales | 90,877 | 52,274 | 15,417 | 6,353 | 16,833 | |
| Seconds | 59,618 | 40,054 | 11,797 | 7,767 | — | |
| Total sales | 1,535,515 | 904,154 | 266,360 | 175,150 | 159,851 | 30,000 |

To translate his quantity forecasts into sales values he used current price levels. Mr Pringle used this information to prepare

the profit and loss forecasts for 1969, 1970 and 1971 (Table 9).
He calculated the materials and wages on the same basis as the
1968 budget. He studied the fixed factory overhead and allowed
for the steps in cost that would result from the increases in output.
In estimating the selling and distribution expenses he recognized
that the company operates its own fleet of vehicles. The small
increase in general administration overhead reflected the fact
that the company had a management staff out of line with its
current level of activity. Bank-overdraft interest was included in
general-administration costs, and this was expected to fall
slightly in 1969 and 1970 and more in 1971. A profit of £75,000
in 1971 appeared to Mr Pringle to be reasonable.

*Table 9*

Forecast Profit and Loss Accounts 1968–71

|  | 1968 | 1969 | 1970 | 1971 |
|---|---|---|---|---|
| Output in dozens | 35,049 | 55,975 | 69,615 | 77,665 |
| *Sales* | £'000 | £'000 | £'000 | £'000 |
| Retail | 480 | 595 | 670 | 758 |
| Contract | 201 | 402 | 562 | 627 |
| Job and seconds | 97 | 108 | 137 | 150 |
|  | 778 | 1,105 | 1,369 | 1,535 |
| *Cost of sales* |  |  |  |  |
| Materials | 288 | 465 | 592 | 645 |
| Wages | 112 | 175 | 215 | 231 |
| Fixed overhead | 150 | 170 | 197 | 205 |
| Cost of output | 550 | 810 | 1,004 | 1,081 |
| Less increase in stock | 24 | 15 | 20 | — |
| Cost of own sales | 526 | 795 | 984 | 1,081 |
| Bought in | 175 | 160 | 160 | 156 |
|  | 701 | 955 | 1,144 | 1,237 |
| Margin | 77 | 150 | 225 | 298 |
| Selling and distribution expenses | 117 | 127 | 132 | 142 |
| General administration | 67 | 67 | 68 | 69 |
| Contingency | 18 | 16 | 15 | 12 |
|  | 202 | 210 | 215 | 223 |
| Profit/(loss) before tax | (125) | (60) | 10 | 75 |

Next he prepared balance-sheet forecasts (Table 10). The increases in stocks, work in progress, creditors and debtors allowed for the build-up in production and sales to October 1971. He assumed that the company would receive subvention payments* to cover the losses in 1968 and 1969 so as to minimize the group's taxation liability. Mr Pringle noted the small reductions in the bank overdraft in 1969 and 1970 and the substantial reduction in 1971, and that Rochester Knitwear did not need to inject additional finance other than the subvention payments.

Before writing his report to Mr Hardie, Mr Pringle examined the return which Rochester Knitwear would receive on its investment in Knitted Garments; £379,000 had been paid for the share capital of Knitted Garments and a further loan of £202,000 made. To this he added the net subvention payments for 1968 and 1969 and calculated the return on investment:

### Return on Parent Company's Investment

|  |  |  | £'000 |
|---|---|---|---|
| Share capital |  |  | 379 |
| Loan from parent company |  |  | 202 |
|  |  |  | 581 |
| *add* Subvention payments |  |  |  |
|  |  | Tax at 40% |  |
|  | Gross | in £ |  |
| 1968 | 125 | 50 |  |
| 1969 | 60 | 24 |  |
|  |  | — | 111 |
| *Parent company's investment* |  |  | £692 |

* When a company has a deficit for tax purposes for any accounting period of the company, and receives a subvention for that period from an associated company which has a surplus for tax purposes in the corresponding period, then in computing the profits or losses of these companies the payment is treated as a trading receipt to one company on the last day of the accounting period in which it has the deficit and is allowed as a deduction to the other company as if it were a trading expense incurred on that day. There must be an agreement allowing for such payments, however.

Return on Parent Company's Investment (*Cont.*)

| Year | Profit £ | Return on investment % |
|------|----------|------------------------|
| 1970 | 10,000 | 1·5 |
| 1971 | 75,000 | 10·5 |
| 1972 onwards | 75,000+ | 10·5+ |

## Table 10
### Forecast Balance Sheet 1968–71

| | As at 31 Dec. 1967 | Increases/decreases | | | | As at 31 Dec. 1971 |
|---|---|---|---|---|---|---|
| | | 1968 | 1969 | 1970 | 1971 | |
| | £'000 | £'000 | £'000 | £'000 | £'000 | £'000 |
| Fixed assets | | | | | | |
| Property | 43 | | | | | 43 |
| Tenants' improvements | 6 | | | | | 6 |
| Plant and machinery | 268 | 38 | 42 | 45 | — | 393 |
| Motor vehicles | 16 | · | | | | 16 |
| Fixtures and fittings | 44 | | | | | 44 |
| Canteen equipment | 10 | | | | | 10 |
| Total cost | 387 | 38 | 42 | 45 | — | 512 |
| Less depreciation | 166 | 40 | 43 | 47 | 50 | 346 |
| Book value | 221 | (2) | (1) | (2) | (50) | 166 |
| Goodwill | 50 | | | | | 50 |
| Current assets (net) | | | | | | |
| Finished stocks | | 24 | 16 | 20 | | |
| Sundry stocks and fittings | 300 | 3 | 2 | 3 | | 464 |
| Yarn and work in progress | | 36 | 29 | 31 | | |
| Debtors/Creditors | 19 | 10 | 10 | 10 | | 49 |
| Subventions | 130 | (130) | (125) | (60) | | |
| | | 125 | 60 | — | | |
| Bank overdraft | (170) | (66) | 9 | 8 | 125 | (94) |
| Net current assets | 279 | 2 | 1 | 12 | 125 | 419 |
| Net assets employed | 550 | — | — | 10 | 75 | 635 |
| Sources of capital | | | | | | |
| Shares | 300 | | | | | 300 |
| Reserves | 48 | | | 10 | 75 | 133 |
| Loan | 202 | | | | | 202 |
| | 550 | — | — | 10 | 75 | 635 |

Mr Pringle completed his calculations on the evening of 23 January, which left him three days in which to write his report and arrange for copies to be circulated to the board of directors three days before their meeting on 30 January. When he arrived at his temporary office in Peterlee next morning, there was a note from Mr Cashmere on his desk.

'Mr Pringle', said the note, 'we have had to revise our sales budget for 1968. I have visited a number of our customers and distributors in Britain and the rest of Europe recently and they have lowered their sales estimate for the second half of 1968. I have revised the retail-sales budget to £429,000, which will increase our budgeted loss by £5,000.

'I have agreed with Mr Cotton that we should not reduce our output, which means that our finished stock at the end of 1968 will increase from £24,500 to £69,500.'

Mr Pringle sat down to write his report.

QUESTIONS

1. What are the main points Mr Pringle should make in his report?
2. Evaluate Mr Pringle's approach
   (a) when examining the budget for 1968;
   (b) when preparing the financial plan to 1971.
3. Can realistic long-range financial plans be developed by hosiery and knitwear companies producing fashion products, and faced with a choice of methods of knitting subject to different rates of technological change?

SUGGESTED BACKGROUND READING

*An Insight into Management Accounting*, Chapters 5 and 7.

# Hardwood, Softwood & Plywood Company*

THE Hardwood, Softwood & Plywood Company are timber traders, sawmillers, manufacturers and general merchants. The company has trading branches located in Belfast, Bath, Cardiff, Greenock, Manchester, Leeds, Newcastle, Birmingham, Nottingham and a further three in London. It also has a number of plants manufacturing plywoods, wallboards, etc., which are sold to trading branches, builders' merchants, furniture manufacturers, other timber merchants, etc. The company was first registered in 1908, and had a turnover in 1969 of £23 million and a profit before taxation of £800,000. The company's net assets employed on 31 December 1969 amounted to £5·35 million (see Table 1).

*Table 1*

Financial Information 1968 and 1969

|  | 1968 | | 1969 | |
|  | £'000 | £'000 | £'000 | £'000 |
|---|---|---|---|---|
| *Turnover* | | 19,935 | | 22,950 |
| Trading profit | | 690 | | 1,115 |
| Directors' emoluments | 56 | | 60 | |
| Depreciation | 118 | | 138 | |
| Interest paid less received | 95 | | 117 | |
| | | 269 | | 315 |
| *Profit before Tax* | | 421 | | 800 |
| Corporation tax | | 130 | | 290 |
| *Net Profit* | | £291 | | £510 |
| Current assets | | | | |
| Stocks | | 3,075 | | 2,785 |
| Debtors | | 4,000 | | 4,838 |
| Bills receivable | | 156 | | 106 |
| Cash | | 326 | | 420 |
| | | 7,557 | | 8,149 |

*This case first appeared in *Accounting and Business Research*, No. 3 summer 1971, pp. 250–57.

*Table 1 (Cont.)*

|  | 1968 |  | 1969 |  |
|  | £'000 | £'000 | £'000 | £'000 |
|---|---|---|---|---|
| Current liabilities |  |  |  |  |
| Creditors | 2,288 |  | 2,513 |  |
| Bills payable | 71 |  | 80 |  |
| Bank overdraft | 1,669 |  | 1,524 |  |
| Corporation tax | 92 |  | 162 |  |
| Ordinary dividend | 120 |  | 147 |  |
|  |  | 4,240 |  | 4,426 |
| *Net current assets* |  | £3,317 |  | £3,723 |
| Fixed assets |  |  |  |  |
| Freehold properties |  | 959 |  | 983 |
| Leasehold properties |  | 205 |  | 200 |
| Plant and machinery |  | 281 |  | 288 |
| Vehicles |  | 57 |  | 87 |
| Furniture |  | 16 |  | 21 |
|  |  | £1,518 |  | £1,579 |
| *Investments* |  | 56 |  | 46 |
| *Net assets employed* |  | £4,891 |  | £5,348 |

Each branch or plant is run by a manager as a profit centre with its own assets employed and profit and loss account. Managers are required to prepare annually for their unit budgets for sales, costs, capital expenditure and assets employed for the forthcoming year by months. Each month returns are made to head office comparing actual with budgeted performance. Mr Teak, the managing director of Hardwood, Softwood & Plywood Company, recognizes that the company has a number of growth opportunities, but is under some pressure from the company's bankers to maintain the company's bank overdraft at its present level. He wishes to secure a more effective allocation of capital to units and to encourage each manager to improve the return on the capital his unit employs. He has developed with Mr Sawdust, the financial director, the concept of *interest-free capital* for this purpose. On 1 December 1969 he sent the following memorandum to all branch and plant managers.

# FORECAST BUDGETS AND MONTHLY ACCOUNTS

My memorandum of 13 November requesting your 1970 forecasts referred to the need for the planned progressive development of each unit and a substantial increased return on the capital that each unit employs. In this connection we are introducing as from 1 January 1970 certain changes in the monthly returns and I should like to give you further information about these.

## 1. BACKGROUND TO CHANGES

The main limiting factor in our expansion is the availability of capital. *We can raise additional permanent capital if there is a sufficiently strong case based on the prospective additional profits that we can achieve with its use.* At present the average rate of return on capital that we employ is too low and this makes it necessary for us over the next year or two to withdraw money from prospectively less profitable units in order to make possible the expansion that we want to see in prospectively more profitable units.

We would like to encourage the manager of each unit to apply for a much larger capital allocation if, by employing more money, he can increase his unit's profitability. There is, of course, a top limit to the amount of capital available which must be watched by us. At the same time we want to encourage him to economize wherever practicable in the use of money both on short term (this means the control of stocks and debtors) and long term (this involves the termination of operations that are insufficiently profitable). In allocating capital for the coming financial year we shall be guided by the prospective profit from its use that the manager indicates in the forecast budget as well as by any longer range development plans.

## 2. PRINCIPAL CHANGES

From 1 January 1970 the monthly accounts for each unit will be drawn up with a view to emphasizing the objectives and limitations that apply to the company as a whole.

Our available resources are obtained as follows:

(*a*) Shareholders' funds represented by issued share capital *and* reserves on which we have to try to produce the highest possible return on a maintainable basis.

(*b*) Fluctuating trade credit from our suppliers.

(*c*) Bank facilities.

The total of these resources is applied principally to

  (i) stocks,

 (ii) debtors,

(iii) fixed assets.

Each unit employs a certain amount of capital (money) which may be regarded as being permanently invested in its business. In future we shall call this permanent capital of each unit its *interest-free capital*. This will consist of its fixed assets plus a rough but effective estimate (which we propose to revise annually or if necessary more frequently) of its normal *minimum* level of stocks and debtors at any time during the year. We shall of course view it in conjunction with your forecast of profitability. Our regular revision of your *interest-free capital* will ensure that changes in the basic hard core of trading capital requirements are taken into consideration.

In addition to this permanent *interest-free capital*, each unit has fluctuating requirements for additional money which in general must come from the group's bank overdraft. We shall fix each unit's maximum capital allocation in relation to its trading possibilities. The money employed by each unit over and above its *interest-free capital* will in future be charged for at a rate of $\frac{1}{2}$ per cent over bank rate subject to a minimum of 5 per cent. Special adjustments will be made as hitherto for exceptional credit terms obtained from suppliers.

In future each unit's maximum capital allocation will be subject to more frequent and substantial change – either upwards or downwards – in the light of its respective requirements and the profitability as set out in its forecast budget. From January 1970 onwards the profit of each unit will be expressed in the monthly accounts as a *percentage annual rate of return on its interest-free capital*. This profit will of course be struck after charging interest on the money used in excess of its *interest-free capital*.

## 3. WHAT ARE THE ADVANTAGES OF THIS NEW METHOD OF OPERATING?

First of all each unit will have a strong incentive to keep its *interest-free capital* down to the lowest possible level in order to maximize the rate of return on it. This means rigorous and continuing control of debtors and stocks.

Secondly the wisdom of taking on a particular business by utilizing the extra capital on which interest is payable will depend upon the gross profitability of that business, upon the stock requirements it creates and the length of credit that has to be given to achieve the business.

Thirdly the new method of analysing your operations will give guide lines for improving the rate of return on *interest-free capital*. The manager of each unit will be giving continuous consideration to the opportunity to expand his unit and conversely to reorganizing or terminating operations that reduce his unit's rate of return on *interest-free capital*, which might release money for expansion in more profitable operations. When opportunities for expansion arise the manager will have to persuade us to increase his maximum capital allocation on the basis of his plan for making that increased capital earn a substantial rate of return.

## 4. HEAD-OFFICE CHARGES

In future we shall extract from the head-office charges that are debited to branches the basic cost of group management – items such as directors' salaries not already apportioned, certain administrative salaries such as statistician, etc. – leaving only the charges which are attributable to you in your accounts. Although they are not all fully under your control this breakdown will simplify your costing.

## 5. MANAGEMENT BONUS SCHEME

All these changes will affect the present management-incentive bonus scheme, which will have to be altered, and we hope to have the revisions ready shortly.

## 6. INTEREST-FREE CAPITAL ESTIMATE

Will you now please prepare your estimate of *interest-free capital* that you require for 1970, on the attached form (Table 2) and submit this figure to Mr Sawdust not later than 1 February.

A. N. TEAK

*Table 2*
Asset Requirements for 1970

|  | Minimum (interest-free) amount £ | Average amount over 12 months £ | Maximum requirement £ |
|---|---|---|---|
| Fixed assets |  |  |  |
| Stocks |  |  |  |
| Book debts and bills receivable |  |  |  |
| Import deposit | NIL |  |  |

*Notes*

1. *Fixed assets*

Estimate net book value at 31 December 1969, and add 50 per cent of proposed additions for 1970. Enter the result in all three columns.

2. *Stocks*

The amount for the middle column should correspond with estimated average stock required in 1970 forecast.

3. *Import deposit*

Import-deposit balances will not form part of the interest-free assets. They will be subject to interest charged monthly in overheads and this cost must be balanced by extra gross-profit margin.

*The interest-free-assets amount* will form the basis for charging interest and for assessing the annual return of net profit.

The completed asset-requirement forms were vetted by Mr Sawdust's staff, and summarized as in Tables 3 and 4. This information was presented to Mr Teak who agreed with Mr Sawdust the maximum capital allocation for each unit. On 11 January 1970 Mr Teak sent the letter printed below to unit managers.

*Table 3*

Budget Forecasts for the Year Ending 31 December 1970
Profitability of Units

|  | Total | Belfast | Bath | Cardiff | Greenock etc. |
|---|---|---|---|---|---|
| Sales and transfers | | | | | |
| Softwoods | | | | | |
| Hardwoods | | | | | |
| Plywoods | | | | | |
| Wallboards and sundries | | | | | |
| Sawing | | | | | |
| | | | | | |
| Gross profits | | | | | |
| Softwoods | | | | | |
| Hardwoods | | | | | |
| Plywoods | | | | | |
| Wallboards and sundries | | | | | |
| Sawing | | | | | |
| | | | | | |
| Percentage of gross profits on sales and transfers | | | | | |
| Overheads | | | | | |
| Own | | | | | |
| H.O. Service Charges | | | | | |
| Wear and Tear | | | | | |
| Interest at 8 per cent on Excess Assets Usage | | | | | |
| | | | | | |
| Net profit | | | | | |
| Interest-free assets | | | | | |
| Annual return of net profit on interest-free assets | | | | | |

*Table 4*

Budget Forecasts for the Year Ending 31 December 1970
Asset Requirements

| | Total | Belfast | Bath | Cardiff | Greenock etc. |
|---|---|---|---|---|---|
| **Minimum (interest-free)** | | | | | |
| Fixed assets | | | | | |
| Stocks | | | | | |
| Book-debts and B/R | | | | | |
| Import deposit | — | — | — | — | — |
| | | | | | |
| **Average** | | | | | |
| Fixed assets | | | | | |
| Stocks | | | | | |
| Book-debts and B/R | | | | | |
| Import deposit | | | | | |
| | | | | | |
| **Maximum** | | | | | |
| Fixed assets | | | | | |
| Stocks | | | | | |
| Book-debts and B/R | | | | | |
| Import deposit | | | | | |
| | | | | | |
| Excess of average usage over minimum (interest-free) | | | | | |
| Interest cost at 8 per cent per annum | | | | | |

# CAPITAL ALLOCATIONS: INTEREST-FREE AND MAXIMUM CAPITALS

At the foot of this note you will see that the interest-free capital for the financial year 1970 and the maximum capital allocated to your branch are shown.

## 1. INTEREST-FREE CAPITAL

We have already discussed this concept in detail and your rate of return on capital will be calculated by relating your net profit to your interest-free capital. This capital should be your normal minimum requirements for the running of the business, including your fixed assets.

## 2. MAXIMUM CAPITAL

In addition to your interest-free capital a further amount of capital is allocated to you which it is our intention that you should utilize *to the full extent* that you can profitably do so. This capital will be available to you at bank rate plus ½ per cent so that in utilizing it you will be able to calculate the marginal costs of its use and ensure that a profit is made over and above the marginal cost of the money.

## 3. 'PEAK' CAPITAL

There will be some occasions when, having exhausted your maximum capital, you have the opportunity of increasing your business and its profitability by the use of a still further quantity of money. This the board encourage you to do provided they have the funds available. No figure of 'peak' capital will be given as availability will depend upon the day-by-day position of the company. However, if you can see your way to do what appears to you to be a profitable business, having calculated the marginal cost of the money at bank rate plus ½ per cent (as well as all other known costs), you are invited to advise us immediately

*Table 5.* Operating Statement: Months to ............

|  | Corresponding period previous year | Total | Belfast | Bath | Cardiff | Greenock etc. |
|---|---|---|---|---|---|---|
| Sales for month |  |  |  |  |  |  |
| Sales to date<br>Transfers to other units |  |  |  |  |  |  |
| Total sales and transfers |  |  |  |  |  |  |
| Forecast sales and transfers |  |  |  |  |  |  |
| Gross profit to date |  |  |  |  |  |  |
| Gross percentage on sales and transfers |  |  |  |  |  |  |
| Forecast gross-profit percentage |  |  |  |  |  |  |
| Interest receivable |  |  |  |  |  |  |
| Overheads: Own<br>H.O. service charges<br>Wear and tear<br>Interest charges |  |  |  |  |  |  |
| Net trading profit |  |  |  |  |  |  |
| *less* Group administrative costs |  |  |  |  |  |  |
| Group net profit |  |  |  |  |  |  |
| Interest-free capital |  |  |  |  |  |  |
| Annual return on interest-free capital |  |  |  |  |  |  |
| Maximum capital allowance |  |  |  |  |  |  |
| Capital employed at month-end:<br>Fixed assets<br>Stocks and work in progress<br>Book-debts and bills received<br>Import deposit |  |  |  |  |  |  |
| Excess C/E over interest-free capital |  |  |  |  |  |  |
| Capital chargeable to interest |  |  |  |  |  |  |
| Percentage of average book debts to average two months sales |  |  |  |  |  |  |
| Book debts include<br>Bills Held<br>Discounted |  |  |  |  |  |  |

of the details of the proposed business, the amount of additional capital required, the period over which it will be outstanding and the estimated net profit which will result from its usage. We will then tell you immediately whether you may have the additional amount and for how long.

*Interest-free capital* £              *Maximum capital* £

                                            A. N. TEAK

During 1970 the units made their normal monthly returns comparing actual with forecast sales, costs, profits, assets employed, etc., and incorporated the interest charge on capital in excess of the interest-free capital. Each month a cumulative operating statement (Table 5) was prepared for Mr Teak. A number of units showed increasing annual returns on interest-free capital, and in most cases units held their capital employed within the maximum capital allowance. A small reduction in the company's bank overdraft was achieved. Mr Teak felt his concept of *interest-free capital* was a good one.

On 10 November 1970 Mr Sawdust requested unit managers to submit their estimates of capital requirements for 1971. In his letter Mr Sawdust gave the following guidance to unit managers:

Valuations are being made of the land and buildings occupied at each unit in the group and the probable result will be the elimination of these assets from the capital employment and a rent charge substituted.

The group are also considering the leasing of lorries, trailers, cranes, fork lifts, etc., and, as leases are made, capital equipment will gradually be reduced and leasing costs substituted in place of depreciation.

New valuations and leasing, however, are not yet finalized and for 1971 fixed assets should be valued at estimated book value at 31 December 1970 plus 50 per cent of proposed additions in 1971.

In the case of *Stocks* and *Book Debts* three assessments are required:

## 1. MINIMUM

Consider *separately* the periods when you anticipate stocks and book debts will be at their lowest totals. Assess these amounts and in the case of *stocks* reduce to the most efficient level that could be attained if goods were strictly available according to the varying replacement times of the products concerned.

For the *book-debts* valuation, take two-monthly period when sales are anticipated to be at their lowest and assess the book debts as at the end of this period. Consider the possible make-up of these sales as to whether a proportion may be for cash against documents and the balance on normal credit arrangements. Ignore any extended credit terms and settle at an ideal amount which could be attained if money was more liquid than it is at present.

## 2. AVERAGE

Experience will guide you on the average requirements in accordance with the anticipated sales over the year.

## 3. MAXIMUM

Peak periods must be examined for the assessment of these maximum requirements. Take into account some element of stock-replacement delay, and in the book debts' computation allow for present-day financial restrictions.

The minimum and maximum asset requirements will be examined at head office as to their feasibility and capability of being financed.

The *minimum* amounts when agreed will be reckoned as the hard-core assets and will carry no interest charge. It will be the base on which net profits will be judged as a percentage.

Assets used in excess of the minimum will be subject to an interest-charge – at present 11 per cent per annum. It is important therefore that units should recoup interest costs in their gross-profit margins.

*Import-deposit balances* will not form part of the interest-free assets. They will be subject to interest charged monthly in overheads and this cost must be balanced by extra gross-profit margins.

## QUESTIONS

1. Do you think Mr Teak's concept of interest-free capital is a good one? Will it (*a*) achieve a more effective allocation of capital to units and (*b*) encourage each manager to improve the return on the capital his unit employs? Is there any conflict between (*a*) and (*b*)?

2. How should the management-incentive bonus be calculated? Should it be based on return on interest-free capital?

3. Does Mr Sawdust's letter of 10 November 1970 influence your assessment of the concept of *interest-free capital*?

4. Can the concept of interest-free capital be employed in companies with a high ratio of fixed to current assets?

## SUGGESTED BACKGROUND READING

1. R. N. Anthony, John Dearden, and R. F. Vancil, *Management Control Systems*, Irwin, Homewood, 1972, Chapter 7.

2. John Dearden, 'The case against R.O.I. control', *Harvard Business Review*, May–June 1969.

3. David Solomons, *Divisional Performance: Measurement and Control*, Irwin, Homewood, 1965, Chapters 3, 4 and 5.

## Wessex Knitting

WESSEX KNITTING, a subsidiary of Nationwide Textiles Ltd, produced single- and double-jersey knitted fabric. In 1969 the company had a turnover of £730,000 and generated a trading profit of £55,000. John Rainbow, the managing director of Wessex Knitting, was concerned about a proposal by Fred Rightway, the financial director of Nationwide Textiles, to transfer Wessex Knitting's freehold land and buildings to Nationwide's property-owning subsidiary, and to rent back the property to Wessex Knitting. John Rainbow explained the situation as follows:

I established Wessex Knitting in a small way in 1957. I recognized that jersey knitting was a growth field, and purchased a freehold site on the outskirts of Dorchester with adequate space for future expansion. I paid £20,000 for the freehold and over the next two years had premises erected costing £40,000. In the early years I let surplus space on a short-term lease. The premises were valued at £100,000 in 1960. I included this figure in our balance sheet at the end of 1960, and have depreciated at 2 per cent per annum straight line since that date.

Pantextile Ltd approached me with a view to joining their group in 1963. At this time I was extremely short of working capital and agreed to their proposal. They provided both capital and security, including a guaranteed outlet for over 50 per cent of my production. They also left me to get on with the job. Each November I prepared a budget for the following year, and provided I achieved my budget, and I always did, they were quite happy. My objective has always been to maximize profit consistent with return on capital. Last year (1969) I made a return of 22 per cent on capital employed (i.e. trading profit to trading assets). I pride myself on being one of the most profitable companies in the group.

At the end of 1968 Pantextile merged with Northern Textiles to form Nationwide Textiles. Although it was described in the financial press as a merger, the former Northern Textiles directors seem to be running things. Fred Rightway was the financial director of Northern Textiles, and the property-owning company was formed by Northern Textiles in 1965. They have valued my freehold land and premises at £250,000, and want to charge Wessex Knitting their standard rental to group companies of 10 per cent of the valuation. I have 65,000 square feet of floor space, and currently it costs 50p a square foot per annum to rent floor space in Dorchester. I am keeping quiet about that! As I was saying, my objective has always been to maximize profits consistent with return on capital. I have made my fortune and I could retire tomorrow, but I obtain satisfaction from running my own show and being one of the most profitable companies in the group. If I accept this proposal to transfer my land and buildings to a property-owning company, I am worried about the effect on my profits and return on capital employed. I expect they will revalue the property each year and increase the rent. I shall lose all the benefit of my enlightened decision to purchase the land in 1957 and to build premises in excess of my immediate requirements.

The accountants at group head office have short memories; they will soon forget about the change in the ownership of the property when examining the trend in my performance. I cannot see any benefit from a transfer to the property-owning company. They will be interfering in the management of Wessex Knitting next. I am seriously considering retiring: I have only five years to go you know.

QUESTION

What advice would you give (a) to John Rainbow and (b) to Fred Rightway?

SUGGESTED BACKGROUND READING

Learned, Christensen, Andrews, and Guth, *Business Policy: Text and Cases*, Irwin, Homewood, Ill. 1969. 'The Accomplishment of Purpose: Organizational Processes and Behaviour', pp. 629–45.

# Bloggs & Cloggs*

JIM BLOGGS and Fred Cloggs planned to set up a limited liability company to do metal spraying. Bloggs was to be the main contributor of capital and Cloggs was to provide the technical expertise.

A search at Companies House revealed that six companies were operating in the field in which Bloggs and Cloggs planned to specialize but only one would be a serious competitor. The last filed return showed that this company made a profit of £27,000 before taxation on a turnover of £85,000. Bloggs and Cloggs expected to achieve a £61,000 turnover in the first year and £80,000 in the second year.

The organization of the company is shown in Figure 1. Two close friends of Cloggs, Jim Simpson and Harold Stepwell, a practising accountant, agreed to become sales director and part-time financial director, and a production manager was to be recruited. Within three months of trading, the labour force was to consist of a supervisor, five male operatives, eight female operatives and a labourer. A wages and salaries budget for the first year was prepared (Table 1).

For metal spraying the company needed equipment and a clean-air installation at a cost of £22,000. Buildings to be acquired would cost £12,500, plus £500 for legal fees. In addition building alterations would involve a further £1,550, fixtures and fittings £350 and other sundry plant and equipment £1,625.

Bloggs and Cloggs also required working capital and the maximum which they, and their fellow directors, could invest was £10,000. So they sought additional finance. To determine their needs they prepared, with the help of Stepwell, a profit and loss and cash flow forecast for the first year's trading (Table 2).

*This case first appeared in *Management Accounting*, February 1972, pp. 45–7.

Armed with their profit and loss and cash forecasts, Bloggs and Cloggs visited Bill Richards, manager of the local branch of Westland Bank, with which they had had personal accounts for several years. Richards listened sympathetically to their request for overdraft facilities but explained that the bank did not provide such facilities for the purchase of fixed assets, particularly specialized plant and equipment, to companies not yet trading. He suggested they might approach Westland Leasing Ltd, the leasing subsidiary of Westland Bank, or Westland Finance Company, which specialized in new-venture capital.

Bloggs and Cloggs approached Westland Finance Company and discussed their requirements with an assistant director. After examination of profit and cash forecasts, Westland Finance offered to lend up to £30,000, secured on the buildings and other fixed assets of the company.

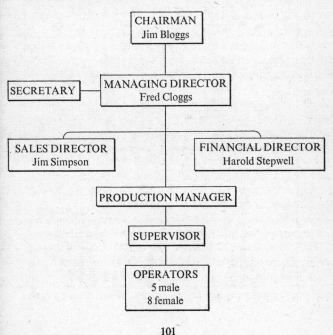

## Table 1
### Wages and Salaries Budget* – Year 1

| | Total | Month (Cash flows) | | | | | | | | | | | |
| --- | --- | --- | --- | --- | --- | --- | --- | --- | --- | --- | --- | --- | --- |
| | | 1 | 2 | 3 | 4 | 5 | 6 | 7 | 8 | 9 | 10 | 11 | 12 |
| | £ | £ | £ | £ | £ | £ | £ | £ | £ | £ | £ | £ | £ |
| **Salaries** | | | | | | | | | | | | | |
| Administrative staff | 900 | 75 | 75 | 75 | 75 | 75 | 75 | 75 | 75 | 75 | 75 | 75 | 75 |
| Manager | 2,600 | 200 | 200 | 400 | 200 | 200 | 200 | 200 | 200 | 200 | 200 | 200 | 200 |
| *Total* | 3,500 | 275 | 275 | 475 | 275 | 275 | 275 | 275 | 275 | 275 | 275 | 275 | 275 |
| **Directors' remunerations** | | | | | | | | | | | | | |
| Bloggs | 2,400 | — | — | — | 200 | 200 | 200 | 200 | 200 | 200 | 200 | 200 | 200 |
| Cloggs | 2,400 | — | — | — | 200 | 200 | 200 | 200 | 200 | 200 | 200 | 200 | 200 |
| Simpson | 2,400 | — | — | — | 200 | 200 | 200 | 200 | 200 | 200 | 200 | 200 | 200 |
| Stepwell | 2,400 | — | — | — | 200 | 200 | 200 | 200 | 200 | 200 | 200 | 200 | 200 |
| *Total* | 9,600 | — | — | — | 800 | 800 | 800 | 800 | 800 | 800 | 800 | 800 | 800 |
| **Wages** | | | | | | | | | | | | | |
| Men | 6,500 | (1)125 | (3)375 | (5)600 | 600 | 600 | 600 | 600 | 600 | 600 | 600 | 600 | 600 |
| Women | 8,800 | — | (8)800 | 800 | 800 | 800 | 800 | 800 | 800 | 800 | 800 | 800 | 800 |
| Supervisor | 1,500 | (1)125 | 125 | 125 | 125 | 125 | 125 | 125 | 125 | 125 | 125 | 125 | 125 |
| Labourer | 825 | — | (1)75 | 75 | 75 | 75 | 75 | 75 | 75 | 75 | 75 | 75 | 75 |
| *Total* | 17,625 | 250 | 1,375 | 1,600 | 1,600 | 1,600 | 1,600 | 1,600 | 1,600 | 1,600 | 1,600 | 1,600 | 1,600 |
| *Total* | 30,725 | 525 | 1,650 | 2,075 | 2,675 | 2,675 | 2,675 | 2,675 | 2,675 | 2,675 | 2,675 | 2,675 | 5,075 |

* Including national insurance, graduated pensions, holiday pay.

## Table 2

### Profit and Loss Account and Cash-flow Statement – Year 1

| | P/L A/C Total £ | 1 £ | 2 £ | 3 £ | 4 £ | 5 £ | 6 £ | 7 £ | 8 £ | 9 £ | 10 £ | 11 £ | 12 £ | Accrued expenses debtors and stocks £ |
|---|---|---|---|---|---|---|---|---|---|---|---|---|---|---|
| | | | | | | | Month (Cash Flows) | | | | | | | |
| **Wages** | 17,625 | 250 | 1,375 | 1,600 | 1,600 | 1,600 | 1,600 | 1,600 | 1,600 | 1,600 | 1,600 | 1,600 | 1,600 | — |
| **Variable overheads** | | | | | | | | | | | | | | |
| Lacquer | 1,800 | — | 150 | 150 | 150 | 150 | 150 | 150 | 150 | 150 | 150 | 150 | 150 | 150 |
| Tape | 1,800 | — | 150 | 150 | 150 | 150 | 150 | 150 | 150 | 150 | 150 | 150 | 150 | 150 |
| Power | 1,500 | — | 125 | 125 | 125 | 125 | 125 | 125 | 125 | 125 | 125 | 125 | 125 | 125 |
| Thinners cleaner | 1,200 | — | 100 | 100 | 100 | 100 | 100 | 100 | 100 | 100 | 100 | 100 | 100 | 100 |
| Jigs and repairs | 1,200 | 200 | 200 | 80 | 80 | 80 | 80 | 80 | 80 | 80 | 80 | 80 | 80 | — |
| Other indirect materials | 1,000 | — | 75 | 75 | 75 | 75 | 75 | 75 | 75 | 75 | 100 | 100 | 100 | 100 |
| Stationery | 750 | — | 150 | 100 | 50 | 50 | 50 | 50 | 50 | 50 | 50 | 50 | 50 | 50 |
| Carriage and packing | 500 | — | 40 | 40 | 40 | 40 | 40 | 40 | 40 | 40 | 40 | 50 | 50 | 40 |
| Sundries | 1,200 | 100 | 100 | 100 | 100 | 100 | 100 | 100 | 100 | 100 | 100 | 100 | 100 | — |
| **Total** | 10,950 | 300 | 1,090 | 920 | 870 | 870 | 870 | 870 | 870 | 870 | 895 | 905 | 905 | 715 |
| **Fixed overheads** | | | | | | | | | | | | | | |
| Directors' remunerations | 9,600 | — | — | — | 800 | 800 | 800 | 800 | 800 | 800 | 800 | 800 | 3,200 | — |
| Staff salaries | 3,500 | 275 | 275 | 475 | 275 | 275 | 275 | 275 | 275 | 275 | 275 | 275 | 275 | — |
| Insurances | 1,680 | 140 | 140 | 140 | 140 | 140 | 140 | 140 | 140 | 140 | 140 | 140 | 140 | — |
| Office expenses | 500 | — | 40 | 40 | 40 | 40 | 40 | 40 | 40 | 40 | 40 | 40 | 40 | 60 |

Table 2 (Cont.)

| | Total | | | | | | | | | | | | |
|---|---|---|---|---|---|---|---|---|---|---|---|---|---|
| Rates | 400 | 200 | — | — | — | — | — | — | 200 | — | — | — | 60 |
| Total | 15,680 | 615 | — | 455 | 655 | 1,255 | 1,255 | 1,255 | 1,255 | 1,455 | 1,255 | 1,255 | 3,655 |
| W.I.P. and stock adjustment | (1,000) | | | | | | | | | | | | (1,000) |
| Cost of sales | 43,255 | 1,165 | 2,920 | 3,175 | 3,725 | 3,725 | 3,725 | 3,925 | 3,725 | 3,725 | 3,750 | 3,760 | 6,160 |
| Net profit before depreciation, interest and taxation | 17,745 | (1,165) | (920) | 1,825 | 1,275 | 1,275 | 1,275 | 1,075 | 2,275 | 2,275 | 2,250 | 2,240 | (225) |
| Sales | 61,000 | — | 2,000 | 5,000 | 5,000 | 5,000 | 5,000 | 5,000 | 6,000 | 6,000 | 6,000 | 6,000 | 4,000 |
| Net internally generated cash | 13,520 | (1,165) | (920) | 1,825 | 1,275 | 1,275 | 1,275 | 1,075 | 2,275 | 2,275 | 2,250 | 2,240 | (160) |
| Capital expenditure | | | | | | | | | | | | | |
| Buildings | 13,000 | 13,000 | | | | | | | | | | | |
| Plant and equipment | 22,000 | 22,000 | | | | | | | | | | | |
| Sundry equipment | 3,525 | 3,525 | | | | | | | | | | | |
| | 38,525 | 38,525 | | | | | | | | | | | |
| External funds | | | | | | | | | | | | | |
| Share capital | 10,000 | 10,000 | | | | | | | | | | | |
| Net cash flow | (15,005) | (29,690) | (920) | 1,825 | 1,275 | 1,275 | 1,275 | 1,075 | 2,275 | 2,275 | 2,250 | 2,240 | (160) |
| Cumulative cash deficit | | (29,690) | (30,610) | (28,785) | (27,510) | (26,235) | (24,960) | (23,885) | (21,610) | (19,335) | (17,085) | (14,845) | (15,005) |

Note: Sales figure of 4,000 in the final column expressed in drs.

The charge for the loan was 18 per cent per annum. Bloggs and Cloggs knew that the loan interest would be allowable as a charge against profit for corporation tax purposes and that the net cost of the loan would be 10·8 per cent i.e. 18 per cent less 40 per cent corporation tax. They noted, too, that the gross interest of £5,400 a year compared favourably with the projected profit before depreciation, interest and taxation in the first year of trading of £17,745.

Shortly after receiving the offer from Westland Finance Company, Bloggs and Cloggs were visited by Bill Bragg, of Westland Leasing Ltd. He was keen to lease the spraying equipment and clean-air system to the new company. His terms were: £410 a month in advance for ten years, plus an additional £410 in the first month. After ten years the company would pay a peppercorn rental of £1 per month in advance.

Bragg pointed out that while the company would sacrifice the capital allowances, i.e. 60 per cent in the first year, and 25 per cent reducing balance in subsequent years, all the rental payments would be allowable as a charge against profits for corporation tax. Bragg was prepared also to lease the buildings to the new company for an initial payment of 10 per cent of the purchase price of £12,500, plus monthly payments in advance of £180 for ten years. At the end of ten years, the company would have an option to renew the lease.

In this case, if it were decided to lease, the company would forgo a capital allowance of 30 per cent in the first year and an annual allowance of 4 per cent per annum straight line in subsequent years. Bloggs and Cloggs were aware that industrial land and buildings in the area had been appreciating at 7 per cent per annum in recent years. Bragg assured them that it was cheaper to lease the assets than pay 18 per cent a year to Westland Finance Company.

Bloggs and Cloggs were not sure which was the cheapest and most suitable method of financing and what its effect would be on break-even volume. They decided to seek Stepwell's advice and sent full details of the Westland Finance Company and Westland Leasing Ltd offers asking him to:

1. Evaluate the alternative methods of financing and make recommendations;
2. complete the profit and loss and cash forecasts for the first year's trading and balance sheet at the end of the first year's trading, assuming that the recommendations in 1 would be accepted;
3. examine the effect of the recommendations on break-even volume.


SUGGESTED BACKGROUND READING

1. *An Insight into Management Accounting*, Chapter 6.
2. A. J. Merrett and Allen Sykes, *Capital Budgeting and Company Finance*, Longmans, London, 1968, Chapter 6.
3. Richard F. Vancil, *Leasing of Industrial Equipment*, McGraw-Hill, New York, 1963.

# Doormouse Ltd

AN EXAMINATION of Doormouse Ltd's profit and loss account for the last year ending 31 December (see Table 1) and balance sheet as at 31 December last (see Table 2) reveals that the company has liquidity and profitability problems. The company is under pressure from Westland Bank to reduce the level of its bank overdraft. In order to improve the profitability of the company, the board of directors is anxious to purchase new machinery costing £138,000. Philip Franks, the company's financial director, has undertaken a financial evaluation of the proposed capital-expenditure project. After discounting the estimated future cash flows (in money terms) at the company's cost of capital (13 per

Table 1

Doormouse Ltd

Summarized Profit and Loss Account

|  | Year ending 31 December | |
| --- | --- | --- |
|  | Last year | This year |
|  | £ | £ |
| Turnover | 4,718,890 | 5,106,945 |
| Net profit before taxation | 240,342 | 174,503 |
| Corporation tax | 114,516 | 81,586 |
|  | 125,826 | 92,917 |
| Minority interests | 8,678 | 6,559 |
| *Profit attributable to parent company* | £117,148 | £86,358 |
| 5% preference dividend | 10,000 | 10,000 |
| Ordinary dividend (gross) | 70,000 | 70,000 |
| Retained profit for year | 37,148 | 6,358 |
|  | £117,148 | £86,358 |

Table 2

Doormouse Ltd

Balance Sheets

*As at 31 December*

| Last year £ | Fixed assets | £ Cost | This year £ Depreciation | £ |
|---|---|---|---|---|
| 484,233 | Freehold property | 684,228 | 133,855 | 550,373 |
| 17,106 | Leasehold property | 24,308 | 8,057 | 16,251 |
| 352,995 | Plant and machinery | 1,229,432 | 921,715 | 307,717 |
| £854,334 | | £1,937,968 | £1,063,627 | £874,341 |
| | *Current assets* | | | |
| 977,383 | Stock | | 1,430,973 | |
| 856,686 | Debtors | | 1,066,164 | |
| 120,613 | Cash | | 37,419 | |
| £1,954,682 | | | £2,534,556 | |
| | *Current liabilities* | | | |
| 374,290 | Creditors | | 522,485 | |
| 270,766 | Bank overdraft | | 682,924 | |
| 63,973 | Corporation tax | | 92,838 | |
| 70,000 | Ordinary dividend (gross) | | 70,000 | |
| £779,029 | | | £1,368,247 | |
| £1,175,653 | *Net current assets* | | | £1,166,309 |
| £2,029,987 | *Net assets employed* | | | £2,040,650 |
| 560,000 | Ordinary share capital | | | 560,000 |
| 200,000 | 5% cumulative preference capital | | | 200,000 |
| 1,089,089 | Capital and revenue reserves | | | 1,110,763 |
| 89,998 | Minority interests | | | 96,557 |
| 90,900 | Corporation tax | | | 73,330 |
| £2,029,987 | | | | £2,040,650 |

cent), the project has a positive net present value of £15,000. He has arrived at the company's cost of capital by adding 4 per cent for inflation to 9 per cent cost of capital in real terms. Nine per cent is the rate of interest Doormouse is paying currently on its bank overdraft.

Franks recognizes that the company has limited cash available for investment purposes, and is investigating the possibility of leasing the machinery by comparing the relative cost of acquiring £100,000 of machinery with fifteen-year life, 1. from internally generated funds, 2. by raising an external loan, and 3. by leasing. He calculates the cost of purchasing from internally generated funds at £64,216 (see Table 3). It will be noted that Franks has assumed that the cash-investment grant (20 per cent) will be received eighteen months after the investment has been made, and that the annual allowance will reduce the amount of corporation tax payable one year later. The annual allowance is 15 per cent per annum reducing balance on the cost of the machinery less the investment grant, and the rate of corporation tax is 45 per cent. Franks has discounted the net cash flow at the company's cost of capital. 'Thirteen per cent per annum is the return we require on internally generated cash. £64,216 is the net cost to the company of financing a £100,000 purchase of machinery from internally generated funds.'

Table 4 shows Franks's calculation of the cost of financing the investment by an external loan at 10 per cent per annum with interest payable every six months. He has recognized that loan interest is an allowable expense for corporation-tax purposes. The purchase of plant is offset in Year 0 by the loan, which is repayable in Year 15. It will be seen that, after discounting the cash flows at 13 per cent, the net cost of financing the purchase from external sources is £16,552.

The loan interest will be paid out of internally generated funds so I have again discounted at 13 per cent. Of course I recognize my borrowing facility is fully extended, but I am interested in comparing the cost of external financing with that of leasing. As I expected an external loan is considerably cheaper than using internally generated funds.

### Table 3

#### Purchase from Internal Sources

| Year | Cash investment £'000 | Investment grant £ | Net annual allowance at 15% per annum £ | Net cash flow £'000 | Present value at 13% Factor | Present value at 13% £'000 |
|---|---|---|---|---|---|---|
| 0 | 100) | | | (100·000) | 1·000 | (100·000) |
| ½ | | | | — | ·939 | — |
| 1 | | | 5,400 | 5·400 | ·882 | 4·763 |
| 1½ | | 20,000 | | 20·000 | ·828 | 16·560 |
| 2 | | | 4,590 | 4·590 | ·777 | 3·566 |
| 2½ | | | | — | ·730 | — |
| 3 | | | 3,901 | 3·901 | ·685 | 2·673 |
| 3½ | | | | — | ·644 | — |
| 4 | | | 3,316 | 3·316 | ·604 | 2·003 |
| 4½ | | | | — | ·567 | — |
| 5 | | | 2,819 | 2·819 | ·533 | 1·503 |
| 5½ | | | | — | ·500 | — |
| 6 | | | 2,396 | 2·396 | ·470 | 1·126 |
| 6½ | | | | — | ·441 | — |
| 7 | | | 2,037 | 2·037 | ·414 | 843 |
| 7½ | | | | — | ·389 | — |
| 8 | | | 1,731 | 1·731 | ·365 | 632 |
| 8½ | | | | — | ·343 | — |
| 9 | | | 1,471 | 1·471 | ·322 | 474 |
| 9½ | | | | — | ·302 | — |
| 10 | | | 1,251 | 1·251 | ·284 | 355 |
| 10½ | | | | — | ·266 | — |
| 11 | | | 1,063 | 1·063 | ·250 | 266 |
| 11½ | | | | — | ·235 | — |
| 12 | | | 904 | 904 | ·221 | 200 |
| 12½ | | | | — | ·207 | — |
| 13 | | | 768 | 768 | ·194 | 149 |
| 13½ | | | | — | ·183 | — |
| 14 | | | 653 | 653 | ·171 | 112 |
| 14½ | | | | — | ·161 | — |
| 15 | | | 3,700 | 3·700 | ·151 | 559 |
| | £(100) | £20,000 | £36,000 | £(44·000) | | (£64·216) |

## Table 4

### Purchase from External Sources

| Year | Net cash flow per table 3 excluding year 0 £ | Loan interest payable at 10% £ | Corporation tax on interest at 45% £ | Net cash flow £ | Present value at 13% Factor | Present value at 13% £ |
|---|---|---|---|---|---|---|
| 0 | — | — | — | — | | |
| ½ | — | (5,000) | — | (5,000) | ·939 | (4,690) |
| 1 | 5,400 | (5,000) | 4,500 | 4,900 | ·882 | 4,320 |
| 1½ | 20,000 | (5,000) | — | 15,000 | ·828 | 12,420 |
| 2 | 4,590 | (5,000) | 4,500 | 4,090 | ·777 | 3,170 |
| 2½ | — | (5,000) | — | (5,000) | ·730 | (3,650) |
| 3 | 3,901 | (5,000) | 4,500 | 3,401 | ·685 | 2,330 |
| 3½ | — | (5,000) | — | (5,000) | ·644 | (3,220) |
| 4 | 3,316 | (5,000) | 4,500 | 2,816 | ·604 | 1,700 |
| 4½ | — | (5,000) | — | (5,000) | ·567 | (2,830) |
| 5 | 2,819 | (5,000) | 4,500 | 2,319 | ·533 | 1,240 |
| 5½ | — | (5,000) | — | (5,000) | ·500 | (2,500) |
| 6 | 2,396 | (5,000) | 4,500 | 1,896 | ·470 | 890 |
| 6½ | — | (5,000) | — | (5,000) | ·441 | (2,210) |
| 7 | 2,037 | (5,000) | 4,500 | 1,537 | ·414 | 640 |
| 7½ | — | (5,000) | — | (5,000) | ·389 | (1,945) |
| 8 | 1,731 | (5,000) | 4,500 | 1,231 | ·365 | 450 |
| 8½ | — | (5,000) | — | (5,000) | ·343 | (1,710) |
| 9 | 1,471 | (5,000) | 4,500 | 971 | ·322 | 310 |
| 9½ | — | (5,000) | — | (5,000) | ·302 | (1,510) |
| 10 | 1,251 | (5,000) | 4,500 | 751 | ·284 | 210 |
| 10½ | — | (5,000) | — | (5,000) | ·266 | (1,330) |
| 11 | 1,063 | (5,000) | 4,500 | 563 | ·250 | 140 |
| 11½ | — | (5,000) | — | (5,000) | ·235 | (1,170) |
| 12 | 904 | (5,000) | 4,500 | 404 | ·221 | 90 |
| 12½ | — | (5,000) | — | (5,000) | ·207 | (1,040) |
| 13 | 768 | (5,000) | 4,500 | 268 | ·194 | 50 |
| 13½ | — | (5,000) | — | (5,000) | ·183 | (910) |
| 14 | 653 | (5,000) | 4,500 | 153 | ·171 | 30 |
| 14½ | — | (5,000) | — | (5,000) | ·161 | (800) |
| 15 | 3,700 | (105,000) | 4,500 | (96,800) | ·151 | (14,617) |
| 15½ | — | (5,000) | — | (5,000) | ·142 | (710) |
| 16 | — | — | 2,250 | 2,250 | ·133 | 300 |
| | £56,000 | £(255,000) | £69,750 | £(129,250) | | £(16,552) |

Franks's calculation of the cost of leasing is shown in Table 5. The terms of the lease are nine half-yearly payments of £11,000 in advance followed by a payment of £9,000 after four and a half

### Table 5

#### Leasing

| Year | Renta £ | Corporation tax at 45% £ | Net cash flow £ | Present value at 13% Factor | £ |
|---|---|---|---|---|---|
| 0 | (11,000) | | (11,000) | 1·000 | (11,000) |
| ½ | (11,000) | | (11,000) | ·939 | (10,329) |
| 1 | (11,000) | 9,900 | (1,100) | ·882 | (970) |
| 1½ | (11,000) | | (11,000) | ·828 | (9,108) |
| 2 | (11,000) | 9,900 | (1,100) | ·777 | (855) |
| 2½ | (11,000) | | (11,000) | ·730 | (8,030) |
| 3 | (11,000) | 9,900 | (1,100) | ·685 | (753) |
| 3½ | (11,000) | | (11,000) | ·644 | (7,084) |
| 4 | (11,000) | 9,900 | (1,100) | ·604 | (664) |
| 4½ | (9,000) | | (9,000) | ·567 | (5,103) |
| 5 | — | 9,000 | 9,000 | ·533 | 4,797 |
| 5½ | — | | — | ·500 | — |
| 6 | — | | — | ·470 | — |
| 6½ | — | | — | ·441 | — |
| 7 | (50) | — | (50) | ·414 | (21) |
| 7½ | — | | — | ·389 | — |
| 8 | (50) | 22 | (28) | ·365 | (10) |
| 8½ | — | | — | ·343 | — |
| 9 | (50) | 22 | (28) | ·322 | (9) |
| 9½ | — | | — | ·302 | — |
| 10 | (50) | 22 | (28) | ·284 | (8) |
| 10½ | — | | — | ·266 | — |
| 11 | (50) | 22· | (28) | ·250 | (7) |
| 11½ | — | | — | ·235 | — |
| 12 | (50) | 22 | (28) | ·221 | (6) |
| 12½ | — | | — | ·207 | — |
| 13 | (50) | 22 | (28) | ·194 | (5) |
| 13½ | — | | — | ·183 | — |
| 14 | (50) | 22 | (28) | ·171 | (5) |
| 14½ | — | | — | ·161 | — |
| 15 | — | 22 | 22 | ·151 | 3 |
| | £(108,400) | £48,776 | £(59,624) | | £(49,167) |

years. From year 7 onwards a peppercorn rent is payable of £50 a year in advance. The calculation shows that the rental payments are allowable as an expense for corporation-tax purposes, but that the company forgoes the investment grant and the capital allowances.

The rental payments would be made out of the internally generated funds so I have discounted the net cash flows at 13 per cent. It will be seen that the net cost of leasing is considerably higher than the cost of an external loan, but lower than the cost of using scarce internally generated funds. Until we are in a position to raise an external loan, I shall recommend to the board of directors that we lease machinery.

As a result of Philip Franks's recommendations, the board of directors decided to lease £138,000 of machinery.

QUESTION

Examine carefully Philip Franks's recommendations.

SUGGESTED BACKGROUND READING

1. *An Insight into Management Accounting*, Chapter 6.
2. A. J. Merrett and Allen Sykes, *Capital Budgeting and Company Finance*, Longmans, London, 1968, Chapter 6.
3. Richard F. Vancil, *Leasing of Industrial Equipment*, McGraw-Hill, New York, 1963, Chapters 4 and 5.

# James Wilson & Son (A)*

NORMAN RICHARDS, the managing director of James Wilson &
Son, made the following comments concerning his company's
management-accounting system:

Before Harold Hawkeye introduced the management-accounting
system the board of directors did not know whether or not the company had made a profit until the auditors produced the figures sometime after the year ended. On some occasions when higher profits were
expected because everyone had been busier than usual the annual
accounts showed a loss. We did not know which of our activities and
garments made profits and which losses. There was no effective financial control. Today the board of directors is much more aware about
what is going on. We receive a monthly report comparing actual
performance against budget. Information is available to show both the
profitability of various departments and the garments they made, and
to assist the management in making decisions.

Wilson's was an old-established company producing knitted
underwear, leisurewear and children's outerwear. They had
premises in Bridge Street and South Street, Milchester, and
recently had opened a new factory in North Ashfleet ten miles
south of Milchester. Underwear and leisurewear was produced at
Bridge Street and knitwear at South Street and North Ashfleet.
The company had a turnover of £1,300,000 in 1971 and some 500
employees. John Sandwich was the production director at Bridge
Street and Peter Goodchild was the director responsible for
production and sales of knitwear. Norman Richards, as well as
being managing director, acted as sales director for underwear
and leisurewear. William Simpson, a city chartered accountant,
was non-executive chairman of James Wilson & Son.

On the fifteenth day of each month the directors received a

* A shortened version of this case appeared in *The Hosiery Trade Journal*,
July 1972, pp. 107–11.

management-accounting report from Harold Hawkeye. It contained a summary of the previous month's operations and the position to date. The report for April 1972 appears in Appendix A. Harold Hawkeye considered his monthly report presented information to the directors in an easily understandable form. In his opinion too many figures could confuse, and he extracted from his management-accounting system those figures necessary to provide the board of directors with an overall picture of the financial situation. If additional information was required by the board of directors relating to a particular aspect of the company's operations special reports were prepared. Harold Hawkeye expressed the following view when questioned on the effectiveness of his approach to reporting at board level:

The board of directors are sympathetic to the need for change and for guidance. They take great interest in the monthly management-accounting report and in the special studies of particular aspects of the company's operations. As you know, we use a computer bureau to provide an analysis of sales and contribution by product and outlet. The information is summarized in the monthly management-accounting report for the board of directors. The purpose of the summary is to show changes in the pattern of distribution in the case of outlet and changes in the product mix in the case of product group. More detailed reports are prepared for the departmental directors showing sales by garment, product group and outlet (see Appendix B). Because of the computer's ability to store data to which rapid access can be obtained, summarized reports are provided to the board of directors, who can then request further analyses. For example, an analysis of sales of athletic garments to multiples by garment size might be requested. We are considering using the Sales Analysis Computer Bureau System for incoming orders to obtain a sales mix and contribution analysis for future sales. As far as costs are concerned, the directors carry out the preparation of the annual budget with enthusiasm. They have developed a more acute cost consciousness and awareness of the use of variances to isolate problems. In addition to the monthly management-accounting report, each director receives a detailed variance report for his department (see Appendix C).

QUESTIONS

1. Evaluate Harold Hawkeye's monthly management accounting report for the board of directors.
2. Evaluate the computer bureau analysis of sales and contribution by product and outlet.

SUGGESTED BACKGROUND READING

1. *An Insight into Management Accounting*, Chapter 7.
2. N. C. Churchill, J. H. Kempster and M. Uretsky, *Computer-Based Information Systems for Management: A Survey*, National Association of Accountants, New York, 1968.
3. I.C.W.A., *The Presentation of Information to Management*, London, 1950.
4. I.C.W.A., *Management Information Systems and the Computer*, London, 1967.

# APPENDIX A

*Management Accounting Report*
*April 1972*

Contents

117  Summary of results
118  Underwear and Leisurewear Department
119    Trading results
119    Overheads and variances
120    Sales by outlet
121    Sales by product
122  Knitwear Department
122    Trading results
122    Overheads and variances
123    Sales by outlet
124    Sales by product
125  Bank overdraft and overheads
126  Average selling prices
126  Capital expenditure
127  Agents' and travellers' sales
128  Export
128  Underwear and Leisurewear Department: Yearly average
       of dozens folded
129  Knitwear Department: Yearly average of dozens examined
129  Number of employees

## SUMMARY OF RESULTS TO 30 APRIL 1972

At 30 April the company is showing a profit of £13,871, which is £4,253 worse than budget.

The biggest factor causing the below-budget profit is the fall-off in sales turnover which is now £28,000 below budget for the group.

The profit to date is made up as follows:

|  | *Actual*<br>£ |
|---|---:|
| Surplus Underwear and Leisurewear Department | 25,875 |
| Deficit Knitwear | (2,390) |
|  | 23,485 |
| *less* Bank interest and pensions | 9,614 |
|  | £13,871 |

### Underwear and Leisurewear Department

Profit in Underwear and Leisurewear Department is £23,846, which is only £428 below budget. The below-budget sales have been offset by savings on the overheads.

### Knitwear Department

Sales are now £21,000 below budget which has resulted in a loss of £9,975, which is £3,800 worse than the budget.

### Comparative figures

|  | *1971*<br>£ | *1972*<br>£ | £ |
|---|---:|---:|---:|
| Sales to date |  |  |  |
| Underwear and Leisurewear Department | 243,357 | 258,964 | +16,000 |
| Knitwear Department | 178,933 | 148,267 | −31,000 |
|  | £422,290 | £407,231 | −15,000 |
| Profit to date |  |  |  |
| Underwear and Leisurewear Department | 24,856 | 23,846 | −1,000 |
| Knitwear Department | (5,614) | (9,975) | −4,000 |
|  | £19,242 | £13,871 | −5,000 |

Compared with this time last year sales are £15,000 down and profit £5,000 down for the company.

*Underwear and Leisurewear Department*

## Trading Results
### Cumulative Figures to 30 April 1972

|  |  | Actual |  | Budget |  |
|---|---|---|---|---|---|
|  |  | £ |  | £ | £ |
| Sales of perfects |  | 258,964 |  | 266,000 | −7,036 |
| Contribution | (28·7%) | 74,466 | (29·5%) | 78,470 | −4,004 |
| less Overheads |  | 50,620 |  | 54,196 | +3,576 |
| Profit/Loss |  | £23,846 |  | £24,274 | £−428 |

Sales are £7,000 below budget but this has been offset by savings on the overheads to give a profit figure to date of £23,846, which is only £428 below budget.

### Month of April 1972: 20 Working Days

|  |  | Actual |  | Budget |  |
|---|---|---|---|---|---|
|  |  | £ |  | £ | £ |
| Sales of perfects |  | 60,122 |  | 68,000 | −7,878 |
| Contribution | (29·8%) | 17,943 | (29·5%) | 20,060 | −2,117 |
| less Overheads |  | 10,446 |  | 11,337 | +891 |
| Profit/Loss |  | £7,497 |  | £8,723 | £−1,226 |

Sales for the month were £7,800 below budget, which accounted for a profit of £7,497, i.e. £1,226 below budget. However, the contribution is 29·8 per cent, i.e. above budget.

### Overheads

|  | Actual | Budget | Saving |
|---|---|---|---|
| Cumulative | 50,620 | 54,196 | 3,576 |

Overheads are £3,600 below budget. The main savings are on:

> Weekly salaries
> Repairs
> Stationery
> Depreciation

There are no large significant items of overspending.

### Variances

The main unfavourable variances are:

|  | £ |
|---|---|
| Folding-room labour | 627 |
| Outside labour | 94 |

Overall variances from standard are favourable.

## Sales by Outlet

| | Month of April 1972 | | Cumulative to 30 April 1972 | | Standard contribution | Contribution per £mu lab* | Increase/decrease in sales since last year |
|---|---|---|---|---|---|---|---|
| | % of total | £ | % of total | £ | % | £mu lab* | % |
| Manufacturers | — | 69 | — | 813 | 8 | 0·8 | −34 |
| Mail order | 21 | 12,502 | 18 | 46,060 | 23 | 2·5 | −9 |
| Wholesale | 22 | 13,259 | 19 | 49,867 | 27 | 3·1 | +46 |
| Multiples | 46 | 27,935 | 50 | 128,927 | 24 | 2·8 | −7 |
| Export | 11 | 6,357 | 13 | 33,297 | 29 | 4·0 | +79 |
| | 100 | 60,122 | 100 | 258,964 | 25 | 3·0 | +6 |
| Budget | | £68,000 | | £266,000 | 29 | | |

Wholesale and export are showing the largest increase in sales.

\* £mu lab = £ of making-up labour

## Sales by Product

| | Month of April 1972 | | Cumulative to 30 April 1972 | | Standard contribution | Contribution per £mu lab | Increase/decrease in sales since last year |
|---|---|---|---|---|---|---|---|
| | % of total | £ | % of total | £ | % | £mu lab | % |
| Leisurewear | 31 | 18,720 | 38 | 97,331 | 22 | 2·1 | −10 |
| Children's knickers | 7 | 4,138 | 8 | 20,390 | 14 | 1·0 | +8 |
| Athletic | 10 | 6,256 | 7 | 17,247 | 23 | 2·1 | −3 |
| Heavy | 1 | 287 | — | 823 | — | — | −53 |
| Womens | 51 | 30,721 | 47 | 123,173 | 29 | 3·8 | +28 |
| | 100 | £60,122 | 100 | £258,964 | 25 | 3·0 | +6 |
| Budget | | £68,000 | | £266,000 | 29 | | |

*Knitwear Department*

### Trading Results

Cumulative figures to 30 April 1972

|  |  | Actual £ |  | Budget £ | Variance £ |
|---|---|---|---|---|---|
| Sales of perfects |  | 148,267 |  | 169,500 | −21,233 |
| Contribution | (29·8%) | 44,216 | (28·6%) | 48,550 | −4,334 |
| less Overheads |  | 54,191 |  | 54,700 | +509 |
| Profit/Loss |  | £(9,975) |  | £(6,150) | £−3,825 |

The actual loss is £3,825 more than budgeted loss. This is due to sales being £21,000 below budget, but the loss is reduced by the high contribution on actual sales (29·8 per cent as against a budget of 28·6 per cent).

### Month of April 1972: 20 Working Days

|  |  | Actual £ |  | Budget £ | Variance £ |
|---|---|---|---|---|---|
| Sales of perfects |  | 17,379 |  | 31,400 | −14,021 |
| Contribution | (29·2%) | 5,083 | (29·1%) | 9,150 | −4,067 |
| less Overheads |  | 11,763 |  | 11,633 | −130 |
| Profit/Loss |  | £(6,680) |  | £(2,483) | £−4,197 |

The loss for the month was £4,197 more than budget. This was due to the extremely low level of sales, which were £14,000 below budget.

### Overheads

|  | Actual | Budget | Saving |
|---|---|---|---|
| To 30 April 1972 | 54,191 | 54,700 | 509 |

Overheads are £509 below budget. The main savings are on:

|  | £ |
|---|---|
| Weekly salaries and non-productive wages | 746 |
| Building and boiler repairs | 182 |
| N.H.I. and G.P.S. | 425 |

The main items of overspending are:

|  | £ |
|---|---|
| Motor and travelling expenses – Mr Goodchild | 462 |
| Training expenses | 268 |

### Variances

The main unfavourable variances are:

|  |  |
|---|---|
| Outside labour | £223 |

Overall variances from standard remain favourable.

## Sales by Outlet

| | Month of April 1972 | | Cumulative to 30 April 1972 | | Standard contribution | Contribution per £ labour | Increase/ decrease in sales since last year |
|---|---|---|---|---|---|---|---|
| | % of total | £ | % of total | £ | % | £ | % |
| Universal Stores | 2 | 318 | 6 | 8,516 | 27 | 2·6 | −66 |
| Universal Mail Order | 18 | 3,216 | 16 | 24,434 | 27 | 2·7 | +37 |
| Homewoods Stores | 13 | 2,278 | 15 | 22,015 | 28 | 2·5 | +97 |
| Other home | 50 | 8,673 | 46 | 68,351 | 27 | 2·8 | −31 |
| Export | 17 | 2,894 | 17 | 24,951 | 29 | 3·1 | −4 |
| | 100 | £17,379 | 100 | £148,267 | 27·6 | 2·8 | −17 |
| Budget | | £31,400 | | £169,500 | 28·6 | | |

1. Total Sales are 17 per cent down on sales for the same period last year.

2. The overall position of sales to Universal Stores and Universal Mail Order is now showing a 23 per cent decrease on sales for the same period last year.

3. Homewoods Stores continue to show an increase (+97 per cent) but both Other home (−31 per cent) and Export (−4 per cent) are shown below last year's comparative sales figures.

## Sales by Product

| | Month of April 1972 | | Cumulative to 30 April 1972 | | Standard contribution | Contribution per £ labour | Increase/decrease in sales since last year |
|---|---|---|---|---|---|---|---|
| | % of total | £ | % of total | £ | % | | % |
| Infants' | 9 | 1,537 | 36 | 53,299 | 29 | 2·6 | −36 |
| Boys' | 31 | 5,311 | 28 | 41,811 | 29 | 3·1 | −19 |
| Girls' | 60 | 10,531 | 36 | 53,157 | 25 | 2·6 | +20 |
| | 100 | £17,379 | 100 | £148,267 | 27·6 | 2·8 | −17 |
| Budget | | £31,400 | | £169,500 | 28·6 | | |

1. During April there has been a large increase in the sale of girls' garments which are now 36 per cent of total sales and level with total sales of infants' garments. However, it should be noted that the increase in sales of girls' garments has not increased the standard contribution or that per £1 of labour, which are both still below the desired level.

# JAMES WILSON & SON (A)

## Bank Overdraft

| | £ |
|---|---:|
| The overdraft per the bank at 30 April was | 126,000 |
| Plus cheques not yet presented | 20,000 |
| Total overdraft | £146,000 |

This is an increase of £19,000 since 31 December 1971.
The reasons for the increase in the overdraft are:

| | £ |
|---|---:|
| 1. Profits | 16,000 |
| 2. Reduction in stock levels | 6,000 |
| | 22,000 |

This has been offset by increases in the overdraft as follows:

| | |
|---|---:|
| 1. Capital expenditure | 4,000 |
| 2. Reduction in creditors | 24,000 |
| 3. Increase in debtors | 13,000 |
| | 41,000 |
| Net increase in overdraft | 19,000 |

The overdraft of £146,000 is the same as the amount forecast for the end of April.

At present the overdraft is following the forecast, and the actual figure at the end of May should be similar to the forecast figure of £144,000.

## Overheads

| | % |
|---|---:|
| *Underwear and Leisurewear Department* | |
| Cumulative overhead rate* to 30 April | 130 |
| Costed rate | 155 |
| *Knitwear Department* | |
| Cumulative overhead rate* to 30 April | 122 |
| Costed rate | 135 |

*As a percentage of direct labour cost.

### Average Selling Prices

The average selling prices per dozen were:

*Underwear and Leisurewear Department*

|  | 1971 | 1972 cumulative to 30 April |
|---|---|---|
|  | £ | £ |
| Children's knickers | 2·5 | 1·4 |
| Leisure | 10·7 | 11·3 |
| Athletic | 2·5 | 2·6 |
| Heavy | 6·0 | 5·1 |
| Women's | 2·5 | 2·6 |
|  | £3·5 | £4·1 |

The average selling price is £4·1 for 1972 because the sale of dozens of leisurewear to 30 April 1972 account for 16 per cent of the total dozens sold, compared with 10 per cent for the whole of 1971.

*Knitwear Department*

|  | 1971 | 1972 cumulative to 30 April |
|---|---|---|
|  | £ | £ |
| Infants' | 8·1 | 8·9 |
| Girls' | 11·8 | 12·2 |
| Boys' | 12·5 | 12·8 |
|  | £9·9 | £10·6 |

### Capital Expenditure

*Underwear and Leisurewear Department*

|  | £ |
|---|---|
| The budget for the year is | 17,354 |
| Expenditure to 30 April was | 2,637 |
| Leaving a balance for the remainder of the year of | £14,717 |

The expenditure during April was £318, which was for an Adamson Dur-kopp lockstitch underbit trimmer complete with unit stand and motor.

*Knitwear Department*

| | £ |
|---|---|
| The budget for the year is | 4,000 |
| Expenditure to 30 April was | 268 |
| Leaving a balance for the remainder of the year of | £3,732 |

The expenditure during April was £268, made up as follows:

| | £ |
|---|---|
| Six tables for press operators | 45 |
| One Avery portable platform scale | 223 |
| | £268 |

### Agents' and Travellers' Sales

| | Cumulative to 30 April 1972 £ | Increase/decrease since last year % |
|---|---|---|
| Own travellers | 145,595 | — |
| Agents | | |
| Johnson | 65,342 | −6 |
| Goodlad | 58,177 | −12 |
| Jackson | 47,851 | +15 |
| Condie | 40,548 | +29 |
| Hunt | 18,850 | +148 |
| Milne | 17,970 | −23 |
| Knowles | 13,856 | −56 |
| Nicholls | 7,532 | −34 |
| | £415,721 | −3 |

The percentage of cumulative sales attributable to our own travellers and agents compared with the same period last year are:

| | 1971 % | 1972 % |
|---|---|---|
| Own travellers | 34 | 35 |
| Agents | 66 | 65 |
| | 100 | 100 |

### Export

#### Cumulative Figures to 30 April 1972

|  | | Actual £ | | Budget £ | |
|---|---|---|---|---|---|
| Sales | | 58,248 | | 59,500 | −1,252 |
| Contribution | (29%) | 17,149 | (31%) | 18,743 | −1,594 |
| less Overheads | | 1,923 | | 1,748 | +175 |
| Surplus | (26%) | £15,226 | (28%) | £16,995 | −1,769 |

Sales are £1,200 below budget, and the actual contribution is 29 per cent compared with the budget of 31 per cent. The surplus is £1,700 below budget.

*Notes*

1. Knitwear Department sales are £10,000 below budget.

2. Underwear and Leisurewear Department's actual contribution is 29 per cent compared with the budget of 35 per cent.

3. Travelling expenses are £218 above budget.

### Underwear and Leisurewear Department

#### Yearly Average of Dozens Folded

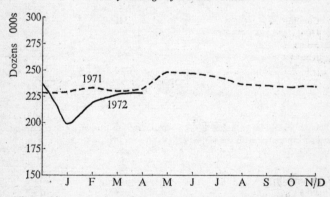

The weekly average dozen folded up to the 30 April 1972 is 4,490 dozens per week compared with 4,735 dozens per week for the same period last year.

*Knitwear Department*

*Yearly Average of Dozens Examined*

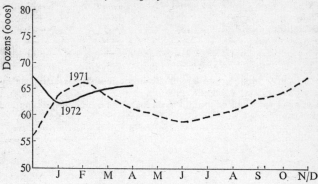

The weekly average dozens examined to end of April 1972 is 1288.
The weekly average dozens examined to end of April 1971 was 1139.

*Number of Employees*

| *Bridge Street* | *30 April 1972* | *Since last month* | *Since 31 December 1971* |
|---|---|---|---|
| Staff | 66 | −1 | +1 |
| Operatives | 181 | — | +1 |
| | 247 | −1 | +2 |

The decrease in staff since last month is due to J. Ring's departure.
The cumulative movement of operatives since 31 December is:

| | *Joined* | *Left* | *Increase/decrease since December* |
|---|---|---|---|
| Folding room | 4 | — | +4 |
| MU department | 9 | 6 | +3 |
| Band room | 4 | 11 | −7 |
| Knitting department | 3 | 2 | +1 |
| | 20 | 19 | +1 |

*Knitwear Department*

|            | 30 April 1972 | Since last month | Since 31 December 1971 |
|------------|---------------|------------------|------------------------|
| Staff      | 65            | +1               | —                      |
| Operatives | 183           | −1               | −13                    |
|            | 248           | —                | −13                    |

The increase in staff since last month is due to engaging a training instructress at North Ashfleet.

The main reduction of operatives since December was on pressing and examining.

## APPENDIX B

An interesting feature of the management-accounting system introduced by Harold Hawkeye was the use of a computer bureau to provide an analysis of sales and contribution by product and outlet.

Contribution was determined by deducting the standard variable cost of a garment from its selling price. The standard variable cost of each garment manufactured was held in a file by the computer. As the sales ledger was posted each day a punched tape was produced on which the following information was recorded:

> Invoice number
> Invoice total
> Purchase tax
> Carriage
> Type of customer/agent
> Garment number
> Size of garment
> Number of dozen per garment
> Value of each garment number

The tapes were submitted to the computer bureau early in the fourth week of the month. The computer produced error messages for the first three weeks. At the end of the fourth week corrections for the first three weeks and the fourth week's tape were submitted.

The computer produced a monthly print-out by department, type of outlet and product group (see Table 1). The product-group totals were further analysed by garment, and the garment totals by size of garment. Thus, for each size of garment, as illustrated in Table 2, the computer prints out:

> Garment number
> Garment size
> Sales in dozens

Standard production cost ⎫
Standard distribution cost ⎬ variable cost only
Standard selling cost ⎭
Standard variable cost
Total contribution
% contribution per £ of make-up labour
Sales in value

The information was summarized in the monthly management-accounting report for the board of directors. Sales in each department were analysed by outlet and product group. The summary reports for the Underwear and Leisurewear Department for June 1971 are shown in Tables 3 and 4. More detailed reports were prepared for the departmental directors showing sales by garment, product group and outlet (see Table 5).

Table 1

Period 6, 1971

Underwear and Leisurewear Department: Outlet 2

| | Size | Quantity (dozens) | Sales | Production cost | Distribution cost | Selling cost | Contribution | % contribution | Contribution per £mu lab | % sales |
|---|---|---|---|---|---|---|---|---|---|---|
| PG 1 | | 4,228·3 | 10,077·10 | 7,077·95 | 177·588 | 604·39 | 2,222·18 | 22 | 1·90 | 14 |
| PG 2 | | 391·0 | 1,806·87 | 1,296·37 | 39·100 | 108·39 | 363·01 | 20 | 1·38 | 3 |
| PG 5 | | 386·6 | 4,488·30 | 2,664·54 | 38·560 | 269·32 | 1,515·88 | 33 | 4·19 | 6 |
| Outlet total | | 5,005·9 | 16,372·27 | 11,038·86 | 255·248 | 982·10 | 4,101·07 | — | 2·29 | — |

Underwear and Leisurewear Department: Outlet 3

| | Size | Quantity (dozens) | Sales | Production cost | Distribution cost | Selling cost | Contribution | % contribution | Contribution per £mu lab | % sales |
|---|---|---|---|---|---|---|---|---|---|---|
| PG 1 | | 2,502·8 | 6,098·65 | 3,247·22 | 99·445 | 366·22 | 2,385·77 | 39 | 4·03 | 9 |
| PG 2 | | 140·4 | 1,499·47 | 913·32 | 14·020 | 89·92 | 482·21 | 32 | 4·25 | 2 |
| PG 3 | | 680·4 | 4,248·72 | 2,938·21 | 28·575 | 254·88 | 1,027·06 | 24 | 2·79 | 6 |
| PG 5 | | 64·2 | 763·68 | 429·61 | 6·340 | 45·76 | 281·97 | 36 | 5·27 | 1 |
| Outlet total | | 3,387·8 | 12,610·52 | 7,528·36 | 148·380 | 756·78 | 4,177·01 | — | 3·71 | — |

## Table 2

### Period 6, 1971

### Underwear and Leisurewear Department

### Outlet 2 Product Group 1

| Style no. | Size (in.) | Quantity (dozens) | Sales | Production cost (standard) | Distribution cost (standard) | Selling cost (standard) | Contribution | % contribution | Contribution per £mu lab | % sales |
|---|---|---|---|---|---|---|---|---|---|---|
| e.g. 5,003 | 36 | 63·0 | 118·20 | 85·05 | 2·646 | 7·09 | 23·42 | 20 | 2·17 | |
| Each style has a number | | No. of dozens sold | Actual value of sale | This is standard and comes from the file i.e. labour cost + material + make-up material + folding material | Carriage + packing (standard). Again this is on file | This is a proportion of the standard cost recovery. This is on file also | Sales – (production + distribution, + selling) | Contribution as a % of sales | Contribution as a multiple of make-up labour in garments | This column refers to group totals only. Group totals' sales as a % of total sales |
| | | ← | | | Totals for group | | | | | |
| | | 4,228·3 | 10,077·10 | 7,077·95 | 177·588 | 604·39 | 2,222·18 | 22 for group | 1·90 | 14 |
| | | | | | | | | ← Weighted average → | | |

## Table 3

### Underwear and Leisurewear Department: Sales by Outlet

| | Month of June 1971 | | Cumulative to June 1971 | | Standard contribution | Contribution per £mu lab | Increase/ decrease in sales since last year |
|---|---|---|---|---|---|---|---|
| | % of total | £ | % of total | £ | % | £mu lab | % |
| Manufacturers | — | | — | 813 | 8 | 0·8 | −51 |
| Mail order | 24 | 16,372 | 20 | 75,695 | 24 | 2·7 | −12 |
| Wholesale | 18 | 12,611 | 19 | 73,847 | 27 | 3·2 | +31 |
| Multiples | 48 | 33,085 | 50 | 187,562 | 24 | 2·6 | −7 |
| Export | 10 | 7,205 | 11 | 41,834 | 28 | 4·0 | +41 |
| | 100 | £69,273 | 100 | £379,751 | 25 | 2·9 | +4 |
| Budget | | £62,000 | | £399,000 | 29 | | |

## Table 4

### Underwear and Leisurewear Department: Sales by Product

| | Month of June 1971 | | Cumulative to June 1971 | | Standard contribution | Contribution per £mu lab | Increase/decrease in sales since last year |
|---|---|---|---|---|---|---|---|
| | % of total | £ | % of total | £ | % | | % |
| Leisurewear | 55 | 37,968 | 42 | 159,049 | 23 | 2·2 | — |
| Children's knickers | 7 | 4,605 | 8 | 30,293 | 17 | 1·7 | +19 |
| Athletic | 12 | 8,409 | 9 | 33,359 | 23 | 2·2 | +12 |
| Heavy | — | 170 | — | 993 | — | — | −158 |
| Women's | 26 | 18,121 | 41 | 156,057 | 29 | 3·8 | +6 |
| | 100 | £69,273 | 100 | £379,751 | 25 | 2·9 | +4 |
| Budget | | £62,000 | | £399,000 | 29 | | |

Table 5 Underwear and Leisurewear Department: Sales Summary

| Period June 1971, Week 4 | | | | Budget | Weeks 29 cumulative | | | |
| Sales £ | % of total | Contribution £ | % of sales | | Sales £ | % of total | Contribution £ | % of sales |
|---|---|---|---|---|---|---|---|---|
| 62,000 | 100 | 18,290 | 29·5 | | 399,000 | 100 | 117,710 | 29·5 |
| | | | | *Manufacturers* | | | | |
| | | | | Leisurewear | | | | |
| | | | | Children's knickers | | | | |
| | | | | Athletic | | | | |
| | | | | Heavy | | | | |
| | | | | Women's | | | | |
| — | — | — | — | | 813 | — | 68 | 8 |
| | | | | *Mail order* | | | | |
| 10,077 | | 2,222 | 22 | Leisurewear | | | | |
| 1,807 | | 363 | 20 | Children's knickers | | | | |
| | | | | Athletic | | | | |
| 4,488 | | 1,516 | 33 | Heavy | | | | |
| | | | | Women's | | | | |
| 16,372 | 24 | 4,101 | 25 | | 75,695 | 20 | 18,209 | 24 |
| | | | | *Wholesale* | | | | |
| 6,099 | | 1,826 | 30 | Leisurewear | | | | |
| 1,499 | | 482 | 32 | Children's knickers | | | | |
| 4,249 | | 1,027 | 24 | Athletic | | | | |
| 764 | | 282 | 36 | Heavy | | | | |
| | | | | Women's | | | | |
| 12,611 | 18 | 3,617 | 29 | | 73,847 | 19 | 20,374 | 27 |

*Table 5 (Cont.)*

Underwear and Leisurewear Department: Sales Summary

|  |  |  |  |  |  |  |  |  |
|---|--:|--:|--:|--:|--:|--:|--:|--:|
| *Multiple* |  |  |  |  |  |  |  |  |
| Leisurewear | 21,534 |  | 4,971 | 23 |  |  |  |  |
| Children's knickers | 1,496 |  | 188 | 12 |  |  |  |  |
| Athletic | 3,777 |  | 848 | 27 |  |  |  |  |
| Heavy | 170 |  | (161) | — |  |  |  |  |
| Women's | 6,108 |  | 1,681 | 27 |  |  |  |  |
|  | 33,085 | 48 | 7,527 | 23 | 187,562 | 50 | 44,267 | 24 |
| *Export* |  |  |  |  |  |  |  |  |
| Leisurewear | 258 |  | — | — |  |  |  |  |
| Children's knickers | (197) |  | 58 | 22 |  |  |  |  |
| Athletic | 383 |  | (49) | — |  |  |  |  |
| Heavy | — |  | 68 | 18 |  |  |  |  |
| Women's | 6,761 |  | 1,581 | 23 |  |  |  |  |
|  | 7,105 | 10 | 1,658 | 23 | 41,834 | 11 | 11,878 | 28 |
| *Total* |  |  |  |  |  |  |  |  |
| Leisurewear | 37,968 | 55 | 9,077 | 24 | 159,049 | 42 | 36,373 | 23 |
| Children's knickers | 4,605 | 7 | 984 | 21 | 30,293 | 8 | 5,199 | 17 |
| Athletic | 8,409 | 12 | 1,943 | 23 | 33,359 | 9 | 7,781 | 23 |
| Heavy | 170 | — | (161) | — | 993 | — | (541) | — |
| Women's | 18,121 | 26 | 5,060 | 28 | 156,057 | 41 | 45,984 | 29 |
|  | 69,273 | 100 | 16,903 | 24 | 379,571 | 100 | 94,796 | 25 |

# APPENDIX C

## Underwear and Leisurewear Department: Variance Report for June 1971

| Item | Variance last month | Variance this month | Variance to date | Person responsible | Reasons given for variance | Action taken |
|------|------|------|------|------|------|------|
| Winding labour | (15) | (15) | (44) | Mr Thomas | Re-winding of yarn for use on 8 feed machines | 3 new multi-feed machines ordered which will eliminate this operation. Number of cores with faults being investigated |
| Cutting usage Dept. 1 | (606) | (458) | (1790) | Mr Robson | — | Check being made of weight per square inch of end patterns |
| Outside labour Dept. 1 | (259) | (412) | (851) | Mr Robson | 1. Flatlocking sent to Dixon and Tomkins due to lack of capacity<br>2. Eyelet fabric being knitted by Morgan James to build up stock to keep bands running<br>3. Interlock fabric knitted by Rockbrook Knitting | 3 Union special tubing machines now ready to go into production, but waiting for trimming and lights to be fixed. These will release capacity on our present flatlockers to enable them to cope with work at present sent to Dodsons<br>3 new multi-feed machines ordered which will have enough capacity to cope with this work and future expected increases in output<br>To make up temporary shortage of fabric |
| Outside labour Dept. 2 | (10) | (10) | (20) | | Wool and Crepe Link by R. Clark & Co. to cover where production shows large fluctuations | Own linkers being kept, supplied before R. Clark & Co. |

Variance Report for June 1971 (*Cont.*)

| Item | Variance last month | Variance this month | Variance to date | Person responsible | Reasons given for variance | Action taken |
|------|------|------|------|------|------|------|
| Direct labour and H.P. Dept. 1 Making-up | (150) | (187) | (581) | Mr Robson | Shirt and Trousers Operators on other work make up on All Welting Section due to new machines being run in | |
| Direct labour and H.P. Dept. 1 Folding | (107) | (74) | (444) | Mr Simpkins | Only two weeks folding jobs. Make up on Press Operatives for doing folding | Steps being taken to reduce number of jobs due to faulty yarn. Classifying of jobs at present not practicable |
| Direct labour and H.P. Dept. 2 Linking and drawthread | (46) | (89) | (229) | Mr Smith | Employing personnel beyond retiring age | |
| Direct labour and H.P. Dept. 2 Folding | (179) | (199) | (577) | Mr Black | Large number of samples and jobs folding. Unmeasured rate paid for sorting | Improved lay-out submitted ready for approval |

*Note*
1. Only adverse variances are shown.
2. Each item will appear each month until the variance is corrected.

# Keepdry Ltd

KEEPDRY LTD produce ladies' nylon raincoats at premises in Handley, Leek and Stone in Staffordshire. Recently the company have been informed that, as a result of a general increase in rates, and a further hardening of the attitude of Insurers against unsprinkled risks, the company's fire insurance premium will increase by approximately £5,000 per annum to £16,500 per annum, and consequential-loss insurance premium by £1,000 per annum to £5,000 per annum. Keepdry's factories are all unsprinkled, and discussions with Insurers have revealed that an investment in sprinkler installations at these establishments would bring reductions in insurance premiums of approximately £10,500 per annum. Although there would be an additional premium in respect of sprinkler leakage cover, approximately £200 per annum, it is clear that the reductions in premiums would more than offset the recently imposed increases.

Keepdry have obtained competitive quotations for sprinkler installations, and the best are:

| Premises | Capital cost | Net annual savings in premiums |
|---|---|---|
|  | £ | £ |
| Handley | 19,100 | 5,300 |
| Leek | 5,900 | 800 |
| Stone | 17,300 | 4,400 |
|  | £42,300 | £10,500 |

The net annual saving in premium is lower for the Leek factory because the water pressure in the area would not guarantee a Class I installation, and therefore Class I insurance premiums. Also the stock holding at Leek is low compared with the Handley and Stone factories. The company's insurers have advised that the trend in premiums is likely to continue upwards. The management of Keepdry Ltd expect the Leek factory to become increasingly important, with correspondingly greater stock holdings.

The sprinkler installations are expected to have a ten-year life and a nil residual value. Keepdry Ltd depreciates equipment on a straight-line basis. The investment will attract a capital allowance of 60 per cent in the first year, and an annual allowance of 20 per cent, reducing balance in subsequent years. The current rate of corporation tax is 40 per cent and the company's cost of capital is 12 per cent per annum.

QUESTION

Undertake a financial evaluation of the proposed investment in sprinkling equipment.

SUGGESTED BACKGROUND READING

*An Insight into Management Accounting*, Chapter 6.

ACKNOWLEDGEMENT

This case is based on material kindly made available by Associated Industrial Consultants Ltd with permission of the National Economic Development Office. It was collected by Associated Industrial Consultants as part of an investment-appraisal study for the Economic Development Committee for the Clothing Industry.

# John Jones Ltd

JOHN JONES LTD, who make up ladies' dresses, have manufacturing, showroom, office and warehousing accommodation at various premises in Manchester, including 101-103 Jones Street and 5 John Street. The Jones Street premises comprise approximately 6,000 square feet on basement and ground floor. The rental for these premises is £3,100 per annum, the rates £2,200 per annum, and the lease expires in four years' time. The John Street premises are also leasehold, the 99-year lease has approximately 87 years to run. The accommodation comprises basement, ground and three upper floors, each of approximately 3,000 square feet. The rental is £1,000 per annum and the rates £4,200 per annum.

During the past five years, John Jones's turnover has increased from around £600,000 per annum to nearly £900,000 per annum, including a small, but expanding export business. Considerable warehousing, handling and distribution problems have resulted from this growth. In addition there is a growing tendency for larger customers to place bulk orders for call-off during a season causing a need for considerable additional warehousing. Recently a subsidiary company has been formed in premises in Alan Road, Manchester, for manufacturing jeans, and in the longer term it is hoped that a considerable increase in both home and export turnover will be achieved. Any increase in turnover will inevitably aggravate the warehousing and handling problems. In order to provide additional manufacturing space, warehouse facilities on one floor of Alan Road will need to be transferred to alternative accommodation.

Existing warehousing accommodation is inadequate. It is spread between Jones Street and various floors at John Street. Almost every available corner is in use, and at times merchandise in stock has overflowed into administrative offices. Because of lack of space merchandise is badly and inefficiently stocked, making access difficult, and in some instances virtually impossible. This results in inefficient order packing and means that during a season many orders may go unfulfilled, resulting not only in a loss of turnover, but in considerable mark-downs at the end of each season. It is estimated that because of this approximately £20,000 to £30,000 sales per season are lost, which, added to the cost of jobbings and mark-downs, could cost the company around £7,500 per annum. The situation has become so serious that further storage space has been taken, on a temporary basis, in a railway warehouse at a rental of £1,200 per annum. This has made little difference to the overall problem, and in some ways, because there are now three warehousing centres, has further aggravated it.

The senior management of John Jones Ltd recently undertook a review of the situation and concluded that, unless urgent and drastic action is taken in the very near future, the activities of the company could possibly come to a standstill. It is felt that new accommodation should be sought in which all showrooms, office and warehouse facilities could be centralized, enabling Jones Street and about half of the John Street accommodation to be disposed of. Alternatively, it is suggested that it might be advantageous to vacate John Street completely, and to transfer the manufacturing facilities to the new premises, in addition to the showroom, office and warehousing operations. This would enable either the whole of John Street to be sublet, or for the company's leasehold interest to be disposed of. John Street is thought to have a market value of £100,000, and subletting could bring in at least 62½p per square foot or upwards of approximately £9,500 per annum. The renewal rental of the Jones Street premises is expected to be in the region of £9,000 to £10,000 per annum based on £3 per square foot for the ground floor, and around £1 per square foot for the basement.

A preliminary search for alternative accommodation has already taken place, and a possible site, currently in the course of redevelopment, has become available at Stretford Road. The developers would be willing to erect on the site custom-built premises of either 20,000 square feet or 30,000 square feet to

John Jones's requirement for entry in one year. Although detailed discussions have not yet taken place, it has been suggested that the property could be offered on a long lease at between 62½p and 75p per square foot. It is not yet known whether the freehold interest could be purchased. Arnold Smith, the managing director of John Jones Ltd, feels that some attempt should be made to quantify the financial effects and implications of the various possible moves. John Jones is a wholly owned subsidiary of Superclothes Ltd and, in the event that one or more moves appeared to be a feasible proposition, Smith would like to seek approval in principle from the Board of Directors of Superclothes Ltd for further investigation of one or more of the various proposals. Further detailed discussions on the terms upon which the new premises could be acquired, and the existing premises disposed of, could be undertaken with the company's various professional advisers. Considerable additional thought would need to be given to the various removal and ancillary costs. The board of directors of Superclothes requires a minimum D.C.F. return of 12 per cent after corporation tax on capital projects, the current rate of corporation tax being 45 per cent.

If the company concentrated all showroom, office and warehouse accommodation in new premises, enabling Jones Street and about half of the John Street premises to be disposed of, 20,000 square feet of new space would be required at an estimated rental of 75p per square foot and 30p per square foot for rates. Legal and professional fees could amount to £3,500, and removal and displacement costs to £4,000. It is not known whether the move would create a redundancy situation, under the Redundancy Payments Act, as each case is decided by the Tribunal on its merits. However, it is certain that some severance or redundancy payments will have to be made, and these are estimated at £2,000. No manpower savings are expected to accrue as a direct result of the move, and transport costs will not be materially affected. If the company were to continue in Jones Street after the current lease expires, the rental of these premises is expected to increase to at least £9,000 per annum. For the remainder of the Jones Street lease it is felt that the premises could hopefully be sublet at a rental of at least £6,000 per annum. Alternatively it is likely that the landlord may be prepared to accept a surrender of the remainder of the lease in view of the desirability of the site. In the event of a floor of Alan Street being released for manufacturing sometime in the future, and the warehouse transferred to new premises, it is felt that the turnover of jeans could be increased by around £50,000 per annum and net profit by £5,000 per annum. The difference between the additional net profit and the additional cash inflow is expected to cover the costs of financing the additional sales in stocks, debtors, etc.

30,000 square feet of new space would be required if Jones Street and John Street were closed completely and the John Street premises sold. Legal and professional fees could amount to around £5,000, and removal and displacement costs to £6,000. Redundancy payments are estimated at £4,000. No manpower savings are likely to accrue as a result of the move. The sale of the John Street premises is expected to realize £90,000. It would be possible to sublet instead of selling the entire premises, but it is felt that the benefits would be marginal. The closure of John Street entirely would have the advantage of releasing nearly £100,000 of assets, thus improving return on capital employed, and enabling the cash to be put to more productive uses. There could be a capital-gains-tax liability on the appreciation on the value of the John Street lease since acquisition, but after charging various expenses on a value of £90,000 this should not be more than £3,000. Betterment Levy is not applicable. At the present time the company is paying 9 per cent interest on a bank overdraft of £350,000. Net realized value of the John Street premises, £90,000 less expenses in connection with legal and professional fees, capital-gains tax, removal costs, redundancy payments, will reduce the level of the company's bank overdraft. It should be possible to release a floor of Alan Road for manufacturing purposes.

QUESTION

You are required by Arnold Smith to undertake a financial

evaluation of the alternative moves, which, if one or more move appeared to be a feasible proposition, he could incorporate in a request for approval in principle from the Board of Directors of Superclothes Ltd.

## SUGGESTED BACKGROUND READING

*An Insight into Management Accounting*, Chapter 6.

## ACKNOWLEDGEMENT

This case is based on material kindly made available by Associated Industrial Consultants Ltd with permission of the National Economic Development Office. It was collected by Associated Industrial Consultants as part of an Investment Appraisal study for the Economic Development Committee for the Clothing Industry.

# Moonshine Ltd*

MOONSHINE LTD has factories and warehouses in Nottingham, Loughborough, Leicester, Beeston, Hucknall, Hinckley, Barrow-on-Soar, Mansfield, Derby, Sutton-in-Ashfield and Macclesfield. The company produces stockings and tights, knitwear, leisure-wear, underwear, socks and swimwear. In 1967 it had a turnover in excess of £16 million. The company is organized into four divisions: hosiery, outerwear, underwear and half-hose. The divisions operate as autonomous units with their own marketing, personnel and finance departments. Each is under the control of a divisional director who is responsible for the profitability of the division. The managing director, Frank Dennison, is supported by a small head-office staff, including the financial director, John Redbrick. Each October divisional directors are required to submit a budget for the following year, including a capital-expenditure forecast, which is examined by Mr Redbrick and approved by Mr Dennison. The divisional directors must seek the authority of the executive committee, a sub-committee of the board of directors of Moonshine Ltd, for capital projects in excess of £25,000. The executive committee consists of Frank Dennison, John Redbrick, Bill Harper (deputy managing director) and the four divisional directors. Capital applications have to be submitted in a standard form to John Redbrick, who is required to examine the applications prior to their consideration by the executive committee. A divisional director speaks for his application at the executive-committee meeting, and usually he is cross-examined by Frank Dennison. He leaves the meeting while a decision on the application is made by the remainder of the committee. John Redbrick prepared for Frank Dennison and

*This case first appeared in the *Hosiery Trade Journal*, March 1972, pp. 85-6, 120-22.

Bill Harper, prior to the meeting of the executive committee, an assessment of capital applications submitted.

The Outerwear Division of Moonshine Ltd produces fully fashioned and cut-and-sewn garments at the following premises:

French Street, Sutton-in-Ashfield, and Simpson Avenue, Nottingham: fully integrated knitting and making-up factories with warehousing space.

Falles Road, Loughborough: a knitting and making-up unit with no warehousing space.

Broad Street, Leicester, Beeston and Hucknall: making-up units with no warehousing space.

Colin Rockcliffe, the divisional director, would like to expand the production of the Outerwear Division and at the same time rationalize operations so as to make best use of available space and labour. He has submitted the following capital application to John Redbrick for approval by the executive committee. Arthur Brownlee, the Outerwear Division accountant, undertook the financial evaluation of the project. Brownlee's working papers are provided in the Appendix.

QUESTIONS

1. What are the major points John Redbrick should make in his assessment of the capital application?
2. In what ways could the capital-application procedure be improved?

SUGGESTED BACKGROUND READING

1. *An Insight into Management Accounting*, Chapter 6.
2. National Economic Development Council, *Investment Appraisal*, H.M.S.O., London, 1972.
3. National Association of Accountants, *Financial Analysis to Guide Capital Expenditure Decisions*, Research Report No. 43, New York, 1967.
4. W. Scott and B. R. Williams, *Investment Proposals and Decisions*, Allen & Unwin, London, 1965.

## CAPITAL APPLICATION
## OUTERWEAR DIVISION EXPANSION

Attached is a capital application (Reference 1968/01) for a scheme to increase production of fully fashioned garments by 750 dozen per week, and cut flat-frame throughout by 375 dozen per week.

The plant, ancillary machines and floor renewals required are as follows:

| | £ |
|---|---|
| 1. Plant | |
| Knitting machinery | |
| 4 Johnson fully fashioned knitting machines | 123,000 |
| 6 Monarch rib-knitting machines for trimmings | 25,500 |
| 2 Snow cable-knitting machines | 9,000 |
| Ancillary machinery, electrical installations etc. | 37,000 |
| 2. Buildings: replacement of 2 floors | 15,000 |
| | £209,500 |

One object of the various projected moves and developments resulting from the proposals is to utilize better the possible female labour available at French Street, Sutton-in-Ashfield, by using Simpson Avenue, Nottingham, space for complete warehousing of Sutton-in-Ashfield's production. At the same time productivity to space ratio will be improved.

IMPLEMENTATION

French Street, Sutton-in-Ashfield, is a fully integrated unit at its maximum capacity of 2,250 plus dozen per week. Labour is relatively free in this area.

Loughborough is committed to an increase of 1,600 dozen per week, which will be attained by July 1968. At this date total knitting capacity of fully fashioned will be 3,850 dozens. Space is available for a further 2×16 section Johnson machines giving a production increase of 320 dozens – total capacity 4,170 dozens. These machines can be installed in September/October making this capacity available by Spring 1969.

French Street has 11,500 square feet of good manufacturing floor space at present used for warehousing. We propose to transfer this operation complete to Simpson Avenue and integrate all divisional warehousing there. The floor space will be laid out for fully fashioned make-up operations. Potential capacity is approximately 1,500 dozen per week.

Simpson Avenue is faced with a difficult labour problem. In order to raise cut make-up capacity, it will be necessary to direct recruitment to that department. Fully fashioned make-up will be frozen at 1,100 to 1,300 dozen per week – its present capacity. If we still have a shortfall in making-up labour, then a retraining programme will be implemented. Labour will be transferred from fully fashioned make-up to cut make-up at Simpson Avenue and the balance of fully fashioned make-up transferred to French Street.

### Phase I

Transfer approximately 750 dozen finished make-up from Broad Street, Leicester, to French Street using machinery, ancillary equipment and trained labour from Leicester. Initially 375 dozen finished make-up at Loughborough would be fed into Broad Street. New machinery would be purchased and labour trained on this site where training facilities are available. Target date August 1968.

### Phase II

Install two Johnson fully fashioned machines at Loughborough together with the required rib-knitting and making-up machinery. These machines will be 21 gauge for Spring 1969 business. Transfer the balance of warehouse from French Street factory to Simpson Avenue and install machinery and recruit labour for French Street factory to increase capacity here for finished make-up by a further 450 dozen per week. Labour available at Loughborough at this time will control the type of business, that is, turned welt or ribbed garments. Target date December 1968.

### Phase III

Recruit trained labour at Leicester for a further 300–375 dozen per week, relieving Simpson Avenue of equivalent quantity, releasing labour at Simpson Avenue for retraining for cut and sewn make-up. This operation would be completed as and when flat-frame knitting and sales exceed making-up capacity at Simpson Street cut and sewn section, Beeston and Hucknall.

### Phase IV

Purchase two Snow cable machines to replace existing eighteen-year-old plant.

COLIN ROCKCLIFFE
Divisional Director

### Capital Application

1. *Division*: Outerwear   Reference: 1968/01
   Date: 10 April 1968

2. *Title of project*: Outerwear Division expansion

3. *Reason for recommending project* (a summary of management's justification given in the covering note)

   To expand production of fully fashioned outerwear by 750 dozens per week and flat-frame outerwear by 375 dozens per week, involving the switching of operations between factories to take advantage of varying labour availability.

4. *Whether included in capital-expenditure forecast submitted in October 1967*

   No, except for £81,900 (see para. 11), now being included as part of this project.

5. *Cost of project*

| | £'000 |
|---|---|
| Plant (before deducting grants) | 194 |
| Buildings (before deducting grants) (see para. 7 note 2) | 15 |
| Allied revenue expenditure | 24 |
| Working capital | 183 |
| Contingency | 20 |
| (less realizations from assets scrapped) | (Nil) |
| *Total for which approval now sought* | 436 |
| *less* Investment grants receivable (25%) | 47 |
| Net expenditure | 389 |

6. *Profit or saving at peak* (most likely assumptions)

<table>
<tr><td></td><td>£'000</td></tr>
<tr><td>(For 6 years from 1970 to 1975)</td><td>97</td></tr>
</table>

7. *Profitability*

| | assumptions most likely | alternative assumptions 'worse' | 'better' |
|---|---|---|---|
| D.C.F. return (after tax)* | 17½% | 14% | 20·5% |
| Traditional return at peak as % of expenditure less grants | 25% | | |
| Pay-back (after tax) | 2 years | | |
| Profit as % of turnover (at peak) | 14% | | |

*To nearest ½ per cent after taking account of any further expenditure under item 10.

*Notes.*

1. When considering the D.C.F. return and the pay-back period, it is important to realize that outflow occurs at the end of our financial year ending 31 December 1968, which is taken as year 0 for the purpose of this project. Sales will commence spring 1969.

2. No amount has been included to represent the value of buildings, apart from the replacement of two floors, as the project only involves the re-siting of operations in space already utilized by the Outerwear Division.

8. *The extent to which alternatives have been considered*
Not applicable.

9. *Underlying assumptions* (price and costs relative to present levels, percentage of capacity working, life)
    (a) most likely
        (i) Production efficiency at rate at present being attained.
        (ii) Costs at present levels, selling prices at 97½ per cent of present levels.
        (iii) Knitting machinery will have seven-year life, constant profit level.
        (iv) Necessary making-up labour is obtained.
    (b) possible variations ('better' and 'worse')
        Better: Selling prices 100 per cent of present levels.
        Worse: Selling prices 95 per cent of present levels.

10. *Probable further expenditure during life of project* to maintain forecast profits (estimate, with explanations necessary)   Nil.

11. *Commitments already made*

| | |
|---|---|
| 2 Johnson F.F. knitting machines | 60,600 |
| 3 Monarch D.R.L./D.R.B. rib-knitting machines | 12,300 |
| New floor – Loughborough | 9,000 |
| | £81,900 |

12. *Is this project part of a larger scheme?* (if so, give details)   No.

13. *Cash-flow schedule* (for the first five years, unless pay-back period longer)
    *on most likely assumptions*

|  | OUTFLOW | | | INFLOW | |
|  | Cost of project £'000 | Grants receivable £'000 | Net expenditure £'000 | Cash profit less net tax payments £'000 | NET CASH FLOW £'000 |
|---|---|---|---|---|---|
| 1968 | 356 | — | 356 | (8) | (364) |
| 1969 | 80 | 47 | 33 | 112 | 79 |
| 1970 | — | — | — | 95 | 95 |
| 1971 | — | — | — | 76 | 76 |
| 1972 | — | — | — | 75 | 75 |
| 19 | | | | | |
| 19 | | | | | |
| 19 | | | | | |

14. *Revenue and costs* (on 'most likely' assumptions at peak)

| | | £'000 | % |
|---|---|---|---|
| Sales | Annual sales or value of production arising directly from this project (at peak) | 684 | 100 |
| Costs | Related costs of production, marketing and distribution | | |
| |     Variable | 531 | 78 |
| |     Depreciation | 22 | 3 |
| |     Other fixed costs | 34 | 5 |
| |     Total | 587 | 86 |
| Profit | At peak | 97 | 14 |

15. *Estimated completion date*
    Early 1969

16. *Application prepared by:*
    Colin Rockcliffe – Divisional Director
    Arthur Brownlee – Divisional Accountant

*Appendix*

## Working Papers

**1. *Effective life of fixed assets***

| | |
|---|---|
| Knitting machinery | 7 years |
| Ancillary machinery | 10 years |
| Buildings | 50 years |
| Fixtures and fittings | 18 years |

**2. *Additional fixed overhead***

| | £'000 | £'000 |
|---|---|---|
| Depreciation (on expenditure less investment grant) | | |
| Knitting machinery | 17 | |
| Ancillary machinery | 4 | |
| Buildings, fixtures and fittings | 1 | |
| | — | 22 |
| Staff | | |
| Selling and distribution | 6 | |
| Factory | 10 | |
| | — | 16 |
| Heating, power, light, space | | 2 |
| Canteen administration | | (say) 6 |
| Transport | | 2 |
| Make-up pay | | 8 |
| | | £56 |

**3. *Additional revenue expenditure***

| | £'000 |
|---|---|
| Training | |
| Knitting-machine operators | 5 |
| Making-up operatives (female) | |
| Simpson Avenue and Hucknall | |
| 100% 55 at £200 | 11 |
| French Street and Loughborough | |
| 50% 80 at £200 | 16 |
| | 32 |
| *less* Grants from Training Board | 20 |
| | 12 |
| Repairs and maintenance | 12 |
| | £24 |

4. *Additional working capital*

|  | £'000 |
|---|---|
| Yarn 3 weeks = 3,375 dozen at £4 | 13 |
| Work in progress 9 weeks = 10,125 dozen at £8 | 81 |
| Finished goods 5 weeks = 5,625 dozen at £10 | 56 |
| Debtors 3 weeks = 3,375 dozen at £13 | 43 |
|  | 193 |
| *less* Increase in creditors | 10 |
|  | £183 |

5. *Estimated additional profits* (*normal year*)

|  | Fully fashioned | Cut and sewn | Total |
|---|---|---|---|
| Dozens per week | 750 | 375 | 1,125 |
| per annum | 36,000 | 18,000 | 54,000 |
| Sales per dozen | £13 | £13 |  |
| per annum | £468,000 | £234,000 | £702,000 |
| Contribution per dozen | £3·5 | £2·5 |  |
| per annum | £126,000 | £45,000 | £171,000 |

|  | Expected | Best | Worst |
|---|---|---|---|
| Sales per dozen | 97½% | 100% | 95% |
|  | £ | £ | £ |
| Sales | 684,450 | 702,000 | 666,900 |
| Variable costs (difference) | 531,000 | 531,000 | 531,000 |
| Contribution | 153,450 | 171,000 | 135,900 |
| Additional fixed overheads | 56,000 | 56,000 | 56,000 |
| *Profit* | £97,450 | £115,000 | £79,900 |

6. *Estimated additional profits* (*years 1–8*)

| Expected | Sales £'000 | Variable £'000 | Depreciation £'000 | Other fixed costs £'000 | Profit £'000 |
|---|---|---|---|---|---|
| Normal year | 684 | 531 | 22 | 34 | 97 |
| Year 0 | nil | nil | nil | 8 | (8) |
| 1 (9 months' sales) | 513 | 398 | 22 | 34 | 59 |
| 2–7 (1970–75) | 684 | 531 | 22 | 34 | 97 |
| 8 (3 months' sales) | 171 | 133 | nil | 5 | 33 |

*Best*

| Year 0 | nil | | (8) |
|---|---|---|---|
| 1 | 526 | | 72 |
| 2–7 | 702 | As above | 115 |
| 8 | 176 | | 38 |

*Worst*

| Year 0 | nil | | (8) |
|---|---|---|---|
| 1 | 500 | As above | 46 |
| 2–7 | 667 | | 80 |
| 8 | 167 | | 29 |

7. *Summary of capital and repairs and maintenance expenditure*

| | Plant £ | Buildings £ | R. and M. £ | Total £ |
|---|---|---|---|---|
| Phase I | 9,361 | 40 | 296 | 9,697 |
| II | 99,752 | 9,000 | 8,850 | 117,602 |
| III | 3,259 | — | — | 3,259 |
| IV | 9,000 | — | — | 9,000 |
| Commitments already made | | | | |
| 2 Johnson F.F. knitting machines | 60,600 | — | — | 60,600 |
| 3 Monarch rib machines | 12,300 | — | — | 12,300 |
| New floor at Loughborough | — | 6,000 | 3,000 | 9,000 |
| | £194,272 | £15,040 | £12,146 | £221,458 |

*Note*

No amount has been included to represent the value of buildings, apart from the replacement of two floors, as the project only involves the re-siting of operations in space already utilized by the Knitted Outerwear Division.

# Schedule of Expenditure and Grants: Form 1

## Part A  Expenditure for Tax Purposes

| PROJECT YEAR | Expenditure before deducting grants | | | | Net expenditure for tax purposes | | | | ALLIED REVENUE EXPENDITURE | WORKING CAPITAL |
| | PLANT | | | BUILDINGS | PLANT | | | BUILDINGS | | |
| | eligible for grant | | not eligible for grant | | eligible for grant (a) | | not eligible for grant (b) | | | |
| | with wear and tear allowance of | | with wear and tear allowance of | | with wear and tear allowance of | | | | | |
| | (1) 15% | (2) 20% | (3) 15% | (4) | (5) 15% | (6) 20% | (7) 15% | (8) (c) | (9) | (10) |
|---|---|---|---|---|---|---|---|---|---|---|
| Contingency | | 10,000 | 14,000 | 5,000 | | 7,500 | 14,000 | 5,000 | 5,000 | 103,000 |
| 0 | | 180,000 | | 15,000 | | 135,000 | | 15,000 | 24,000 | |
| 1 | | | | | | | | | | 80,000 |

(a) Seventy-five per cent of columns 1 and 2 outside a Development Area, 55 per cent within a Development Area.
(b) Repeat figures from column 3.
(c) The same as in column 4 if outside a Development Area, if within a Development Area, normally 75 per cent of column 4.

## Schedule of Expenditure and Grants: Form 1 (*Cont.*)

### Part B  Estimated Cash Outflow

| | (11) | (12) | (13) | (14) | (15) | (16) | (17) | (18) |
|---|---|---|---|---|---|---|---|---|
| | Expenditure before deducting grants | | | GRANTS *receivable* | | | | |
| | PLANT | | BUILDINGS (f) | PLANT (g) | BUILDINGS (h) | ALLIED REVENUE EXPENDITURE | WORKING CAPITAL | TOTALS to Form 3 11+12+13 +16+17 −14−15 |
| PROJECT YEAR | eligible for grant (d) | not eligible for grant (e) | | | | | | |
| 0 | 190,000 | 14,000 | 20,000 | — | — | 29,000 | 103,000 | 356,000 |
| 1 | | | | (47,500) | — | | 80,000 | 32,500 |

(d) The sum of columns 1 and 2 above.

(e) The same as column 3 above.

(f) The same as column 4 above.

(g) Twenty-five per cent of column 11 of the previous year if the project is outside a Development Area, 45 per cent if the project is within a Development Area.

(h) Nil if the project is outside a Development Area, normally 25 per cent of column 13 if the project is within a Development Area.

*Note:* The grants are not lagged in Part A, but are lagged one year in Part B.

## Schedule of Tax Allowances and Recoveries*
### Form 2

| | (1) | (2) | (3) | (4) | (5) | (6) | (7) | (8) | (9) | (10) | (11) | (12) |
|---|---|---|---|---|---|---|---|---|---|---|---|---|
| | NET EXPENDITURE (from Cols. 5–10 of Form 1) | | | | | | NET TAX SAVED RESULTING FROM EXPENDITURE | | | | | |
| | PLANT | | | BUILD-INGS | ALLIED REVENUE EXPENDI-TURE | WORKING CAPITAL | PLANT PURCHASED Year 0 | | | BUILDINGS PURCHASED Year 0 | ALLIED REVENUE EXPENDI-TURE | TOTALS to Form 3 col. 5 |
| | eligible for grant | | not eligible for grant | | | | eligible for grant | | not eligible for grant | | | |
| | with wear and tear allowance of | | | | | | with wear and tear allowance of | | | | | |
| PROJECT YEAR | 15% | 20% | 15% | | | | 15% | 20% | 15% | Year 0 | | |
| 0 | | 142,500 | 14,000 | 20,000 | 29,000 | 103,000 | — | | | | | |
| 1 | | | | | | 80,000 | | 12,100 | 2,700 | 1,400 | 12,300 | 28,500 |
| 2 | | | | | | | | 9,700 | 500 | 200 | | 10,400 |
| 3 | | | | | | | | 7,800 | 400 | 200 | | 8,400 |
| 4 | | | | | | | | 6,200 | 300 | 200 | | 6,700 |
| 5 | | | | | | | | 4,900 | 300 | 200 | | 5,400 |
| 6 | | | | | | | | 4,000 | 300 | 200 | | 4,500 |
| 7 | | | | | | | | 3,200 | 200 | 200 | | 3,600 |
| 8 | | | | | | | | 2,500 | 200 | 700† | | 2,900 |
| 9 | | (9,000) | (4,000) | (12,000) | — | (183,000) | | 6,300† | (600)† | | | 6,400 |
| TOTAL | | 133,500 | 10,000 | 8,000 | 29,000 | — | | 56,700 | 4,300 | 3,500 | 12,300 | 76,800 |

*Recoveries (i.e. scrap and residual values of plant and buildings and recoveries of working capital) should be entered as appropriate in columns 1–6 in the final year of the project.
† Balancing allowance/(charge).

# Cash Flow Schedule (Worst): Form 3

## A: Cash outflow

| YEAR | CASH OUTFLOW from Form 1 Col. 18 £'000 | DISCOUNTED AT 10% Factor | Resultant | DISCOUNTED AT 15% Factor | Resultant |
|---|---|---|---|---|---|
| 0 | 356 | 1·0 | 356 | 1·0 | 356 |
| 1 | 33 | 0·909 | 30 | 0·870 | 28 |
| TOTALS (A) | 389 | | 386 | | 384 |

## B: Cash inflow

| YEAR | (1) Profit £'000 | (2) Depreciation £'000 | (3) PROFIT BEFORE DEPRECIATION £'000 | (4) TAX at 42·5% on previous year of col. 3 £'000 | (5) TAX SAVED on allowances (from Form 2 col.12) £'000 | (6) Recovery of capital (from final year of cols. 1–6 Form 2) £'000 | (7) NET CASH INFLOW 3+5+6−4 £'000 | DISCOUNTED AT 10% Factor | Resultant £'000 | DISCOUNTED AT 15% Factor | Resultant £'000 |
|---|---|---|---|---|---|---|---|---|---|---|---|
| 0 | (8) | | (8) | (3) | — | | (8) | 1·0 | (8) | 1·0 | (8) |
| 1 | 46 | 22 | 68 | 29 | 28 | | 99 | 0·909 | 90 | 0·870 | 86 |
| 2 | 80 | 22 | 102 | 43 | 10 | | 83 | 0·826 | 69 | 0·756 | 63 |
| 3 | 80 | 22 | 102 | 43 | 8 | | 67 | 0·751 | 50 | 0·658 | 44 |
| 4 | 80 | 22 | 102 | 43 | 7 | | 66 | 0·683 | 45 | 0·572 | 38 |
| 5 | 80 | 22 | 102 | 43 | 5 | | 64 | 0·621 | 40 | 0·497 | 31 |
| 6 | 80 | 22 | 102 | 43 | 5 | | 64 | 0·564 | 36 | 0·432 | 28 |
| 7 | 80 | 22 | 102 | 43 | 4 | | 63 | 0·513 | 32 | 0·376 | 24 |
| 8 | 29 | — | 29 | 43 | 3 | 208 | 197 | 0·467 | 92 | 0·327 | 64 |
| 9 | | | | 12 | 6 | | (6) | 0·424 | (2) | 0·284 | (2) |
| TOTALS | 547 | 154 | 701 | 296 | 76 | 208 | 689 | | 444 | | 368 |

TOTALS (B)

| | |
|---|---|
| NET PRESENT VALUE | 58 |  (16) |

D.C.F. rate of return is by interpolation = 14·0% (to nearest ½%)

# Cash Flow Schedule (Expected): Form 3

## A: Cash outflow

| YEAR | CASH OUTFLOW from Form 1 col. 18 £'000 | DISCOUNTED AT 15% Factor | Resultant | DISCOUNTED AT 20% Factor | Resultant |
|---|---|---|---|---|---|
| 0 | 356 | 1·0 | 356 | 1·0 | 356 |
| 1 | 33 | 0·870 | 28 | 0·833 | 27 |
| TOTALS (A) | 389 | | 384 | | 383 |

## B: Cash inflow

| YEAR | (1) Profit £'000 | (2) Depreciation £'000 | (3) Profit before depreciation £'000 | (4) Tax at 42·5% on previous year of col. 3 £'000 | (5) Tax saved on allowances (from Form 2 col. 12) £'000 | (6) Recovery of capital (from final year of cols. 1–6 Form 2) £'000 | (7) Net cash inflow 3+5+6−4 £'000 | DISCOUNTED AT 15% Factor | Resultant £'000 | DISCOUNTED AT 20% Factor | Resultant £'000 |
|---|---|---|---|---|---|---|---|---|---|---|---|
| 0 | (8) | — | (8) | — | — | | (8) | 1·0 | (8) | 1·0 | (8) |
| 1 | 59 | 22 | 81 | (3) | 28 | | 112 | 0·870 | 97 | 0·833 | 93 |
| 2 | 97 | 22 | 119 | 34 | 10 | | 95 | 0·756 | 72 | 0·694 | 66 |
| 3 | 97 | 22 | 119 | 51 | 8 | | 76 | 0·658 | 50 | 0·579 | 44 |
| 4 | 97 | 22 | 119 | 51 | 7 | | 75 | 0·572 | 43 | 0·482 | 36 |
| 5 | 97 | 22 | 119 | 51 | 5 | | 73 | 0·497 | 36 | 0·402 | 29 |
| 6 | 97 | 22 | 119 | 51 | 5 | | 73 | 0·432 | 32 | 0·335 | 24 |
| 7 | 97 | 22 | 119 | 51 | 4 | | 72 | 0·376 | 27 | 0·279 | 20 |
| 8 | 33 | — | 33 | 51 | 3 | 208 | 193 | 0·327 | 63 | 0·233 | 45 |
| 9 | | — | | 14 | 6 | | (8) | 0·284 | (2) | 0·194 | (2) |
| TOTALS | 666 | 154 | 820 | 351 | 76 | 208 (TOTALS B) | 753 | | 410 | | 347 |
| NET PRESENT VALUE | | | | | | | | | 26 | | (36) |

D.C.F. rate of return is by interpolation = 17·5% (to nearest ½%)

## Cash Flow Schedule (Best): Form 3

### A: Cash outflow

| YEAR | CASH OUTFLOW from Form 1 col. 18 £'000 | DISCOUNTED AT 15% Factor | DISCOUNTED AT 15% Resultant | DISCOUNTED AT 20% Factor | DISCOUNTED AT 20% Resultant |
|---|---|---|---|---|---|
| 0 | 356 | 1·0 | 356 | 1·0 | 356 |
| 1 | 33 | 0·870 | 28 | 0·833 | 27 |
| TOTALS (A) | 389 | | 384 | | 383 |

### B: Cash inflow

| YEAR | (1) Profit £'000 | (2) Depreciation £'000 | (3) PROFIT BEFORE DEPRECIATION £'000 | (4) TAX at 42·5% on previous year of col. 3 £'000 | (5) TAX SAVED on allowances (from Form 2 col. 12) £'000 | (6) Recovery of capital (from final year of cols. 1–6 Form 2) £'000 | (7) NET CASH INFLOW 3+5+6−4 £'000 | DISCOUNTED AT 15% Factor | DISCOUNTED AT 15% Resultant £'000 | DISCOUNTED AT 20% Factor | DISCOUNTED AT 20% Resultant £'000 |
|---|---|---|---|---|---|---|---|---|---|---|---|
| 0 | (8) | — | (8) | — | — | | (8) | 1·0 | (8) | 1·0 | (8) |
| 1 | 72 | 22 | 94 | (3) | 28 | | 125 | 0·870 | 109 | 0·833 | 104 |
| 2 | 115 | 22 | 137 | 40 | 10 | | 107 | 0·756 | 81 | 0·694 | 74 |
| 3 | 115 | 22 | 137 | 58 | 8 | | 87 | 0·658 | 57 | 0·579 | 50 |
| 4 | 115 | 22 | 137 | 58 | 7 | | 86 | 0·572 | 49 | 0·482 | 41 |
| 5 | 115 | 22 | 137 | 58 | 5 | | 84 | 0·497 | 42 | 0·402 | 34 |
| 6 | 115 | 22 | 137 | 58 | 5 | | 84 | 0·432 | 36 | 0·335 | 28 |
| 7 | 115 | 22 | 137 | 58 | 4 | | 83 | 0·376 | 31 | 0·279 | 23 |
| 8 | 38 | — | 38 | 58 | 3 | 208 | 191 | 0·327 | 62 | 0·233 | 45 |
| 9 | | — | | 16 | 6 | | (10) | 0·284 | (3) | 0·194 | (2) |
| TOTALS | 792 | 154 | 946 | 401 | 76 | 208 | 829 | | 456 | | 389 |
| TOTALS (B) | | | | | | | | | | | |
| NET PRESENT VALUE | | | | | | | | | 72 | | 6 |

D.C.F. rate of return is by interpolation = 20·5% (to nearest ½%)

## *Portobello Knitwear Company**

JAMES BROWNLEE, the managing director of Portobello Knitwear Company, was faced with a difficult situation. The company, which manufactured fully fashioned knitted outerwear, produced a trading loss of £65,000 during the first six months of 1970. Worldwide demand for fully fashioned knitwear was falling, selling prices were under severe downward pressure, and Portobello's incoming order position was unsatisfactory. The company had spare knitting capacity, particularly 21 gauge, and excessive stocks of finished garments.

Portobello Knitwear Company was a wholly owned subsidiary of Vauxhall Hosiery Ltd. The parent company manufactured and distributed ladies' hosiery under the brand name 'Vauxhall'. The factory, office and warehouse of Vauxhall Hosiery were located in North London. Portobello Knitwear had a factory and warehouse in Leicester. They knitted fully fashioned knitwear on 21-gauge, 15-gauge and 9-gauge machines using natural and man-made fibres. 'Vauxhall' branded knitwear was produced for distribution by Vauxhall Hosiery from their North London warehouse. Contract and export sales were distributed direct to customers from the Leicester warehouse.

Early in July 1970 James Brownlee requested John Johnston, his financial director, to prepare a report on the company's current trading position, including recommendations for improving profitability during the second half of 1970. He had finished reading Johnston's report (see Appendix A) and was contemplating Johnston's proposal to produce 60,000 branded cashmere garments for a package offer to multiple stores. Normally only a small proportion of the company's garments were knitted from cashmere; Courtelle, Tricel and Crimplene were

*This case first appeared in the *Hosiery Trade Journal*, May 1972, pp. 86–90.

more extensively used. If the cashmere garments had been sold, they could have contributed £45,000 in the second half of 1970. However, the unit contribution was only 31·25 per cent of direct cost, and for branded retail garments a mark-up of 40 per cent was normally added to direct cost to arrive at a target selling price. (Examples of the calculation of target selling prices for branded garments are shown in Appendix B.) The target average selling price for the special offer of cashmere garments of £3·15 compared favourably with the target selling for style 7426, a gent's cashmere long-sleeve pullover, of £3·95. The special promotion need not have affected future planning of design of garments, and the company could have reverted to their normal type of garments and pricing rules in 1971.

## QUESTIONS

1. Are you satisfied with Mr Johnston's report?

2. Should Mr Brownlee have accepted Mr Johnston's proposal to utilize his spare 21-gauge capacity to produce the cashmere garments?

3. Evaluate Portobello's pricing rules for establishing target selling prices.

## SUGGESTED BACKGROUND READING

*An Insight into Management Accounting*, Chapters 8 and 9.

# APPENDIX A

*Profit Forecast July–December 1970*

This report is in six sections.

1. First half-year: Comparison of contract and export confirmed deliveries with actual deliveries and effect of delivery shortfall on total contribution.
2. Second half-year: Forecast of perfect unit sales and total contribution.
3. 1970: Forecast of unit sales and total contribution.
4. 1970: Summary of total contribution forecast versus anticipated expenses.
5. Second half-year: Unit sales forecast compared with available production capacity.
6. Proposals for improving 1970: Total contribution forecast.

## 1. FIRST HALF-YEAR: COMPARISON OF CONTRACT AND EXPORT CONFIRMED DELIVERIES WITH ACTUAL DELIVERIES AND EFFECT OF DELIVERY SHORTFALL ON TOTAL CONTRIBUTION

*Source:* Confirmed delivery programme for weeks 1 to 26 inclusive issued by Mr Cannock (production director).

*Assumption:* The unit-delivery shortfall when delivered will produce an average contribution per unit in line with the average-contribution realization on January–June deliveries.

| | Confirmed units 000s | Delivery units (approximate) 000s | Unit shortfall 000s | Total contribution value of shortfall £'000 |
|---|---|---|---|---|
| (a) Contract | | | | |
| 21 Gauge | 68·1 | 82·8 | — | — |
| 15 Gauge | 6·6 | 1·9 | 4·7 | 1·9 |
| 9 Gauge | 46·9 | 35·9 | 11·0 | 5·0 |
| *Total* | 121·6 | 120·6 | 15·7 | 6·9 |

|  | Confirmed units 000s | Delivery units (approximate) 000s | Unit shortfall 000s | Total contribution value of shortfall £'000 |
|---|---|---|---|---|
| (b) Export |  |  |  |  |
| 21 Gauge | 8·3 | 9·3 | — | — |
| 9 Gauge | 103·6 | 75·5 | 28·1 | 17·5 |
| Total | 111·9 | 84·8 | 28·1 | 17·5 |

The loss of total contribution resulting from unit delivery shortfall is £24,400.

## 2. SECOND HALF-YEAR: FORECAST OF PERFECT UNIT SALES AND TOTAL CONTRIBUTION

|  | Unit sales 000s | Total contribution £'000 |
|---|---|---|
| (a) Branded |  |  |
| 21 Gauge | 125·0 | 66·3 |
| 15 Gauge | 15·0 | 14·2 |
| 9 Gauge | 20·0 | 20·7 |
|  | 160·0 | £101·2 |
| (b) Contract |  |  |
| 21 Gauge | 125·0 | 32·1 |
| 15 Gauge | 0·3 | 0·1 |
| 9 Gauge | 25·0 | 11·2 |
|  | 150·3 | £43·4 |
| (c) Export |  |  |
| 21 Gauge | 31·5 | 18·5 |
| 9 Gauge | 100·0 | 62·1 |
|  | 131·5 | £80·6 |
| Total |  |  |
| 21 Gauge | 281·5 | 116·9 |
| 15 Gauge | 15·3 | 14·3 |
| 9 Gauge | 145·0 | 94·0 |
|  | 441·8 | £225·2 |

The second-half-year forecast of unit sales was prepared by Mr Hemlock (sales director) and refers only to the sale of perfect garments. Total contribution is based on average contribution (approximate) realized on sales of perfect garments in first half-year. The forecast total contribution for second half-year is £225,000.

### 3. 1970: FORECAST OF UNIT SALES AND TOTAL CONTRIBUTION

|  | Unit sales 000s | Total contribution £'000 |
|---|---|---|
| Branded | 378·4 | 196·0 |
| Contract | 331·0 | 81·8 |
| Export | 218·8 | 136·2 |
| Total | 928·2 | 414·0 |
| *less* |  |  |
| Jobbing loss |  | 9·3 |
| Direct expenses various incurred in first half-year |  | 8·6 |
|  |  | 17·9 |
| Adjusted total (I) | 928·2 | 396·1 |
| Assume complete delivery of first half-year contract and export unit delivery shortfall | 43·8 | 24·4 |
| Adjusted total (II) | 972·0 | 420·5 |

### 4. 1970: SUMMARY OF TOTAL CONTRIBUTION VERSUS ANTICIPATED EXPENSES

|  | £ |
|---|---|
| Anticipated total expenses for 1970 per annual budget | 476,000 |
| Total contribution forecast for 1970 | 420,500 |

Assuming no jobbing loss or adverse direct expenses various

will occur in second half of 1970; the *additional* contribution required in second half year

| | |
|---|---|
| (a) to achieve 'breakeven' | £55,500 |
| (b) to produce £20,000 profit | £75,500 |

## 5. SECOND HALF-YEAR: UNIT SALES FORECAST COMPARED WITH AVAILABLE PRODUCTION CAPACITY

(a) Conservative production capacity (C.P.C.)

| | Unit sales forecast (U.S.F.) 000s | Conservative production (perfects) 000s | C.P.C. (seconds) 000s | Excess perfects production capacity 000s |
|---|---|---|---|---|
| 21 gauge | 281·5 | 343·9 | 42·5 | 62·4 |
| 15 gauge | 15·3 | 22·3 | 2·5 | 7·0 |
| 9 gauge | 145·0 | 157·2 | 8·3 | 12·2 |

(b) Maximum production capacity (M.P.C.)

| | Unit sales forecast (U.S.F.) 000s | Maximum production (perfects) 000s | M.P.C. (seconds) 000s | Excess perfects production capacity 000s |
|---|---|---|---|---|
| 21 gauge | 281·5 | 429·9 | 53·1 | 148·4 |
| 15 gauge | 15·3 | 27·4 | 3·0 | 12·1 |
| 9 gauge | 145·0 | 170·4 | 9·0 | 25·4 |

*Note*

1. Both C.P.C. and M.P.C. are based on 23 weeks' production (source document was produced in November/December 1969 by Mr Cannock).

2. Second half-year U.S.F. relates to perfect garments only (see (b) above).

3. Average seconds production rate assumed as follows: 21 gauge (11 per cent), 15 gauge (10 per cent) and 9 gauge (5 per cent).

## 6. PROPOSALS FOR IMPROVING 1970: TOTAL CONTRIBUTION FORECAST

*Current Situation.* In all probability Portobello Knitwear will incur total expenses around £476,000 in 1970, but will recover only £420,500 if current forecasts of unit sales and total contribution are achieved.

### Objective

(a) To produce an additional contribution of £55,500 to ensure that the total contribution generated by sales will equate with the total expenses incurred, i.e. £55,500 additional contribution must be produced if the company is to break even.

(b) For Portobello Knitwear to make a profit of £20,000, £75,500 additional contribution is required.

### SOURCES OF ADDITIONAL CONTRIBUTION

(a) *Leicester Stock Holding at 11 July 1970.* The volume of free stock currently held in Leicester warehouse represents an investment of some £29,000 (direct labour and materials). This stock should be cleared as quickly as possible by company sales personnel. If priced to produce an average contribution of £0·15 on 21-gauge garments and £0·30 on 9-gauge garments, disposal of this free stock would produce an additional contribution as follows:

|  | 21 gauge | 9 gauge | Total |
|---|---|---|---|
| Unit stock | 26,400 | 10,600 | 37,000 |
| Contribution | £3,900 | £3,100 | £7,000 |

(b) *Seconds Stock.* Current seconds stock at North London is some 13,000 garments. In view of market-price levels, it would be unrealistic to offer seconds to the trade at prices designed to provide full recovery of production overheads attributable to seconds. The current policy of distributing seconds in the branded sales form, unless comparable prices are obtainable from other outlets, should be maintained to ensure best possible prices and best means of control. Approximate unit sales of perfect garments in the first half of 1970 were as follows:

|  | Units 000s | Units as % of total |
|---|---|---|
| Botany | 14·1 | 11 |
| Courtelle | 47·6 | 36 |
| Tricel | 54·6 | 40 |
| Crimplene | 17·7 | 13 |
| Total | 134·0 | 100 |

Provided Fred Hemlock agrees (and he shows some enthusiasm) the distribution of seconds could be approached as follows.

50-Garment Package and Deal

| Fibre | Quantity £ | Average direct cost per unit £ | Contribution per unit £ | Unit selling price £ | Total selling price £ |
|---|---|---|---|---|---|
| Botany | 5 | 0·82½ | 0·12½ | 0·95 | 4·75 |
| Courtelle | 20 | 0·70 | 0·14 | 0·84 | 16·75 |
| Tricel | 20 | 0·74 | 0·16 | 0·90 | 18·00 |
| Crimplene | 5 | 0·95 | 0·15 | 1·10 | 5·50 |
| Total | 50 | 0·75 | 0·15 | 0·90 | £45·00 |

Trade discount of $2\frac{1}{2}$ per cent reduces the selling price to £43·87½ and the unit selling price to £0·87½ (contribution £0·12½). The purchase tax payable on the discounted average selling price is £0·12, hence the average total cost (including purchase tax) to the retailer would be £0·99½. Assuming a 50 per cent mark-up, the average retail selling price would be £1·49½. The current stock of seconds at North London is 13,000 garments. If each garment produces an average unit contribution of £0·12½, the additional contribution derived from the sale of seconds would be £1,600 (approximately).

(c) *North London Perfects Stock.* The current stock of branded perfects amounts to some 126,000 garments (20 July 70). Average stock movements into North London warehouse should be 8,000 perfects per week (i.e. in line with weekly knitting-order dozenage).

Assuming that deliveries of current branded styles to North London warehouse continue at this level for ten weeks, after which deliveries would be restricted to Spring 1971 stock, the stocks of perfect garments at North London would be around 206,000 garments. Total unit sales forecast for the second half-year from North London warehouse is 160,000 perfect branded garments. Provided this U.S.F. is achieved, this would leave a stock balance of current styles (which will automatically be discontinued at the end of the year) of 46,000. If these garments are disposed of at an average unit contribution of 5 per cent of the selling price, the additional contribution would amount to £11,500.

(d) *Second Half-Year: Excess Production Capacity.* Section 5 shows that perfects production capacity will exceed the perfect unit sales forecast as follows:

|  | 21 gauge | 15 gauge | 9 gauge |
|---|---|---|---|
| Minimum | 62,400 | 7,000 | 12,200 |
| Maximum | 148,400 | 12,100 | 25,400 |

Total second-half-year production capacity, inclusive of seconds, is as follows:

|  | C.P.C. 000s | M.P.C. 000s | Assumed realistic (½ way) 000s | Perfects 000s | Seconds 000s |
|---|---|---|---|---|---|
| 21 gauge | 386·9 | 483·0 | 434·7 | 386·9 | 47·8 |
| 15 gauge | 24·8 | 30·4 | 27·6 | 24·8 | 2·8 |
| 9 gauge | 165·5 | 179·4 | 172·0 | 163·4 | 8·6 |

Contract sales will be needed to achieve the required volume of output, but the average unit contribution will probably be lower than in first half-year because of active competition.

|  | U.S.F. perfects 000s | Realistic capacity perfects 000s | Seconds 000s | Excess capacity perfects 000s | Average unit contribution £ | Total contribution £'000 |
|---|---|---|---|---|---|---|
| 21 gauge | 281·5 | 386·9 | 47·8 | 105·4 | 0·20 | 21·1 |
| 15 gauge | 15·3 | 24·8 | 2·8 | 9·5 | 0·40 | 3·8 |
| 9 gauge | 145·0 | 163·4 | 8·6 | 18·4 | 0·40 | 7·4 |
| Total |  |  |  | 133·3 | 0·242 | £32·3 |

### (e) Second Half-Year Seconds

|  | Sales 000s | Assumed average unit contribution £ | Additional contribution £'000 |
|---|---|---|---|
| 21 gauge | 47·8 | 0·125 | 6·0 |
| 15 gauge | 2·8 | 0·20 | 0·6 |
| 9 gauge | 8·6 | 0·20 | 1·7 |
| Total | 59·2 | 0·140 | £8·3 |

### (f) Summary – Second Half-Year: Sources of Additional Contribution

| Source | Additional contribution £'000 |
|---|---|
| (a) Leicester free stock | 7·0 |
| (b) Current seconds stock | 1·6 |
| (c) North London stock of perfects in excess of U.S.F. | 11·5 |
| (d) Excess of perfects production capacity | 32·3 |
| (e) Seconds production | 8·3 |
| Total | 60·7 |
| less Additional contribution required to break even | 55·5 |
| Profit | £5·2 |

(g) *Alternative Means of Utilizing Second-Half-Year Excess 21-Gauge Production Capacity.* The excess 21-gauge production capacity presents a most severe problem, mainly because of general over-production in the United Kingdom and intense downward pressure on prices as a result of this. The prices that have to be obtained to give the average unit contributions contained in (d) above may be difficult to achieve. It is proposed as an alternative that a special offer of cashmere and/or lambswool garments be considered. We would aim at a retail selling price of £5·47½, which is considerably lower than competitors' prices and would give the retailer a 50 per cent mark-up. Assuming a production run of 60,000 perfect cashmere garments in five styles, three sizes, six colours, the product could be offered to twenty retail groups, in the form of 250 dozen 'packages'. Each package would consist of, say:

> 75 dozen long-sleeve turtle necks
> 50 dozen long-sleeve round necks
> 50 dozen long-sleeve golfers
> 50 dozen long-sleeve cardigans
> 25 dozen long-sleeve polo necks

250 dozen to 20 retail groups = 60,000 units

*Pricing assumptions*

|                                         | £                 |
| --------------------------------------- | ----------------- |
| Average selling price (gross)           | 3·22½             |
| Average selling price (net) (2½%)       | 3·15              |
| Average direct material                 | 2·12              |
| Average direct labour                   | 0·28              |
| Average direct cost                     | 2·40              |
| Average unit contribution               | 0·75              |
| Purchase tax payable                    | 0·43              |

Retail selling price, allowing 50% mark-up = £3·22½ + £0·43 + 50%
= £5·47½

If the package is used by the retailer as a special Christmas promotion at a price of £4·97½, the yield to the retailer is still 28 per cent. Despite the fact that we have not yet approached the retail stores and have not therefore obtained any orders for these garments, I am confident that the sales can be achieved because of the lower mark-up on a lower direct cost. The benefits derived from bulk buying of cashmere would reduce our average direct material per garment from £2·50 per garment to £2·12. 60,000 garments sold at an average unit contribution of £0·75 gives an additional contribution of £45,000.

(h) *Revised Additional Contribution Second Half-Year* 1970. If this alternative usage of excess perfects production capacity at 21 gauge were adopted, the additional contribution for the second half-year 1970 would be as follows:

| Source | Additional contribution £'000 |
| --- | --- |
| (a) Leicester free stock | 7·0 |
| (b) Current seconds stock | 1·6 |
| (c) North London stock of perfects in excess of second half U.S.F. | 11·5 |
| (d) Excess perfects production capacity* | 65·3 |
| (e) Seconds production | 8·3 |
| Total | £93·7 |

*See section (d) above. Adopting alternative usage of excess 21-gauge perfects production capacity.

|  | Unit sales 000s | Average contribution per unit £ | Total contribution £'000 |
|---|---|---|---|
| 21 gauge – cashmere | 60·0 | 0·75 | 45·0 |
| – contract | 45·4 | 0·20 | 9·1 |
| 15 gauge | 9·5 | 0·40 | 3·8 |
| 9 gauge | 18·4 | 0·40 | 7·4 |
| Total | 133·3 | 0·49 | £65·3 |

(i) *Summary* 1970 *Total Contribution Assuming Achievement of* (g)

|  | Total contribution £'000 |
|---|---|
| 1970 forecast as in section 3 | 420·5 |
| Second-half-year forecast of additional contribution | 93·7 |
| 1970 total | 514·2 |
| 1970 anticipated expenses | 476·0 |
| 1970 profit | £38·2 |

JOHN JOHNSTON
Financial Director
25 July 1970

# APPENDIX B

*Cost Information for Pricing Decisions – Examples*

### 15 Gauge. Style 6507

Type: Ladies          Yarn: 2/28 Dyed Courtelle
Garment: Cardigan       Neck: V
Shoulder: Raglan        Sleeve: Long
                           Pockets: Two

|  | Material | Wages | Total | Cumulative total | Unit cost |
|---|---|---|---|---|---|
|  | £ | £ | £ | £ | £ |
| Knit | 149·772 | 20·553 | 170·325 | 170·325 | 0·7096 |
| Finish |  | 48·728 | 48·728 | 219·053 | 0·9127 |
| Dye |  | 4·000 | 4·000 | 223·053 | 0·9293 |
| Trim |  | 1·460 | 1·460 | 224·513 | 0·9354 |
| Pack | 4·108 | 2·000 | 6·108 | 230·621 | 0·9609 |
|  | £153·880 | £76·741 | £230·621 | £230·621 | 0·9609 |

*Direct cost per 20 dozen*

Contribution 40%     0·3844

£1·3453

*Target selling price*    £1·35

### 21 Gauge. Style 7351

Type: Ladies          Yarn: 1/14 Cashmere
Garment: Jumper        Neck: Round
Shoulder: Fashioned    Sleeve: Long T.B.C.

|  | Material | Wages | Total | Cumulative total | Unit Cost |
|---|---|---|---|---|---|
|  | £ | £ | £ | £ | £ |
| Knit | 479·400 | 24·400 | 503·800 | 503·800 | 2·0992 |
| Gauge |  | 14·914 | 14·914 | 518·714 | 2·1613 |
| Mill |  | 8·000 | 8·000 | 526·714 | 2·1946 |
| Finish |  | 18·007 | 18·007 | 544·721 | 2·2697 |
| Trim |  | — | — |  |  |
| Pack | 4·108 | 2·000 | 6·108 | 550·829 | 2·2951 |
|  | £433·508 | £67·321 | £550·829 | £550·829 | 2·2951 |

*Direct cost per 20 dozen*

Contribution 40%     0·9180

£3·2131

*Target selling price*    £3·21

## 21 Gauge. Style 7426

Type: Gents
Garment: Pullover
Shoulder: Fashioned

Yarn: 1/14 Cashmere
Neck: 12/1 Polo
Sleeve: Long T.B.C.

| | Direct cost per 20 dozen | | | | Unit cost |
| | Material | Wages | Total | Cumulative total | |
|---|---|---|---|---|---|
| | £ | £ | £ | £ | £ |
| Knit | 603·689 | 20·951 | 624·640 | 624·640 | 2·6027 |
| Gauge | | 14·825 | 14·825 | 639·465 | 2·6644 |
| Dye/Mill | | 8·000 | 8·000 | 647·465 | 2·6978 |
| Finish | | 22·419 | 22·419 | 669·884 | 2·7912 |
| Trim | | | | | |
| Pack | 4·108 | 2·000 | 6·108 | 675·992 | 2·8166 |
| | £607·797 | £68·195 | £675·992 | £675·992 | 2·8166 |
| | | | | Contribution 40% | 1·1266 |
| | | | | | £3·9432 |

Target selling price £3·95

## 9 Gauge. Style 6416

Type: Gents
Garment: Pullover
Shoulder: Raglan

Yarn: 2/8 Shetland
Neck: Round
Sleeve: Long
Strip: Cuffs and ribs

| | Direct cost per 20 dozen | | | | Unit cost |
| | Material | Wages | Total | Cumulative total | |
|---|---|---|---|---|---|
| | £ | £ | £ | £ | £ |
| Knit | 144·774 | 18·805 | 163·579 | 163·579 | 0·6816 |
| Finish | | 41·905 | 41·905 | 205·484 | 0·8562 |
| Dye/Mill | | 4·000 | 4·000 | 209·484 | 0·8728 |
| Trim | | | | | |
| Pack | 4·108 | 2·000 | 6·108 | 215·592 | 0·8983 |
| | £148·882 | £66·710 | £215·592 | £215·592 | 0·8983 |
| | | | | Contribution 40% | 0·3593 |
| | | | | | 1·2576 |

Target selling price £1·25

# Urban Underwear Company*

URBAN UNDERWEAR COMPANY produces a wide range of knitted underwear. The greater part of the company's output is for a large multiple-store group, Superstores Ltd, and the company generally makes goods to a price. The management of Urban Underwear appreciates that, however efficient it may be in producing its products, it will never be in a position to obtain satisfactory profits if it is making and selling lines within its range of products that do not bring a good return to the company for the time and money expended in producing such lines. Tom Drybones, the managing director of Urban Underwear, has requested Rex Hollingwood, the company's new management accountant, to prepare a set of financial guidelines for selecting lines for its range of products. Hollingwood's proposals are set out in the following memorandum.

Dear Mr Drybones,

### Production Selection

1. In order to be able to realize a satisfactory price the management must endeavour to select those lines which it deems to be most profitable and acceptable to the market. In the past cost estimates have been produced in a format which is misleading in that the true profitability cannot be seen.

2. At the planning stage cost standards for all direct costs for all product lines will be prepared. Work study will be employed to determine required-labour input, waste allowances for materials will be agreed with production management and standard material costs determined, and overhead-recovery rates will be calculated at the forecast level of activity. Currently the overhead-recovery rates are 150 per cent of knitting labour for the

*This case first appeared in the *Hosiery Trade Journal*, January 1972, pp. 5–47.

Knitting Department, 70 per cent of the make-up labour for the Making-up Department and 50 per cent of total direct labour for administration overheads. All the information will then be available to prepare acceptable cost estimates for management.

3. The technique of marginal costing should be used in determining the profitability of a style. Marginal costing segregates all fixed costs (e.g. rent, rates, depreciation) from variables (those which vary in sympathy with activity), and makes the point that, regardless of the activity achieved by a company, the fixed costs will remain unaltered.

4. Cost estimates should be prepared for all styles being produced. The true test of profitability is to relate the *contribution to the fixed overheads allocated to a style*, and not, as often the case, by expressing the net profit to sales. The method that should be adopted for completing a cost estimate (Table 1) is as follows:

*Table 1*

Costing of Men's Printed Hipster Briefs
Style 53

|  | £ | £ |
|---|---|---|
| Gross selling price | 4·00 | |
| Selling expenses and discount (5%) | 0·20 | |
|  |  | 3·80 |
| Direct costs |  |  |
|     Yarn (including Dyeing and Printing) | 1·80 | |
|     Knitting Labour | 0·15 | |
|     Making-up Labour | 0·40 | |
|     Get-up | 0·15 | |
| *Total direct costs* |  | 2·50 |
| Contribution |  | 1·30 |
| Overheads recovered |  |  |
|     Knitting overheads (150% knit labour) | 0·22 | |
|     Making-up overhead (70% making-up labour) | 0·28 | |
|     Administration overhead (50% total direct labour) | 0·28 | |
|  |  | 0·78 |
| *Net profit* |  | £0·52 |

*Profitability assessment*    $\dfrac{\text{Contribution}}{\text{Overheads}} = \dfrac{1\cdot30}{0\cdot78} = 166\cdot7\%$

(a) Insert gross selling price (price is usually dictated by Superstores Ltd).

(b) Calculate percentage allowance for selling expenses and discount allowed to customers, and loss from estimated percentage of substandard goods.

(c) By deduction of (b) from (a) the net selling price is known.

(d) Calculate all direct costs for production of style (these costs will have been determined at the planning stage for direct labour and materials). The total of all direct costs when deducted from the net selling price will show the expected *contribution* for the 'costed' style. From the *total contribution* generated by our total sales we must recover our overheads and earn our net profit.

(e) Overhead costs will be calculated for the style using the budgeted overhead-recovery rates which have been calculated.

(f) The contribution now expressed as a percentage over the fixed overheads attributed to the style will give a *profitability assessment*. The higher this percentage turns out to be the more profitable the style is to produce.

In the past we have related the net profit margin to sales but this is not a true guide in assessing profitability. Two different styles may have similar total costs yet one may take longer to produce than the other. The cost estimates in Table 2 illustrate this point. If a 10-per-cent addition were added to the total costs for both styles and were sold at those selling prices, or if Superstores were prepared to pay £3·85 for each dozen garments, the two styles would not be equally profitable since style 53 would record a profitability assessment of 149 per cent while style 58 would only record 133 per cent.

By costing in this manner, we can immediately see the following points:

(a) The minimum cost (i.e. direct cost) at which it is better to produce and sell, rather than to have idle capacity. In periods of trade depression it would be more advantageous to produce and sell style 53 at a net selling price of direct cost say plus £0·05 rather than not produce, the reason being that at least the company by selling at £2·55 per dozen is making a contribution of

£0·05 towards fixed overheads and profit, which it would not have made otherwise.

(b) The profitability percentage which indicates the likely total contribution expressed as a percentage of fixed costs if all lines produced were of this particular profitability ratio. For example, the cost estimate illustrated in Table 1 indicates a profitability assessment of 167 per cent. If the budgeted overheads were £100,000, 167 per cent on all products would indicate a total contribution of £167,000 or a net profit of £67,000.

*Table 2*

Costing of Men's Printed Hipster Briefs
Comparison of Styles 53 and 58

|  | *Style 53* | | *Style 58* | |
|  | *Cost per dozen* | | *Cost per dozen* | |
|  | £ | £ | £ | £ |
|---|---|---|---|---|
| Yarn (including dyeing and printing) | 1·80 | | 1·31 | |
| Knitting labour | 0·15 | | 0·40 | |
| Making-up labour | 0·40 | | 0·28 | |
| Get-up | 0·15 | | 0·15 | |
| Total direct costs | | 2·50 | | 2·14 |
| Overheads | | | | |
|   Knitting (150% of knit labour) | 0·22 | | 0·60 | |
|   Making-up (70% of making-up labour) | 0·28 | | 0·20 | |
|   Administration (50% total direct labour) | 0·28 | | 0·34 | |
| Total overheads | | 0·78 | | 1·14 |
| Total cost | | 3·28 | | 3·28 |
| Selling expenses and discount (5% S.P.) | | 0·19 | | 0·19 |
| Net profit (10% of S.P.) | | 0·38 | | 0·38 |
| Gross selling price | | £3·85 | | £3·85 |

*Profitability assessment*

Style 53    $\dfrac{(0\cdot78 + 0\cdot38)}{0\cdot78} = 148\cdot7\%$

Style 58    $\dfrac{(1\cdot14 + 0\cdot38)}{1\cdot14} = 133\cdot3\%$

5. By looking at the different profitability assessments shown for all the various styles, management can decide which styles to promote, which styles to redesign and which to exclude from its range altogether. Of course from the point of view of marketing and relations with Superstores, it may be necessary to consider whether a garment with a low-profit assessment is wanted in the range. In this way the management will know when it is producing such garments for Superstores.

REX HOLLINGWOOD
Management Accountant

## QUESTION

Carefully examine Rex Hollingwood's proposals for product selection (a) when Urban Underwear has idle capacity, and (b) when Urban Underwear has a shortage of yarn, of knitting labour, and/or of making-up labour.

## SUGGESTED BACKGROUND READING

*An Insight into Management Accounting*, Chapters 8 and 9.

# Kettle Knitwear Ltd

You have discussed recently with Arnold French, the managing director of Kettle Knitwear Ltd, the method he employs to determine the selling prices of the fully fashioned knitted outerwear his company produces. The form he uses to calculate the total cost and selling price of a style of garment is illustrated in Table 1. The overhead-recovery percentages are determined annually in the following manner:

1. Costs are classified under four headings: occupation expenses, labour expenses, administration expenses, direct expenses. Total occupation expenses is apportioned to productive departments on the basis of floor space occupied, total labour expenses on the basis of number of personnel and administrative expenses on the basis of the direct wages in each productive department. The direct expenses, such as depreciation and supervisors' wages, are allocated directly to productive departments.

2. Total overheads of each productive department are calculated as a percentage of departmental direct wages for expected weekly output to give departmental overhead-recovery percentages.

Within the normal range of activity, i.e. expected weekly output plus or minus 10 per cent, the overhead costs are fixed in relation to variations in output.

In your discussions Arnold French maintained that he is happy so long as he is getting a $12\frac{1}{2}$ per cent mark-up on total cost, and that he does not like to see any of his products falling below this mark-up. Subsequently you examined a number of the selling price decisions made by Arnold French. You discovered that frequently he does not fix the selling price of a style of garment at total cost plus $12\frac{1}{2}$ per cent, but increases it to a slightly higher level. The final selling price of a garment appears to be based on his subjective judgement. At a later meeting he explained that he does this where he believes there has been some extra input of skill in make-up or design, and the market can bear the extra price. At this meeting he outlined some of his current problems. He has a shortage of skilled labour for the fully fashioned knitting department and of female labour to put trimmings onto garments. You recognized that he should take these factors into account when deciding which garments to produce, and when making his selling-price decisions. When you suggested that his approach to costing and pricing decisions could distort the return on the effort put into a garment, when making a range with different amounts of input in terms of labour and materials, Mr French accepted this could be so but doubted whether there are any significant distortions in practice. He invited you to examine a sample of his selling-price decisions to test your beliefs. Appendix A contains a summary of the information you have collected.

QUESTIONS

1. Analyse the information you have collected and prepare a report for Mr French.

2. What additional information would you require in order to decide which garments Kettle Knitwear should produce?

SUGGESTED BACKGROUND READING

*An Insight into Management Accounting*, Chapters 8 and 9.

## Table 1
### Cost Sheet

Style No. 7317
Type: Long-Line Halter Polo with Belt

Yarn: Matt Tricel Bonde

| Department | Overhead % | Direct labour £ | Overheads £ | Yarn £ | Trim and packaging £ | Dye and print £ | Total £ |
|---|---|---|---|---|---|---|---|
| Flat-knit ribs | 304 | 0·04 | 0·12 | — | — | — | 0·16 |
| Run on steam iron, etc. | 110 | 0·26 | 0·28 | — | — | — | 0·54 |
| F.F. knit | 128 | 0·62 | 0·79 | 4·13 | — | — | 5·54 |
| Pre-dye make-up | 145 | 0·29 | 0·42 | — | 0·11 | — | 0·82 |
| Flat-knit trim | 304 | 0·09 | 0·26 | 1·54 | — | — | 1·89 |
| Dye/Scour | — | — | — | — | — | 2·13 | 2·13 |
| Print | — | — | — | — | — | — | — |
| Post-dye make-up | 121 | 1·04 | 1·21 | — | 0·07 | — | 2·32 |
| Press and counter | 287 | 0·19 | 0·53 | — | 0·20 | — | 0·92 |
| | | £2·53 | £3·61 | £5·67 | £0·38 | £2·13 | £14·32 |

### Cost summary

Cost per garment £1·38

| | £ |
|---|---|
| Factory cost brought down | 14·32 |
| Seconds allowance | 0·34 |
| Pack and dispatch | 0·04 |
| Sub total | 14·70 |
| Profits 12½% | 1·83 |
| Total per dozen | £16·53 |

## APPENDIX A

Style No. 7726
Type: Short-Sleeve Raglan V-Neck Jumper
Yarn: Tricel

|  | Total £ | F.F. knit* £ | Trim* £ |
|---|---|---|---|
| Direct labour | 2·81 | 0·44 | 0·20 |
| Overheads | 4·20 | | |
| Yarn | 3·41 | | |
| Trim and packing | 0·38 | | |
| Dye and print | 1·73 | | |
| Factory cost | 12·53 | | |
| Seconds and dispatch | 0·33 | | |
| Total cost | 12·86 | | |
| Profit 12½% | 1·61 | | |
| Total per dozen | £14·47 | | |
| Cost per garment | 1·21 | | |
| Selling price | 1·25 | | |

*Labour included in total direct labour.

Style No. 7728
Type: Long-Line Halter-Neck Polo Jumper
Yarn: Matt Tricel Bonde

|  | Total £ | F.F. knit £ | Trim £ |
|---|---|---|---|
| Direct labour | 2·53 | 0·62 | 0·09 |
| Overheads | 3·61 | | |
| Yarn | 5·67 | | |
| Trim and packing | 0·38 | | |
| Dye and print | 2·13 | | |
| Factory cost | 14·32 | | |
| Seconds and dispatch | 0·38 | | |
| Total cost | 14·70 | | |
| Profit 12½% | 1·83 | | |
| Total per dozen | £16·53 | | |
| Cost per garment | 1·38 | | |
| Selling price | 1·47½ | | |

### Style No. 7825
### Type: Short-Sleeve Raglan Windsor Cardigan
### Yarn: Tricel

|                       | Total £ | F.F. knit £ | Trim £ |
|-----------------------|---------|-------------|--------|
| Direct labour         | 3·20    | 0·45        | 0·21   |
| Overheads             | 4·78    |             |        |
| Yarn                  | 3·66    |             |        |
| Trim and packing      | 0·88    |             |        |
| Dye and print         | 1·73    |             |        |
| Factory cost          | 14·25   |             |        |
| Seconds and dispatch  | 0·38    |             |        |
| Total cost            | 14·63   |             |        |
| Profit 12½%           | 1·82    |             |        |
| Total per dozen       | £16·45  |             |        |
| Cost per garment      | 1·37    |             |        |
| Selling price         | 1·45    |             |        |

### Style No. 8321
### Type: Short-Sleeve Raglan Round-Neck Jumper
### Yarn: Tricel

|                       | Total £ | F.F. knit £ | Trim £ |
|-----------------------|---------|-------------|--------|
| Direct labour         | 2·78    | 0·44        | 0·04   |
| Overheads             | 3·86    |             |        |
| Yarn                  | 2·64    |             |        |
| Trim and packing      | 0·61    |             |        |
| Dye and print         | 1·72    |             |        |
| Factory cost          | 11·61   |             |        |
| Seconds and dispatch  | 0·30    |             |        |
| Total cost            | 11·91   |             |        |
| Profit 12½%           | 1·49    |             |        |
| Total per dozen       | £13·40  |             |        |
| Cost per garment      | 1·12    |             |        |
| Selling price         | 1·19    |             |        |

Style No. 8605
Type: Short-Sleeve Jumper
Yarn Tricel

|                      | Total<br>£ | F.F. knit<br>£ | Trim<br>£ |
|----------------------|-----------|----------------|-----------|
| Direct labour        | 3·13      | 0·44           | 0·14      |
| Overheads            | 4·48      |                |           |
| Yarn                 | 3·20      |                |           |
| Trim and packing     | 0·31      |                |           |
| Dye and print        | 1·73      |                |           |
| Factory cost         | 12·85     |                |           |
| Seconds and dispatch | 0·34      |                |           |
| Total cost           | 13·19     |                |           |
| Profit 12½%          | 1·65      |                |           |
| Total per dozen      | £14·84    |                |           |
| Cost per garment     | 1·24      |                |           |
| Selling price        | 1·27½     |                |           |

Style No. 8721
Type: Long-Sleeve Domino Lumber
Yarn: Tricel

|                      | Total<br>£ |      | F.F. knit<br>£ | Trim<br>£ |
|----------------------|-----------|------|----------------|-----------|
| Direct labour        | 2·22      |      | 0·57           | 0·01      |
| Overheads            | 3·26      |      |                |           |
| Yarn                 | 3·74      |      |                |           |
| Trim and packing     | 0·75      |      |                |           |
| Dye and print        | 1·98      |      |                |           |
| Factory cost         | 11·95     |      |                |           |
| Seconds and dispatch | 0·32      |      |                |           |
| Total cost           | 12·27     |      | 12·27          |           |
| Profit 12½%          | 1·54      | 10%  | 1·23           |           |
| Total per dozen      | £13·81    |      | £13·50         |           |
| Cost per garment     | 1·15      |      | 1·12           |           |
| Selling price        |           |      | 1·13           |           |

### Style No. 8767
### Type: Long-Sleeve Raglan Round-Neck Jumper
### Yarn: Tricel

|  | Total £ | F.F. knit £ | Trim £ |
|---|---|---|---|
| Direct labour | 2·25 | 0·79 | 0·01 |
| Overheads | 3·22 |  |  |
| Yarn | 3·40 |  |  |
| Trim and packing | 0·77 |  |  |
| Dye and print | 1·98 |  |  |
| Factory cost | 11·62 |  |  |
| Seconds and dispatch | 0·31 |  |  |
| Total cost | 11·93 |  |  |
| Profit 12½% | 1·49 |  |  |
| Total per dozen | £13·42 |  |  |
| Cost per garment | 1·12 |  |  |
| Selling price | 1·22½ |  |  |

### Style No. 8794
### Type: Long-sleeve Raglan Cardigan
### Yarn: Tricel

|  | Total £ | F.F. knit £ | Trim £ |
|---|---|---|---|
| Direct labour | 3·57 | 0·57 | 0·15 |
| Overheads | 4·69 |  |  |
| Yarn | 4·36 |  |  |
| Trim and packing | 0·54 |  |  |
| Dye and print | 2·38 |  |  |
| Factory cost | 15·54 |  |  |
| Seconds and dispatch | 0·41 |  |  |
| Total cost | 15·95 |  |  |
| Profit 12½% | 1·99 |  |  |
| Total per dozen | £17·94 |  |  |
| Cost per garment | 1·49 |  |  |
| Selling price | 1·65 |  |  |

Style No. 9006
Type: Short-Sleeve Raglan Round-Neck Jumper
Yarn: Botany Wool

| | Total £ | F.F. knit £ | Trim £ |
|---|---|---|---|
| Direct labour | 1·95 | 0·47 | 0·03 |
| Overheads | 2·87 | | |
| Yarn | 4·26 | | |
| Trim and packing | 0·37 | | |
| Dye and print | 1·44 | | |
| Factory cost | 10·89 | | |
| Seconds and dispatch | 0·29 | | |
| Total cost | 11·18 | | |
| Profit 12½% | 1·40 | | |
| Total per dozen | £12·58 | | |
| Cost per garment | 1·05 | | |
| Selling price | 1·06 | | |

Style No. 9035
Type: Short-Sleeve Raglan Round-Neck Jumper with Zip
Yarn: Botany Wool

| | Total £ | F.F. knit £ | Trim £ |
|---|---|---|---|
| Direct labour | 2·21 | 0·47 | 0·11 |
| Overheads | 2·92 | | |
| Yarn | 4·14 | | |
| Trim and packing | 0·80 | | |
| Dye and print | 1·44 | | |
| Factory cost | 11·51 | | |
| Seconds and dispatch | 0·30 | | |
| Total cost | 11·81 | | |
| Profit 12½% | 1·48 | | |
| Total per dozen | £13·29 | | |
| Cost per garment | 1·11 | | |
| Selling price | 1·12½ | | |

Style No. 9039
Type: Long-Sleeve Raglan Round-Neck Jumper
Yarn: Botany Wool

|  | Total £ | F.F. knit £ | Trim £ |
|---|---|---|---|
| Direct labour | 3·43 | 0·55 | 0·19 |
| Overheads | 5·10 | | |
| Yarn | 5·94 | | |
| Trim and packing | 0·37 | | |
| Dye and print | 1·72 | | |
| Factory cost | 16·56 | | |
| Seconds and dispatch | 0·44 | | |
| Total cost | 17·00 | | |
| Profit 12½% | 2·12 | | |
| Total per dozen | £19·12 | | |
| Cost per garment | 1·59 | | |
| Selling price | 1·62½ | | |

Style No. 9069
Type: Long-Sleeve Raglan Halter-Neck Polo Jumper
Yarn: Botany Wool

|  | Total £ | F.F. knit £ | Trim £ |
|---|---|---|---|
| Direct labour | 2·37 | 0·85 | 0·15 |
| Overheads | 3·55 | | |
| Yarn | 6·39 | | |
| Trim and packing | 0·37 | | |
| Dye and print | 1·73 | | |
| Factory cost | 14·41 | | |
| Seconds and dispatch | 0·39 | | |
| Total cost | 14·80 | | |
| Profit 12½% | 1·85 | | |
| Total per dozen | £16·65 | | |
| Cost per garment | 1·39 | | |
| Selling price | 1·40 | | |

Style No. 9321
Type: Short-Sleeve Shirt Dress
Yarn: Matt Tricel Bonde

|  | Total £ | F.F. knit £ | Trim £ |
|---|---|---|---|
| Direct labour | 4·62 | 1·70 | 0·17 |
| Overheads | 6·70 | | |
| Yarn | 6·78 | | |
| Trim and packing | 0·43 | | |
| Dye and print | 3·21 | | |
| Factory cost | 21·74 | | |
| Seconds and dispatch | 0·58 | | |
| Total cost | 22·32 | | |
| Profit 12½% | 2·79 | | |
| Total per dozen | £25·11 | | |
| Cost per garment | 2·09 | | |
| Selling price | 2·15 | | |

Style No. 9429
Type: Short-Sleeve Raglan V-Neck Cardigan
Yarn: Matt Tricel Bonde

|  | Total £ | F.F. knit £ | Trim £ |
|---|---|---|---|
| Direct labour | 2·94 | 0·45 | 0·04 |
| Overheads | 3·82 | | |
| Yarn | 3·55 | | |
| Trim and packing | 0·52 | | |
| Dye and print | 1·90 | | |
| Factory cost | 12·73 | | |
| Seconds and dispatch | 0·33 | | |
| Total cost | 13·06 | | |
| Profit 12½% | 1·63 | | |
| Total per dozen | £14·69 | | |
| Cost per garment | 1·22 | | |
| Selling price | 1·27½ | | |

# James Wilson & Son (B)*

MR HAWKEYE, the management accountant of James Wilson & Son of Milchester, calculated three possible costed selling prices for a garment. Wilson's was an old-established company producing knitted underwear, leisurewear and children's outerwear. They had premises in Bridge Street and South Street, Milchester, and recently had opened a new factory in North Ashfleet, ten miles south of Milchester. Underwear and leisurewear were produced at Bridge Street and knitwear at South Street and North Ashfleet. The company had an annual turnover of £1,300,000 and some 500 employees.

The three methods Mr Hawkeye employed to calculate costed selling prices for a garment are illustrated in Table 1. The weight of yarn per dozen garments was determined from production samples and a fixed percentage was added for waste. Yarn cost was obtained by multiplying the yarn weight by the standard cost per pound of yarn (Mr Hawkeye operated a standard costing system). For needles there was a recovery based on past experience, and trimmings were charged at standard cost. Labour-time standards and piece rates were established by the work-study engineer, and the time allowances were multiplied by the standard wage rates. If times or piece rates had increased in a department since the standards were established, percentage addition for holiday/increase was raised. Overheads were included by multiplying the total labour cost by the overhead-recovery rate for the factory in which the garment was to be produced. The sum of the two columns represented total cost and variable cost. For example, the total cost of the boy's jersey was £16·08 and variable cost £12·66.

---

*This case first appeared in *The Hosiery Trade Journal*, February 1972, pp. 87–8.

The three costed selling prices were determined by the following additions to total or variable cost:

1. Total cost plus 8·5 per cent gave a costed selling price of £17·45 for the boy's jersey.

2. Variable cost plus 43 per cent gave a costed selling price of £18·10 for the boy's jersey.

3. Variable cost plus three times making-up labour gave a costed selling price of £17·50 for the boy's jersey.

The mark-ups of 8·5 per cent and 43 per cent were calculated by Mr Hawkeye in the following manner.

### Knitwear Division Budget 1970

| | |
|---|---|
| Budgeted sales | £510,000 |
| Estimated capital employed, with fixed assets valued on an assumed current-cost basis | £270,000 |
| Required return on capital employed | 15% |
| Required profit | £40,000 |
| Fixed overheads | £112,000 |

$$\text{Mark-up on total cost} = \frac{\text{required profit}}{\text{total cost}} \times 100$$
$$= \frac{£40,000}{£(510,000-40,000)} \times 100$$
$$= 8·5\%$$

$$\text{Mark-up on variable cost} = \frac{\text{required total contribution}}{\text{total variable cost}} \times 100$$
$$= \frac{£152,000}{£358,000} \times 100$$
$$= 43\%$$

The factor that frequently limited Wilsons' capacity to manufacture additional garments was making-up labour. The company had a making-up capacity equivalent to a standard cost for making-up labour of £50,000. To achieve the budgeted contribution of £152,000 it had to obtain £3 contribution for every £1 standard making-up labour. Therefore, the third pricing rule was variable cost plus three times making-up labour.

Mr Hawkeye used his costed selling prices in the following manner:

I recommend to Mr Simpson, the sales manager, the highest costed selling price produced by the three methods. Everyone's criterion is then met. Mr Simpson cannot always negotiate the highest selling price and sometimes has to come down below the lowest costed selling price, but I am very unhappy with any selling price below total cost. For example, as you are no doubt aware, maxi-cardigans are very fashionable at the present time, and last month we introduced them to our knitwear range. For the maxi-cardigan in Table 1, I recommended a selling price of £33·45 per dozen to Mr. Simpson, and, in the event, he has sold twelve dozen at £40 per dozen. Business is hard to come by at the moment, and our North Ashfleet factory, which produces the maxi-cardigans, is working on short time. I could not recommend the price of £30·05 based on making-up labour, the total cost per dozen is £30·81 and we would not recover our overheads.

Each quarter I produce an analysis of sales which distinguishes between:

1. Sales below total cost.
2. Sales between total cost and lowest desirable selling price.
3. Sales between desirable selling price on labour and desirable selling price on variable cost.
4. Sales above highest desirable selling price.

QUESTION

Consider the strengths and weaknesses of Mr Hawkeye's method of calculating costed selling prices.

SUGGESTED BACKGROUND READING

*An Insight into Management Accounting*, Chapter 9.

Table 1. Illustration of Calculation of Costed Selling Prices

| | Boy's jersey size 26 in. | | Baby's cardigan size 18 in. | | Maxi cardigan size 36 in. | |
|---|---|---|---|---|---|---|
| | lb. | £ | lb. | £ | lb. | £ |
| **Yarn usage per dozen** | | | | | | |
| Weight | 8·88 | | 2·26 | | 16·44 | |
| Waste | 0·56 | | 0·16 | | 1·03 | |
| | | 9·44 | | 2·38 | | 17·47 |
| **Cost per dozen** | | | | | | |
| Yarn cost | 7·08 | 7·10 | 1·93 | 1·95 | 14·15 | 14·17 |
| Draw thread and swatches | 0·02 | 0·06 | 0·02 | 0·06 | 0·02 | 0·06 |
| Needles | 0·13 | | 0·03 | | 0·50 | |
| Buttons | 0·26 | | 0·25 | | 0·30 | |
| Sewing/Tabs/Tapes | 0·90 | | | | | |
| Plastic | | 1·29 | | 0·28 | — | 0·80 |
| Bags/Boxes | | 0·15 | | 0·13 | | 0·30 |
| Knitting labour | 0·66 | | 0·46 | | 2·80 | |
| Making-up labour | 1·62 | | 0·89 | | 2·29 | |
| Holiday pay/Increase (24%) | 2·28 | 2·83 (24%) | 1·35 (24%) | 1·60 | 5·09 (11%) | 5·65 |
| Carriage/Packing | 0·55 | 0·18 | 0·25 | 0·16 | 0·56 | 0·18 |
| Overheads | 11·61 (12½%) 3·42 | 11·61 | 4·18 (12½%) 2·03 | 4·18 | 21·16 (13½%) 7·63 | 21·16 |
| Commission discount (7%) | 15·03 / 1·05 | | 6·21 / 0·43 | | 28·79 / 2·02 | |
| Total cost/Variable cost +8·5%/43% | 16·08 / 1·37 | 12·66 / 5·44 | 6·64 / 0·56 | 4·61 / 1·99 | 30·81 / 2·64 | 23·18 / 9·97 |
| Costed selling price per dozen | £17·45 | £18·10 | £7·20 | £6·60 | £33·45 | £33·15 |
| Variable cost + 3 making-up labour | £17·50 | | £7·30 | | £30·50 | |

# James Wilson & Son (C)

JAMES WILSON & Son of Milchester was an old-established-manufacturer and distributor of knitted underwear, leisurewear and children's outerwear. Homewoods Stores, a large multiple retail-stores group, was an important customer of James Wilson & Son. When negotiating contracts with Homewoods Stores the company was normally a price taker. The Homewoods buyer stated the price he was prepared to pay for a style of garment, and Mr Simpson, the company's sales manager, had to decide whether or not to supply the garment at the stated price. Mr Hawkeye, the company's management accountant, had gained the impression, from remarks made by Mr Simpson, that the Homewoods buyer was prepared occasionally to negotiate higher prices for certain garments. With other garments he indicated clearly that there was no room for negotiation, and became aggravated if requests for higher prices were made.

Mr Hawkeye felt that James Wilson & Son must develop a pricing strategy which would enable Mr Simpson to negotiate the highest selling prices from the Homewoods buyer. On Mr Hawkeye's request, his assistant prepared two tables, Table 1: Current Selling Prices to Homewoods Stores and Table 2: Homewoods Stores Current Retail-Selling Prices. The information for both tables was obtained from Homewoods' remittance advices, which showed retail-selling prices. If the information had not been available on the remittance advices, Mr Hawkeye had planned to visit Homewoods' Milchester store and note the selling prices of the garments manufactured by Wilsons.

QUESTION

What advice, if any, should Mr Hawkeye give to Mr Simpson concerning pricing negotiations with Homewoods Stores?

*Table 1*

Current Selling Prices to Homewoods Stores

| Type | Size (in.) | Garment No. | Current selling price per dozen £ |
|------|-----------|-------------|-----------------------------------|
| Matinee coat | | 1307 | 5·05 |
| ,, | | 1186 | 5·00 |
| Cardigan | 18–20 | 1382 | 5·10 |
| ,, | 22–24 | 1382 | 6·15 |
| Jumper | 18–20 | 1383 | 5·75 |
| ,, | 22–24 | 1420 | 6·45 |
| Jumper suit | 20–22 | 1257 | 14·05 |
| ,, | 20–22 | 1434 | 13·35 |
| ,, | 26–28 | 1257 | 15·85 |
| ,, | 26–28 | 1434 | 16·35 |
| Lumber | 18–20 | 1292 | 5·80 |
| ,, | 18–20 | 1420 | 5·80 |
| ,, | 18–20 | 1490 | 6·00 |
| ,, | 18–20 | 1365 | 6·05 |
| ,, | 18–20 | 1293 | 6·35 |
| ,, | 22–24 | 1292 | 6·45 |
| ,, | 22–24 | 1383 | 6·60 |
| ,, | 22–24 | 1490 | 7·12½ |
| ,, | 22–24 | 1293 | 7·22½ |
| ,, | 22–24 | 1367 | 7·27½ |
| Buster suit | 22–24 | 1431 | 10·25 |
| Boy's pullover | 24–26 | 3043 | 10·00 |
| ,, | 28–30 | 3043 | 11·55 |
| ,, | 32–34 | 3043 | 13·30 |
| Pram set | 12–14 | 1436 | 11·90 |
| Walking suit | 20–22 | 1065 | 13·10 |
| ,, | 20–22 | 1034 | 13·10 |
| ,, | 24–26 | 1065 | 15·42½ |
| ,, | 24–26 | 1034 | 15·42½ |

198

## *Table 2*

Homewoods Stores Current Retail-Selling Prices

| Type of garment | Size (in.) | Retail-selling price £ |
|---|---|---|
| Matinee coat | 10 | 0·62½ |
| Cardigan | 18–20 | |
| Jumper | 18–20 | 0·75 |
| Lumber | 18–20 | |
| Cardigan | 22–24 | |
| Jumper | 22–24 | 0·85 |
| Lumber | 22–24 | |
| Buster suit | 22–24 | 1·30 |
| Boy's pullover | 24–26 | |
| Pram set | 12–14 | 1·50 |
| Boy's pullover | 28–30 | |
| Walking suit | 20–22 | 1·65 |
| Jumper suit | 22–24 | 1·75 |
| Boy's pullover | 32–34 | 1·85 |
| Walking suit | 24–26 | 1·90 |
| Jumper suit | 26–28 | 2·00 |

# Milky Dairies Ltd*

IN THIS case study some specific examples of the application of marginal costing in the dairy industry are given. The examples are based on products, prices and costs in the industry in 1960,† and the changes since that date do not affect the principles applied. Before discussing detailed examples a brief introduction to the nature of cost accounting in the dairy industry is provided.

## THE NATURE OF COST ACCOUNTING IN THE DAIRY INDUSTRY IN 1960

The distribution of milk starts from the farms. The farmers sell their milk to the Milk Marketing Board (M.M.B.), who resell the milk to the dairymen at a fixed price. The M.M.B. arrange for the milk to be delivered from the farms to the dairies, or the dairyman may collect the milk from the farms himself. If the dairyman collects the milk from the farms he will receive a collection allowance from the M.M.B. The milk may come to the dairy in churns or it may be collected from the farms by a bulk tanker. If the milk arrives at the dairy in churns, the dairyman has to have a milk-reception point, where he can tip the churns and wash them for returning to the farms. The M.M.B. pay the dairyman an ex-farm allowance for performing this function. It should be noted that the full cost of the churns is borne by the dairyman. When the milk is collected in bulk from the farms it is only necessary to pump the milk into the storage tanks and 'steam out' the tanker.

The raw milk is thus collected from the farms and reaches the storage tanks in the dairies. At this point two types of dairyman

* This case study is derived from John Sizer,'Marginal Costing in the Dairy Industry', *Accountancy*, December 1967, pp. 789–98.

† In the examples d. equals *old* penny. The old penny was replaced by the new penny (p) in 1971. One new pence (p) equals 2.4d., i.e. £1 equals 240d. and 100p.

can be distinguished. They are the *depot proprietor*, who is usually located in the country; he receives milk from the surrounding farms and then consigns it in tankers to town dairies. He may heat-treat and bottle milk, and sell it wholesale and retail. He may also manufacture into milk products any milk which is surplus to the town dairies' liquid requirements. He is basically a collecting point for milk in rural districts from which milk can be consigned to town dairies in highly populated areas. The other type is the *town dairyman*, who sells milk wholesale and retail. He receives his raw milk from the farms, any deficit coming from the depot proprietor. During the months when milk yields are high he may receive milk in excess of his requirements from the farms, and he will send the surplus to other town dairies or to depot proprietors for manufacture. The M.M.B. will pay allowances to town dairies and depot proprietors according to how they handle the milk they receive. This case study is mainly concerned with a town dairy and the allowances a town dairyman received from the M.M.B.

From the raw-milk storage tanks the milk will pass through the sterilized or pasteurized processing and bottling lines and into storage prior to distribution. The town dairyman sells his milk to three broad classes of customers:

1. *Retail customers*, i.e. householders in the main. The maximum retail selling price is prescribed by the government in the statutory instrument which is for the time being in force.
2. *Shops, schools and canteens*: these are sales at a price less than the maximum retail selling price, i.e. semi-retail sales, and usually have separate transport from the retail sales.
3. *Other milkmen*, i.e. wholesale sales. These are sales to other dairymen who resell the milk to retail customers or to shops. The maximum wholesale prices are laid down each month by the M.M.B.

Broadly speaking, electric vehicles of all sizes are used for retail distribution, though occasionally small diesel vehicles are used; small and medium-sized diesel vehicles and large electric vehicles are used for shop distribution; for distribution to other milkmen medium-sized and large diesels and tractor units with trailers are employed.

The M.M.B. pay allowances to the town dairyman according to the type of sale he makes. They pay heat-treatment allowances on all milk sold retail and semi-retail. They also pay wholesale allowances on all sales to other milkmen.

To summarize, the dairyman buys his milk at a fixed price from the M.M.B. and sells at maximum prices to wholesale and retail customers, but usually sells below maximum retail price to shops, canteens, schools, etc. He receives rebates from the M.M.B. at varying rates for retail and semi-retail and wholesale sales. The gross margin for any sale will depend upon the class of customer and the type of milk, and may be calculated as follows:

|  | d. |
|---|---|
| Maximum selling price | x |
| *less* Cost of milk | x |
|  | x |
| *plus* Rebate from M.M.B. | x |
| Gross margin | x |

By careful study of the various rebates and maximum selling prices it is possible to split the gross margin into a remuneration for the dairy function and a remuneration for the distribution function. When there are frequent changes in margins this split may become somewhat arbitrary. The dairy remuneration varies according to the type of process, i.e. pasteurized or sterilized, and the type and size of container, i.e. pint, half-pint or third-pint bottles or cartons. The distribution remuneration varies according to the type of customer, i.e. retail, shops or other milkmen, the type of milk and the type and size of container. This division, though somewhat arbitrary, enables the cost accountant to have separate profit centres for the dairy functions and the distribution functions. It gives both the dairy and distribution managements a feeling of earning profits and makes them profit- as well as cost-conscious. The profit centres of a typical town dairy and the source of revenue for each centre may be summarized as follows:

| *Profit centre* | *Source of revenue* |
|---|---|
| 1. Collection from farms: | |
|   (a) by M.M.B. | — |
|   (b) by own transport | Collection allowance |
| 2. Milk reception: | |
|   (a) in churns | Ex-farm allowance |
|   (b) in bulk tanker | — |
| 3. Processing and bottling: | |
|   (a) pasteurized | Dairy remuneration |
|   (b) sterilized | ,, ,, |
| 4. Distribution | |
|   (a) retail | Distribution remuneration |
|   (b) shops | ,, ,, |
|   (c) other milkmen | ,, ,, |

Given these fixed margins for processing and distribution, the maximization of profits in the dairy industry depends to a considerable degree on the control of costs. The dairy industry has a high fixed cost to total cost ratio, approximately 50 per cent. In the dairy two of the principal items of cost are usually fixed, i.e. depreciation of the processing and bottling plant and dairy wages up to normal capacity. With the trend towards increased auto-mation in the processing and handling of milk in the dairy, the fixed cost to total cost ratio is continually increasing. The principal variables are bottles and closures. On the distribution side the drivers' wages, traction batteries for electric vehicles, vehicle depreciation, licences and insurances are fixed. For a retail vehicle which operates on a set route each day it may be argued that all the costs of operating the vehicle are fixed, in the sense that any additional customers on that route, if the vehicle is not fully loaded, could be supplied without incurring any additional distribution costs. There would be an increase in drivers' wages if incentive schemes are operated. It will be appreciated that with this high ratio of fixed costs the marginal benefits of increasing the gallonage processed in the dairy and filling up distribution vehicles are very high. By thinking in marginal costing terms the dairyman should be able to follow a policy of maximizing profit by fully utilizing his processing and distribution capacity.

## DETAILED APPLICATIONS OF MARGINAL COSTING

After this brief introduction to the nature of the cost and revenue functions in the dairy industry, some detailed applications of marginal costing in Milky Dairies Ltd are considered. In these examples the technique of calculating marginal effects of additional gallonage on the profits of the firm is illustrated, and one or two other examples of marginal costing applications in the dairy industry are given.

### 1. PURCHASE OF SMALL 'OTHER MILKMAN'

Milky Dairies delivers milk retail in Miltown, a small rural town, which it supplies from its dairy in Bigtown. They have recently purchased the retail round of Smith, who also delivered retail in Miltown and used to purchase his milk from another dairy. The management of Milky Dairies required an estimate of the additional profit per year resulting from the purchase of Smith's retail round. The estimate is shown in Table 1.

It will be seen that the first step is to calculate the additional annual sales in gallons of the various types of milk, allowing for a 15 per cent loss of customers to competitors. The next step is to calculate the additional profit at Bigtown Dairy, i.e. the additional dairy remuneration less the marginal cost of processing and bottling the additional gallonage. To this figure is added the additional profit on Miltown distribution, which is the distribution remuneration less variable distribution costs, mainly additional wages. It is assumed that no additional wages and vehicle costs will be incurred on transport from Bigtown to Miltown. The additional gallonage will be used to fill up existing rounds in Miltown, and it will be transported with the existing gallonage from Bigtown to Miltown. This example clearly shows the marginal effects of filling up existing capacity in the dairy and on distribution. Approximately 118 daily retail gallons have been purchased, and, with a normal purchase price in 1960 of £20 a daily gallon, it would have cost approximately £2,360 to generate additional profits before tax of £1,094 per annum.

### Table 1
#### Profit at Miltown on Purchase of Smith's Round

| | | | | Gallons |
|---|---|---|---|---|
| Sales per year (assuming a 15% loss on purchase) | | | | |
| Channel Island | | | | 3,448 |
| T.T. Pasteurized | | | | 176 |
| Pasteurized | | | | 32,532 |
| | | | | 36,156 |

| | | *d.* | £ | £ |
|---|---|---|---|---|
| Profit at Bigtown on bottling | | | | |
| Dairy remuneration | | | | |
| Channel Island | | 6·125 | 88 | |
| T.T. | | 5·625 | 4 | |
| Pasteurized | | 5·625 | 492 | |
| | | | 584 | |
| *less* Variable and semi-variable processing costs | | | | |
| 36,156 gallons at 1·76d. | | | 266 | |
| | | | | 318 |

| | | *d.* | £ | |
|---|---|---|---|---|
| Profit at Miltown on distribution: | | | | |
| Distribution remuneration: | | | | |
| Channel Island | | 16·500 | 222 | |
| T.T. | | 16·000 | 12 | |
| Pasteurized | | 14·000 | 1,898 | |
| | | | 2,132 | |
| *less* Variable distribution costs | | | | |
| 36,156 gallons at 9·000d. | | | 1,356 | |
| | | | | 776 |

| | | | | £ |
|---|---|---|---|---|
| *Additional profit per year before tax* | | | | £1,094 |

## 2. PURCHASE OF LARGE 'OTHER MILKMAN'

A. Dairyman Ltd already purchases his sterilized milk from Milky Dairies but pasteurizes at his own dairy in Townsville. Milky Dairies are considering purchasing A. Dairyman Ltd and require an estimate of the additional profit they will earn if they close down A. Dairyman's Townsville dairy and do all the processing in their existing dairy.

In Table 2 the additional gallonage and the additional dairy

### Table 2
### Estimated Annual Profit on Purchase of A. Dairyman Ltd
A. Dairyman already purchases his sterilized milk from our dairy
and pasteurizes at his own dairy at Townsville

| | Daily gallons sold | Yearly gallons sold | Remuneration Dairy per gallon | per year | Distribution per gallon | per year |
|---|---|---|---|---|---|---|
| | | | d. | £ | d. | £ |
| Other milkmen | | | | | | |
| Sterilized | 170 | 62,050 | Already processed | | 3·000* | 776 |
| Channel Island pints | 80 | 29,200 | 6·000 | 730 | 3·000 | 365 |
| T.T. pints | 570 | 208,050 | 6·000 | 5,201 | 2·625 | 2,276 |
| Pasteurized pints | 1,150 | 419,750 | 6·000 | 10,494 | 0·625 | 1,093 |
| Thirds pasteurized | 15 | 5,475 | 9·625 | 220 | 0·625 | 14 |
| Bulk pasteurized | 220 | 80,300 | 1·000 | 335 | 1·000 | 335 |
| | 2,205 | 804,825 | | | | |
| Retail | | | | | | |
| T.T. pints | 80 | 29,200 | 6·000 | 730 | 16·625 | 2,023 |
| Pasteurized pints | 167 | 60,955 | 6·000 | 1,524 | 12·625 | 3,206 |
| | 247 | 90,155 | | 19,234 | | 10,088 |
| | 2,452 | 894,980 | | | | |

| Additional dairy costs | Yearly gallons | Variables and semi-variables Per gallon | £ |
|---|---|---|---|
| Sterilized | 62,050 | | already processed |
| Channel Island, T.T. and pasteurized | 747,155 | 2·000 | 6,226 |
| Thirds | 5,475 | 3·400 | 78 |
| Bulk | 80,300 | 0·270 | 90 |
| | 894,980 | | 6,394 |
| Additional dairy wages | | | Nil† |
| | | | 6,394 |

| Additional ex-farm income | | | | |
|---|---|---|---|---|
| Variables, etc. | | | | |
| 2,282 × 365 days × 0·234d. | 812 | | | |
| less Remuneration at 0·375d. | 1,301 | Cr. 489 | 5,905 | |
| *Additional dairy profit* | | | 13,329 | |

Additional distribution costs

| | | |
|---|---|---|
| Gallons delivered to Other Milkmen and Townsville Depot at 2d. per gallon (2,282 × 365 days) | 6,941 | |
| N.B. Sterilized already delivered | | |
| Retail deliveries in Townsville at 12d. per gallon (247 × 365 days) | 4,508 | 11,449 |
| *Distribution loss* | | (£1,361) |

*Table 2 (Cont.)*

SUMMARY

|  |  £ |
|---|---|
| Dairy profit | 13,329 |
| Distribution loss | (1,361) |
| *Additional profit per year before tax* | £11,968 |

\* 2d. cut no longer given plus 1d. additional rebate as sales to Other Milkmen now under 150 gallons per day.

† The Townsville Dairy is at present operating below normal capacity on its pasteurized processing and bottling line (approximately 5½ hours per day) and the additional gallonage on the purchase of A. Dairyman Ltd would not increase the total throughput above normal capacity gallonage (8 hours per day). Because of the guaranteed weekly wage, the dairy is at present staffed for normal capacity gallonage, and there should be no increase in dairy wages on the purchase of A. Dairyman Ltd.

and distribution remuneration per year have been calculated. Points to note on this part of the estimate are:

1. There is no additional dairy remuneration on the sterilized milk because this is already processed by Milky Dairies.

2. Although the sterilized milk will be sold to the same other milkmen as A. Dairyman sells it to, there will be an additional 3d. per gallon distribution remuneration. Milky Dairies gives A. Dairyman a 2d. per gallon cut, a quantity discount, and this is A. Dairyman's remuneration for delivering to the smaller other milkmen. The M.M.B. price structure, and rightly so, does not provide any remuneration for performing this function. Milky Dairies would also receive an additional 1d. per gallon wholesale rebate from the M.M.B., because the gallons per day sold to these individual other milkmen would all be less than 150.

From the additional dairy remuneration is deducted the additional processing and bottling costs, i.e. the additional gallonage at the marginal cost per gallon, to give the estimated increase in dairy profit. It is assumed that there will be no increase in dairy wages because the additional gallonage will not bring the total gallonage above normal capacity. It will be seen that there is also some ex-farm income because the additional gallonage can again be handled at marginal cost. Marginal cost is assumed to be constant over the higher output range. This provides a margin of safety, as marginal cost probably falls as output is increased.

To calculate the increase in distribution profit, the additional distribution costs have been deducted from the additional distribution revenue. It will be seen that there is little marginal benefit to distribution. The gallonage previously processed by A. Dairyman would have to be transported to Townsville and this could probably be done on existing vehicles. But the retail deliveries in Townsville would have to be made on additional vehicles with additional drivers at full cost. The net result is a distribution loss of £1,361 per annum. This is partly accounted for by the M.M.B. price structure which does not encourage other milkmen sales. The M.M.B. do not like to have a middleman between the processing dairy and the retail or semi-retail customer.

The distribution loss is, however, offset by the additional dairy profit which includes the marginal benefit of the additional throughput. The estimated additional profit before tax of £11,968 will assist the management in arriving at a purchase consideration for A. Dairyman Ltd.

## 3. THE MERGER

Milky Dairies Ltd is contemplating a merger of their Bigtown dairy with a smaller competitor in Bigtown, A.B.C. Dairies (Bigtown) Ltd. It is intended to close down the dairy of A.B.C. Dairies (Bigtown) Ltd, and expand the capacity of Milky Dairies' Bigtown dairy to process and bottle the additional gallonage. The management require an estimate of the additional profits resulting from purchasing A.B.C. Dairies (Bigtown) Ltd and integrating their gallonage into the Bigtown dairy.

The calculation is shown in Table 3. In the first section the additional dairy profit has been calculated. The contribution per gallon has been determined for each type of milk and this has been multiplied by the A.B.C. Dairies annual gallonage to give the additional margin per year. From this margin has been deducted the extra fixed costs, including dairy wages, resulting from the expansion of normal capacity. The daily production in bottles after the integration is shown in a separate section at the end of the calculation. The additional fixed costs would be based on increasing normal capacity to meet the requirements of this volume of daily production.

In the second section the additional distribution profit resulting from the merger has been calculated. It is not merely a question

## Table 3

### Estimation of Additional Profits on Purchase of A.B.C. Dairies (Bigtown) Ltd and Integrating in Our Bigtown Dairy

1. Additional dairy profit – Bigtown

|  | Sterilized pints | T.T. pints | Pasteurized pints | Bulk | Total |
|---|---|---|---|---|---|
| Additional daily gallons | 500 | 450 | 1,290 | 37 | 2,277 |
|  | d. | d. | d. | d. |  |
| Dairy remuneration | 6·250 | 5·750 | 5·750 | 1·000 |  |
| less Variable and semi-variable processing costs | 3·040 | 1·860 | 1·860 | 0·370 |  |
| Contribution | 3·210 | 3·890 | 3·890 | 0·630 |  |
| | | | | | £ |
| Additional margin per year on above gallonage | £2,439 | £2,662 | £7,632 | £35 | 12,768 |

less Extra fixed expenses (including dairy wages) to cover above gallonage – £50 per week ............ 2,600

Additional dairy profit ............ 10,168

2. Additional distribution profit – Bigtown

|  | Gallons per day | Remuneration d. | Variable cost d. | Additional variable margin d. | £ |
|---|---|---|---|---|---|
| **Retail** |  |  |  |  |  |
| Sterilized | 100 | 16·375 | 4·000 | 12·375 | 1,882 |
| T.T. Pasteurized | 350 | 16·875 | 4·000 | 12·875 | 6,853 |
| Pasteurized | 940 | 12·875 | 4·000 | 8·875 | 12,688 |
| Bulk pasteurized | 37 | 8·000 | 0·500 | 7·500 | 422 |
|  | 1,427 |  |  |  | £21,845 |
| **Shops** |  |  |  |  |  |
| Sterilized | 200 | 12·375 | 3·000 | 9·375 | £2,852 |
| **Other Milkmen** |  |  |  |  |  |
| Sterilized | 120 | 7·375 | 1·500 | 5·875 | 1·072 |
| ,, (2¼d. cut) | 80 | 5·125 | 1·500 | 3·625 | 441 |
| T.T. Pasteurized | 100 | 2·750 | 1·500 | 1·250 | 190 |
| Pasteurized | 350 | 0·750 | 1·500 | Dr. 0·750 | Dr. 399 |
|  | 650 |  |  |  | £1,304 |
|  | 2,277 |  |  |  | £26,001 |

*Table 3 (Cont.)*

2 . Additional distribution profit – Bigtown (*Cont.*)

|  | £ | Total |
|---|---|---|
| *less* Additional fixed expenses | | |
| Rent and rates, etc., for parking and charging space for 20 vehicles | 520 | |
| Additional checker | 650 | |
| Additional vehicle depreciation | 2,000 (see below) | |
| Additional licences and insurance | 400 | |
| Additional drivers' wages | 8,000 | |
| | £11,570 | |
| *Additional distribution profit* | | 14,431 |

3. Additional ex-farm income (net)

|  | £ | |
|---|---|---|
| Variable cost | | |
| 1,900 daily gallons at 0·190d. * | 549 | |
| Fixed costs | nil | |
| | 549 | |
| *less* Remuneration at 0·375d. | 1,084 | |
| | | 535 |

| | |
|---|---|
| *Total additional profit centre profits* | 25,134 |
| *less* Additional branch controlled administration overheads | 1,731 |
| *Additional profit per year before tax* | **£23,403** |

\* Average daily ex-farm intake.

Bigtown daily production in bottles after integration

| | Quarter ending 30 September 1960 | | Daily A.B.C. Dairy | Total daily |
|---|---|---|---|---|
| | Total | Per day | | |
| Pints sterilized | 4,555,680 | 50,619 | 4,000 | 54,619 |
| Pints T.T. and pasteurized | 2,350,224 | 26,114 | 13,920 | 40,034 ⎫ |
| Thirds pasteurized * | 1,591,920 | 17,688 | — | 17,688 ⎭ 57,722 |
| $\left(\frac{90}{35} \times 24 \times 25,783\right)$ | | | | |
| | 8,497,824 | 94,421 | 17,920 | 112,341 |

Sterilized: Plant is now bottling at 6,000 bottles per hour.
Pasteurized: A new filler capper with 8,000-bottles-per-hour capacity would be needed, and is allowed for in the additional fixed dairy expenses.
   \* Only delivered to schools during 35 days in the quarter.

### Table 3 (Cont.)

Additional vehicle depreciation

| Type of | No. required | Estimated cost per vehicle £ | total £ | Estimated life (years) | Depreciation per annum £ |
|---|---|---|---|---|---|
| Electric barrows | 10 | 400 | 4,000 | 8 | 500 |
| 1-ton electrics | 6 | 900 | 5,400 | 8 | 675 |
| 2-ton electrics | 4 | 1,237·5 | 4,950 | 6 | 825 |
| | 20 | | £14,350 | | £2,000 |

It is assumed that the usage of the vehicles will be spread evenly over their estimated lives.

of filling up existing vehicles, the whole of the retail distribution will require reorganizing, rounds will have to be merged and new rounds will be created. It is estimated that twenty additional electric vehicles will be required for retail rounds, and that the additional shop and other milkmen gallonage can be distributed on existing vehicles at variable running cost. In the calculation the existing variable running cost per gallon has been deducted from the remuneration per gallon to give the additional variable margin. From the total additional variable margin has been deducted the additional fixed costs resulting from increasing the retail fleet by twenty electric vehicles for new retail rounds.

The additional ex-farm income is calculated in the third section. It will be noted that this figure is based on the average daily ex-farm intake of A.B.C. Dairies, who received some of their raw milk from depots.

The estimated increase in branch-controlled administrative overheads, which are normally a fixed cost, are deducted from the total additional profits from all profit centres.

This example illustrates how a marginal-costing approach can be used to calculate the effect of a complicated merger of two dairies, and to present the calculation in a form which is clearly understandable to management.* By calculating separately the

---

*The estimate of additional profits can easily be converted into a cash-flow statement and the effects of taxation introduced. Similar statements could be prepared for future years to provide the basis for discounted-cash-flow calculations, for appraising the acceptability of the proposed merger. In this example the management simply required an estimate of the additional profits per year before tax.

effect on each profit centre, it will be possible for the responsible management to consider whether the additional fixed costs included are accurate. The variable costs are based on present performance and there is little possibility of there being an increase in variable costs per gallon. If anything there will be a reduction in variable costs. It is therefore the additional fixed expenses which are of paramount importance, and by using this marginal-costing presentation their impact is shown separately. The management is thus able to see the estimates of the additional fixed costs and check that they are correct.

# 4. SCHOOL MILK

Cut-price school milk is usually profitable if it utilizes surplus capacity in the dairy and is delivered on existing vehicles at marginal running cost, i.e. a few extra miles at variable running cost. Milky Dairies deliver school milk to near-by Littletown from their Bigtown dairy, and in doing so use an additional vehicle and driver. The management question the wisdom of this action and ask the accountant to estimate the profitability of the round.

An estimate of the weekly profit on Littletown Schools is shown in Table 4. It will be seen that in calculating the gross margin per gallon allowance has been made for the price cut given off the maximum retail selling price per gallon. The additional gallonage is processed and bottled at marginal cost but there are no marginal benefits on the distribution and the full cost of a vehicle and driver have to be charged against the round. There is a small contribution to administrative overheads, but when administrative overheads are allocated to the round there is a weekly loss. Regardless of whether the administrative overheads are charged or not, the round is not making a satisfactory contribution to company profits. When the tender comes up for renewal the dairy must seriously reconsider their pricing policy.

*Table 4*

Weekly profit Littletown Schools

| | Pasteurized Pints | Pasteurized Thirds | Total |
|---|---|---|---|
| Gallons per week | 100 | 438 | 538 |
| | d. | d. | £ |
| Maximum legal selling price | 60·000 | 60·000 | |
| *less* Cost of milk from M.M.B. | 42·500 | 42·500 | |
| | 17·500 | 17·500 | |
| *less* Price cut | 6·000 | 4·250 | |
| | 11·500 | 13·250 | |
| *Add* Rebate 6 from M.M.B. | 1·750 | 1·750 | |
| Gross margin | 13·250 | 15·000 | |
| *less* Variable and semi-variable processing costs | 1·880 | 3·090 | |
| | 11·370 | 11·910 | 26·48 |

| | | £ | |
|---|---|---|---|
| *less* Vehicle cost | | 12·59 | |
| Driver's wages | | 13·25 | 25·84 |
| Contribution to administrative overheads | | | £0·64 |
| Allocated administrative overheads | | | £4·52 |
| Weekly loss (by absorbing costing) | | | £3·88 |

# 5. WHERE TO PROCESS?

Milky Dairies Ltd own dairies in a number of towns and, because of the differences in the age and size of the plants and buildings, they are not equally efficient. Some dairies have lower processing costs.

Dairy B is a low-cost dairy and has surplus capacity on its sterilized processing and bottling line. Dairy A is a high-cost dairy and is located fifty miles from Dairy B. The director responsible for Dairies A and B is considering transferring 8,400

*Table 5*

Comparisons of Costs of Processing 8,400 Gallons Sterilized
Pints per Week for Dairy A at Dairies A and B

| | Dairy B | | Dairy A | |
|---|---|---|---|---|
| *Processing costs and profits* | d. | d. | d. | d. |
| Dairy remuneration | | 6·50 | | 6·50 |
| Variable and semi-variable costs | | | | |
| Bottles | 1·05 | | 1·05 | |
| Closures | 0·91 | | 0·91 | |
| Crates | 0·15 | | 0·15 | |
| Milk loss | 0·30 | | 0·55 | |
| Electricity | 0·13 | | 0·15 | |
| Fuel | 0·41 | | 0·63 | |
| Water | 0·09 | 3·04 | 0·14 | 3·58 |
| Processing margin per gallon | | 3·46 | | 2·92 |
| | | £ | | £ |
| Processing margin per week | | 122 | | 101 |

*Haulage from Dairy B to storage yard*
(12 loads per week 700 gallons per load = 1 additional tractor unit)

| Vehicle costs | £ | |
|---|---|---|
| Licence and insurance | 1·70 | |
| Depreciation: tractor unit and tractor | 5·12 | |
| Fuel and oil (1,200 miles at 45·5d. and 12 m.p.g.) | 18·96 | |
| Tyres (1,200 miles at 1·94d.) | 9·70 | |
| Repairs (1,200 miles at 2·31d.) | 11·55 | |
| | 47·03 | |
| Driver's wages | 18·00 | |
| | £65·03 | 65 |

*Haulage from Dairy A to storage yard*

| (100 yards down road) | | £ | |
|---|---|---|---|
| Wages of extra man | | 15 | |
| Vehicle costs and contingencies | | 5 | 20 |
| Profit on milk before distribution and overheads | | £57 | £81 |

gallons of sterilized pints per week from Dairy B, the low-cost dairy, to Dairy A, the high-cost dairy, and reducing production at Dairy A by a similar quantity. He now asks the accountant whether this would be profitable to the company.

The calculation is shown in Table 5. The marginal processing cost has been deducted from the dairy remuneration for each dairy to give the processing margin per gallon and the total processing margin per week. From the processing margin of Dairy B, the low-cost dairy, is deducted the cost of hauling twelve loads per week of 700 gallons per load from Dairy B to Dairy A's storage yard. This would require an additional tractor unit and trailer plus driver, and must be charged at total cost. From the processing margin of Dairy A, the high-cost dairy, is deducted the cost of storing the additional gallonage in a yard owned by the company, which is located 100 yards from the dairy. The premises of Dairy A are not large enough to garage all vehicles and store all the bottled milk overnight. If the milk were processed at Dairy B, it could be delivered direct to the storage yard and the cost of haulage to the storage yard would be saved.

It will be seen that the additional profit in Dairy B is more than offset by the higher haulage from Dairy B to the storage yard, and that it would not be advisable to transfer the processing of 8,400 gallons of sterilized pints per week to Dairy B. This calculation could have been made purely in terms of differences in costs rather than profits, but the management usually like to think in terms of profits rather than costs.

# 6. QUOTATIONS

The last example of marginal costing in the dairy industry to be examined is an application of marginal pricing.

The X.Y.Z. Company Ltd have invited Milky Dairies and a number of other dairies to submit quotations for the supply of milk to their Uptown factory and staff canteen, their Downtown depot and their offices. The manager of the Milky Dairies Bigtown dairy has asked the accountant for his recommendations on minimum selling prices and suggested selling prices.

The accountant's recommendations are set out in Table 6. He deals first with the pasteurized pints, T.T. pasteurized pints, pasteurized bulk and sterilized pints, since these are standard lines and additional gallonage can be processed at marginal cost. It will be seen that to the cost of milk has been added the variable processing and distribution costs to give the marginal cost per gallon. The accountant has then added a minimum contribution of 5d. per gallon to give the minimum selling prices. He has also given suggested selling prices, which are slightly higher than the minimum selling prices. These prices will be based on his previous experience and knowledge of tender prices to this class of customer. This is a good example of a 'secondary' pricing decision,* where the suggested prices have been based on marginal cost data.

In arriving at his minimum selling price for the half-pint cartons, it will be noted that the accountant has included fixed processing costs for normal capacity output, i.e. he has based his recommendation partly on absorption cost data. Why is this? This is not a 'secondary' pricing decision, it is closer to a 'primary' pricing decision. Half-pint cartons are not very well established in the British dairy industry, and Milky Dairies have only a very low sales gallonage of this type of container. The present gallonage is not fully recovering fixed processing costs, and the accountant feels that any additional sales must be charged with their share of fixed processing costs, as well as the minimum contribution of 5d. per gallon, in arriving at a minimum selling price.

It is hoped that the reader is now convinced of the suitability of marginal costing techniques as an aid to the accountant when he is called upon to advise the management on the effect of volume changes on costs and profits, and when he has to make recommendations on pricing policy.

* John Sizer, 'The Accountants' Contribution to the Pricing Decision' *Journal of Management Studies*, Vol. 3, No. 2, May 1966, pp. 129–50.

## Table 6

### Quotations for X.Y.Z. Company Limited – Bigtown

| | Uptown factory (including staff canteen) | | | | Downtown depot | Office |
|---|---|---|---|---|---|---|
| | ½ pint cartons | Pasteurized pints | Pasteurized bulk | Sterilized pints | T.T. Pasteurized pints | Pasteurized pints |
| | d. | d. | d. | d. | d. | d. |
| Cost of milk from M.M.B. | 45·375 | 45·375 | 45·375 | 45·375 | 45·375 | 45·375 |
| less Rebate | 1·750 | 1·750 | 1·750 | 1·750 | 1·750 | 1·750 |
| Cost of milk | 43·625 | 43·625 | 43·625 | 43·625 | 43·625 | 43·625 |
| Processing expenses | | | | | | |
| Variable | 19·900 | 1·380 | 0·020 | 2·410 | 1·380 | 1·380 |
| Semi-variable | 0·800 | 0·490 | 0·010 | 0·610 | 0·490 | 0·490 |
| Fixed | 6·175* | nil | nil | nil | nil | nil |
| | 70·500 | 45·495 | 43·655 | 46·645 | 45·495 | 45·495 |
| Variable distribution costs | 3·000 | 3·000 | 3·000 | 3·000 | 2·000 | 2·000 |
| Marginal cost | 73·500 | 48·495 | 46·655 | 49·645 | 47·495 | 47·495 |
| Minimum contribution | 5·000 | 5·000 | 5·000 | 5·000 | 5·000 | 5·000 |
| | 78·500 | 53·495 | 51·655 | 54·645 | 52·495 | 52·495 |
| Minimum selling price per gallon | 78·5 (5d. per carton) | 53·5 | 51·5 | 54·5 | 52·5 | 52·5 |
| Maximum cut per gallon | 17·5 | 10·5 | 12·5 | 13·5 | 15·5 | 11·5 |
| Full retail price per gallon | 96·0 | 64·0 | 64·0 | 68·0 | 68·0 | 64·0 |
| Suggested selling price per gallon | 80d. | 54d. | 52d. | 56d. | 56d. | 54d. |

* Normal capacity fixed processing costs per Bigtown dairy standard processing costs of 1 January 1960.

QUESTIONS

1. Is it advisable to establish separate profit centres for the dairy functions and the distribution functions?

2. Do you agree that the maximization of profits in the dairy industry depends to a considerable degree on the control of costs? Will a dairyman by thinking in marginal-costing terms be able to follow a policy of maximizing profit by fully utilizing his processing and distribution capacity?

3. What are the key assumptions in each of the six applications of marginal costing described in the case?

4. A 15 per cent loss of sales gallons on purchase has been assumed in Table 1. You have learnt from the sales manager of the dairy in Bigtown that 'while we normally lose 15 per cent of sales gallons when we purchase a retail round, in two in twenty cases we lose 20 per cent and in one in twenty cases it is as high as 25 per cent'. Revise Table 1 to take account of this additional information.

5. Do you agree that it is the additional fixed expenses that are of paramount importance in the merger example?

6. When the school-milk tender comes up for renewal, what factors should Milky Dairies take into consideration when reviewing their pricing policy?

7. Critically examine the approach and calculations in example 5.

8. In some of the examples 'Milky Dairies make the mistake of employing short-run techniques to evaluate the effect of long-run decisions.' Is this the case?

9. Are you 'now convinced of the suitability of marginal-costing techniques as an aid to the accountant when called upon to advise management on the effects of volume changes on costs and profits, and when he has to make recommendations on pricing policy'?

SUGGESTED BACKGROUND READING

1. *An Insight into Management Accounting*, Chapters 8 and 9.
2. S. Dixon, *The Case for Marginal Costing*, General Edu-

cational Trust of the Institute of Chartered Accountants in England and Wales, London, 1966.

3. Gordon Shillinglaw, 'The Concept of Attributable Cost', in David Solomons (ed.), *Studies in Cost Analysis*, Sweet & Maxwell, London, 1968, pp. 134–47.

## Diversified Engineering Ltd

ARNOLD KOPF founded Diversified Engineering Ltd in Loughborough in 1961, and was its chairman and managing director
at the end of 1969. The company's growth since 1961, though
somewhat haphazard, was guided by Kopf's experience, knowledge and expertise.

Initially the company specialized in metal spraying, in association with a local plating company, Sunnyhill Plating Ltd, and
carried out a certain amount of machine-tool work. Further
scope was seen for a specialized metal-spraying service concen-
trating on industrial repair work, and some jobbing sub-contract
work. The company purchased secondhand metal-spraying
equipment, machine tools and shotblasting equipment. Floor
space of 2,200 square feet was leased. In practice programming
of metal-spraying work proved difficult because of the un-
predictability and the urgent nature of repair work. Towards
the end of 1961 the company took over from Sunnyhill Plating
the manufacture of certain plastic products. A further diversi-
fication into heat treatment took place during 1962. Sunnyhill
Plating obtained a contract requiring heat-treatment work, and
Diversified Engineering carried this out with a salt bath. It
became necessary to acquire equipment for hardening and inspection, and this was purchased out of retained profits and by
hire purchase. Trade in hardening expanded rapidly. At the same
time the metal-spraying activities were extended to include high-
temperature processes. Although these processes were highly
specialized, a satisfactory demand arose.

In 1963 efforts began to market plastic products. Unfortunately
their quality was poor due to lack of expertise and ignorance of
standards. Anticipated orders did not materialize and the limited
work undertaken proved unprofitable. A stimulus to increased
plastics production resulted from an order to manufacture a

special automatic electroplating plant. The manufacture of this plant involved both plastic fabrications and machining work, but was organized inefficiently and a low profit resulted. The plant sold for £5,000 and took six months to build. No advance payments were received, and the contract put considerable strain on the company's liquid resources. Towards the end of 1963 an induction-hardening machine was acquired, and the company secured a contract from one of its heat-treatment customers for £450 worth of work a month. Successful efforts were made to obtain new customers.

Through 1963 and 1964 the company was stretched to the limit of its physical resources. The factory area had been extended to 4,000 square feet by leasing the remainder of the building. Financially the company performed well and in September 1964 repaid the balance of a bank overdraft. Labour proved difficult to obtain, and a more serious problem of supervision and administration arose. No one aspect of the business was large enough to justify a full-time supervisor who could also carry out inspection and production paperwork. Arnold Kopf attempted to segregate administrative and technical functions with the appointment of an administrative assistant who also acted as a company representative. Much of the company's metal-spraying business was gained through personal contact. The administrative assistant left in April 1967, and an under-manager, Simon Pike, was appointed. He was made responsible for non-specialist technical matters leaving Arnold Kopf to supervise administration and more specialized technical matters.

In May 1967 a competitor appeared: a small company specializing in heat treatment which cut prices to obtain business. Diversified Engineering's trade was affected quite seriously by the temporary loss of a number of customers. Lost trade became more significant towards the end of 1967, when the company occupied 25,000 square feet of production space and office accommodation in new premises. The movement of plant and equipment took nine months. During the period ending December 1969 the company introduced no new processes, but concentrated on consolidating its existing activities. Heat treatment (both salt bath and induction) was expanded, as was the volume of plastics work. Metal spraying was fairly static, partly because little time was devoted to soliciting customers. Little additional machining work was brought in from outside the company, but additional work was generated internally, partly by the manufacture of electroplating plants, which tended to occur at irregular intervals.

The organization of the company reflected its reliance on Arnold Kopf's experience, commercial knowledge and technical expertise. Although Kopf delegated many of the day-to-day technical problems to Simon Pike, he normally investigated the more difficult or specialist technical problems himself. The larger part of Kopf's work was administrative. He prepared many of the quotations required (although many jobs were taken without quotation). He also undertook the costing of many of the complex, unusual or specialist jobs. The costing of the routine work was undertaken by Pike with the assistance of a cost clerk. The Bath Hardening Shop was supervised by a productive foreman, and any problems were normally dealt with by Pike. He also undertook much of the supervision of induction hardening, metal spraying and machining, but all technical research and experimentation was under Kopf's control. The plastics section was controlled by a working foreman, who normally was in charge of induction hardening, metal spraying and machining. This foreman efficiently organized the plastics section, and was consulted frequently over quotations for future jobs. Arnold Kopf supervised the manufacture of electroplating plants. The securing of business was carried out almost exclusively by Kopf, but he was assisted frequently by Sunnyhill Plating Ltd.

Kopf increasingly became concerned about the company's profit performance and liquidity position. Turnover and work in progress expanded between 1967 and 1969, but a net loss of £4,115 was made in 1967, which rose to £12,311 in 1968. The company's liquidity position had deteriorated with a bank overdraft of £10,317 on 31 October 1968 and net current liabilities of £8,250. Kopf partly attributed the trading losses to the move to larger premises and an increase in administrative staff, but nevertheless decided to initiate an investigation into the profitability of Diversified Engineering's various activities. He invited a local management consultant, Bernard Quick, to carry out the investigation and examine future prospects.

After visiting the company and discussing its development and organization with Arnold Kopf, Quick was able to agree with Kopf that the activities of Diversified Engineering Ltd could be divided into five main groups of manufacturing processes:

Salt-bath hardening and heat treatment
Induction processes
Metal spraying and shotblasting
Plastics
Machining

A sixth group 'special operations' was a derivative of two of the groups of manufacturing processes, i.e. plastics and machining. The company maintained the minimum of accounting records. Kopf was able to supply Quick with trading and profit and loss accounts for years ending, and balance sheets as at, 31 October 1966, 1967 and 1968 (see Tables A and B, pp. 246 and 247). In order to ascertain the revenue attributable to each activity, he analysed sales invoices by activity and customer. This analysis revealed the importance of each customer to an activity, the geographical distribution of customers, and the nature of work (jobbing or batch). An analysis of costs was derived from advice notes and invoices, the purchases ledger, and the half-year profit and loss account ending 30 April was extended for a full year with Kopf's assistance. He segregated for each activity direct materials, direct labour and departmental expenses. He classified the remaining costs as general overheads.

The following is a summary of the information Bernard Quick gathered during his investigation.

## GENERAL OVERHEAD COSTS AND ALLOCATION

An analysis of general overheads into fixed and variable elements is shown in Table 1. The general overheads have been apportioned to activities on the basis of the number of 'productive workers' employed by each activity. The term 'productive workers' is defined as those directly engaged in the manufacturing process, and excludes clerical staff, labourers and drivers. There are sixteen productive workers, and the charge per worker is £1,542.

*Table 1*

Analysis of General Overheads

| | £ | £ |
|---|---|---|
| Fixed costs | | |
| Administration and office salaries | 8,100 | |
| Rent | 3,050 | |
| Rates | 1,365 | |
| Insurance | 500 | |
| Electricity (light and heat) | 606 | |
| Bank charges | 400 | |
| Equipment hire | 50 | |
| Audit fees | 380 | |
| Professional charges | 28 | |
| Sundry trade expenses | 600 | |
| Repairs | 50 | |
| Foreman's wages (part allocation) | 700 | |
| | | 15,829 |
| Variable costs | | |
| Laundry | 350 | |
| National Health Insurance | 5,000 | |
| Transport (part allocation) | 1,100 | |
| E.I.T.B. levy | 406 | |
| | | 6,856 |
| Semi-variable costs | | |
| Stationery | 300 | |
| Telephones | 450 | |
| Labourers | 1,000 | |
| Advertising | 200 | |
| | | 1,950 |
| Total | | £24,635 |

*Notes*

1. The cost of transport has been divided equally between heat treatment and general overhead.
2. The foreman spends approximately 50 per cent of his time supervising and the remainder on productive work in the plastics department. He has been counted as a productive worker for overhead-allocation purposes.

224

## SALT-BATH HARDENING AND HEAT TREATMENT

The operations for this group of processes involve placing metal components into baths of molten salts (about 800 – 1,100°C.) and leaving them immersed for several hours. On removal the components are quickly quenched (i.e. cooled in water or oil) at a specific temperature and hardened. In addition metal components may be placed in a dry tempering furnace and subsequently moved to a tempering tank. The processes are scientifically complicated, but have been organized so that they can be carried out by unskilled personnel.

During the year ending 31 October 1969 the turnover from these processes amounted to £27,328. Two local customers accounted for 46·3 per cent and 32·1 per cent of the turnover and a third, situated some 35 miles away, contributed 10·8 per cent. A further four customers accounted for over £300 each and six for sales over £100 each. An analysis of the geographical distribution of sales shows:

| Distance from factory | No. of customers | Total turnover £ | % of total |
|---|---|---|---|
| Less than 5 miles | 17 | 22,026 | 80·6 |
| 5 miles to 25 miles | 21 | 1,923 | 7·1 |
| 25 miles to 60 miles | 6 | 3,342 | 12·2 |
| Further than 60 miles | 2 | 37 | 0·1 |
| | 46 | £27,328 | 100·0 |

The three major customers place orders regularly: batches of the same type of components are received daily or weekly, and the flow of work can be planned. A large number of customers do not trade regularly, and do not require very similar components.

| No. of dealings with customers in the year | No. of customers | Turnover £ | % of total |
|---|---|---|---|
| Twice or less | 13 | 69 | 0·25 |
| 2–5 times | 11 | 308 | 1·00 |
| 6–10 times | 6 | 211 | 0·75 |
| More than 10 times | 16 | 26,740 | 98·00 |
| | 46 | £27,328 | 100·0 |

An analysis of sales to customers who dealt more than ten times shows:

| Sales per customer | | No. of customers |
|---|---|---|
| More than | £9,000 | 2 |
| „ | £2,000 | 1 |
| „ | £300 | 4 |
| „ | £200 | 1 |
| „ | £100 | 3 |
| Less than | £100 | 5 |
| | | 16 |

There is a local competitor, and it is doubtful whether volume of business could be expanded locally without a certain amount of price cutting. Work could be sought from further afield, notably engineering towns with low hardening capacity such as Coventry and Birmingham.

Quotations aim at a net profit of 30 per cent of selling price for jobbing work and 20 per cent for batch work. Table 2 is a profit and loss account for the Heat Treatment Department. The investment in plant and equipment is summarized in Table 3. The life of a heat-treatment bath is virtually unlimited: the only expense incurred after purchase is maintenance and replacement of pots. If operated fifty hours per week, a salt bath can normally be expected to recover its cost in about ten months. At present, a fifty-hour week is worked within the department, but in periods of low demand a forty-hour week is normal. Over the twelve-month period turnover varied considerably:

| Month | Customer A £ | Customer B £ | Others £ | Total £ |
|---|---|---|---|---|
| 1 | 1,056 | 719 | 632 | 2,407 |
| 2 | 651 | 91 | 439 | 1,181 |
| 3 | 1,244 | 874 | 492 | 2,610 |
| 4 | 1,044 | 614 | 595 | 2,253 |
| 5 | 1,032 | 809 | 376 | 2,217 |
| 6 | 1,320 | 670 | 303 | 2,293 |
| 7 | 1,150 | 633 | 394 | 2,177 |
| 8 | 1,174 | 329 | 466 | 1,969 |
| 9 | 898 | 1,128 | 598 | 2,624 |
| 10 | 609 | 1,181 | 451 | 2,241 |
| 11 | 1,562 | 1,245 | 465 | 3,272 |
| 12 | 903 | 492 | 689 | 2,084 |
| | £12,643 | £8,785 | £5,900 | £27,328 |

*Table 2*

Heat Treatment Department
Trading Account

| | £ | £ |
|---|---|---|
| Sales | | 27,328 |
| | | |
| Variable process costs | | |
| Gas | 3,401 | |
| Salts | 1,208 | |
| Quenching oil | 203 | |
| Cleaning mediums | 80 | |
| Effluent treatment | 139 | |
| Wire | 42 | |
| Protective clothing | 150 | |
| Electric arc extraction | 155 | |
| Pots | 344 | |
| Baskets | 145 | |
| Maintenance | 69 | |
| | | 5,936 |
| Fixed process costs | | |
| Transport | 1,100 | |
| Inspection | 500 | |
| Labourers | 2,300 | |
| | | 3,900 |
| | | |
| Total departmental expenses | | 9,836 |
| Direct labour | | 5,230 |
| General overhead allocation | | 4,626 |
| | | |
| *Total expenses* | | £19,692 |
| | | |
| *Net profit* | | £7,636 |
| | | |
| % profit to sales | | 27·9% |

The three large salt-bath furnaces are working at full capacity (7,500 furnace hours per year), but capacity could be increased by the acquisition of an additional furnace at a cost of £800 or by the introduction of shift working. If an additional furnace were acquired process variable costs would increase proportionately to the increase in capacity. An additional van would have to be obtained for general deliveries, and the lorry would be transferred wholly to heat-treatment work. The lorry costs £1,800 per annum to operate. Additional inspection will cost £150, but labourers probably could be kept at the present level with some reorganization. In order to attract additional business a further £250 of advertising would be necessary. The direct labour force could be maintained at its present level, but would be fully stretched. They would earn £750 additional bonus in a year. The present supervision should prove adequate. As the present labour force would be maintained, the general overhead allocation to the department would not change. With the extra furnace, the total department revenue at full capacity (10,000 furnace hours) would rise to £36,400.

The introduction of longer working through shift methods

*Table 3*

Heat Treatment Department
Fixed Assets

| Item | Purchase date | Cost £ |
|---|---|---|
| Salt bath (large) | 1964 | 650 |
| „ „ | 1965 | 800 |
| „ „ | 1966 | 800 |
| „ (small) | 1963 | 150 (secondhand) |
| Tempering furnace | 1963 | 100 (secondhand) |
| 4 quench tanks | 1963 | 400 |
| 2 oil tempering tanks | 1963 to 1969 | 120 |
| 2 washing tanks | | 70 |
| Inspection equipment | 1967 and 1969 | 480 |
| Hoists | 1967 | 150 |
| Cooling tower | 1967 | 300 |
| Storage tank and effluent tester | 1967 | 200 |
| Pollution-extraction system | 1967 | 900 |
| Plumbing | 1967 | 800 |
| Alteration to building: fireproofing | 1967 | 1,000 |
| | | £6,920 |

would enable production to be increased without further capital expenditure. By staggering working hours the labour could be used more effectively. This should allow a total of ninety-five hours per week working on each furnace compared with the present fifty hours per week. Process variable costs will be 190 per cent of their present level (£5,936). Inspection time would be increased, but much of the process inspection during the evening shift would be carried out by the operator. There would be additional final inspection, and the cost would increase to £600. The transport requirement would increase significantly, and the lorry would be fully utilized by the department. One labourer would be transferred to the night shift and paid at a premium of $1\frac{1}{4}$. The total labourer cost would rise to £2,700. Additional advertising would be necessary at a cost of £250.

The cost of direct labour would rise by about 14 per cent. If no extra labour were recruited there would be two productive workers paid at normal rates, and one paid on a nightshift premium of $1\frac{1}{4}$. The direct labour cost would rise to £5,800. However, with an increase of 90 per cent in the working hours of each furnace, there would probably be some further increase in direct labour cost. Employment of a further worker could be avoided by using two furnaces only on the night shift, but productive hours would be reduced from 14,250 to 12,000 per year. If an extra worker were recruited to allow the third furnace to operate for ninety-five hours per week, the extra revenue generated would be £8,200 per year. The additional direct labour cost would be £2,320, process variable cost would increase by £1,760 and overheads by £1,542. However, the extra man would reduce overheads per man to £1,452 per year. This reduction could be attributed to the extra employee, and set off against the extra costs. The benefit would be £360 (four men at £90), and the added cost would be reduced to £5,250, which would give a profit of £3,000 if an extra man is acquired. Even if three men are capable of operating the furnaces, it is probable that extra labour would be required to prepare work for processing and dispatch. The projected sales for 14,250 hours working are £51,900.

## INDUCTION PROCESSES

These processes involve a machine passing a high-frequency, high-amperage electric current through a copper coil, which normally is tubular. Cooling water is pumped through the coil. Metal inserted within the coil heats very quickly at the surface but the interior remains cool. If cooled quickly with water the surface becomes very hard, but if allowed to cool slowly the surface will soften. The machines may also be used for brazing components (normally circular) cheaply and quickly.

The coil of the machine has to be designed specially for each job, and this requires a large degree of experimentation. The process is economical for large batches or production runs only, and it is essential that the coils are efficient in both speed of operation and in use of electricity. Normally automatic or semi-automatic fixtures are employed to allow the use of semi-skilled labour.

The induction processes contributed £7,143 to turnover in the year under review. An analysis of turnover shows that one customer (also the largest customer for heat treatment) contributed 68 per cent of the turnover. Three other customers represented 12, 9·5 and 5·5 per cent of turnover, a fifth company contributed nearly £200, and the remaining six customers during the year less than £100 each. Six customers traded eight or more times during the year and between them contributed £7,076. The over-dependence on one customer is at present being removed through a successful search for new contracts.

The company has expanded its induction processes as rapidly as possible without any proper profitability assessments. Competition is sparse: one large customer for whom shafts are treated is situated 115 miles away. Items are small, are processed in bulk, and transport is not always a significant cost compared with the processing charge for the batch. The company do have some difficulty in pricing work undertaken. They have no clear idea of competitors' charges. They feel a high mark-up is required to justify setting up the machines and making the complex coils. A profit of 30 to 40 per cent of sales value is aimed for.

The trading account (Table 4) shows a net profit of 35·5 per cent of sales.

Table 4

Induction Processes Department
Trading Account

|  | £ | £ |
|---|---|---|
| Sales |  | 7,143 |
|  |  |  |
| Electricity | 300 |  |
| Materials | 230 |  |
| Maintenance | 209 |  |
| Tooling | 200 |  |
| Depreciation | 300 |  |
| Inspection | 250 |  |
|  |  |  |
| *Total departmental expenses* |  | 1,489 |
| Direct labour |  | 1,580 |
| General overhead allocation |  | 1,542 |
|  |  |  |
| *Total expenses* |  | 4,611 |
|  |  |  |
| *Net profit* |  | £2,532 |
|  |  |  |
| % net profit to sales |  | 35·5% |

Two induction machines were in use throughout the year and a third was installed during the year. The plant inventory for the induction processes is summarized in Table 5. The shaft-hardening

Table 5

| Machine | Purchase date | Cost £ |
|---|---|---|
| Delapena induction | 1963 | 2,000 |
| 8.D.M. induction | 1965 | 850 (secondhand) |
| 8.D.M. induction | 1969 | 1,350 (secondhand) |
| Shaft-hardening machine | 1967 | 400 |
|  |  | £4,600 |

machine was built by the company, and would have cost £2,500 if purchased externally. The life of an induction machine, if used for fifty hours per week, is normally ten to twelve years.

The company views this area of activity as offering the greatest growth potential. A reputation for good quality has been established which has proved more useful than giving a minimum-price quotation. Potentially there is a very large market which would embrace not only the East Midlands and northern Home Counties but also the Birmingham area. At the present time it is thought doubtful whether the process efficiency could be improved, but capacity is under-utilized, and there is room for improvement on the capital turnover ratio of 3·5 times per annum. The two machines were not fully used because of irregular work flow and development work on anticipated jobs.

One skilled man is engaged in setting up the machines and carrying out much of the work. The balance of the work is performed by an unskilled operator who in the last year spent approximately 50 per cent of her time on the process. If machine capacity is expanded a larger proportion of work could be undertaken by unskilled operatives, leaving the setting-up and testing to the skilled operator. At the present level of operations (1,500 hours per machine year) the profit per machine is £1,200. The capacity of $1\frac{1}{2}$ operators is 3,000 hours per year. Further capacity could be obtained by the acquisition of a new machine at a cost of £2,000, but shift working will not be possible in the near future. The machines frequently develop faults which require skilled attention. Shift working will be practical only if there is adequate work to justify a second complete staff.

## METAL SPRAYING

This process involves spraying metal in either powder or wire form onto a metallic component using a spraying gun. The process is a specialist one and is not widely known. The service has been offered by the company since its formation, and a reputation for good quality has been established. Although a number of companies carry out their own spraying, there is little com-

petition within a fifty-mile radius. The process can be for two
purposes: 1. Protection of components against corrosion (low-
value metal spraying). 2. Reclamation of expensive components
(high-value metal spraying).

## 1. LOW-VALUE METAL SPRAYING

Components are shot- or sand-blasted, and sprayed with zinc
or copper to prevent corrosion. Sales of this process amounted
to £3,497. An analysis of sales shows:

| Frequency of customer dealing per annum | No. of customers | Turnover £ |
|---|---|---|
| 1 or 2 times | 40 | 265 |
| 2 to 5 times | 19 | 463 |
| 6 to 10 times | 3 | 167 |
| More than 10 times | 7 | 2,602 |
| | 69 | £3,497 |

One customer accounted for £1,600, a second £606, and five
others over £100. A distance from factory analysis shows:

| Customer distance from factory | Turnover £ |
|---|---|
| Less than 5 miles | 424 |
| 5 miles to 25 miles | 829 |
| 25 miles to 60 miles | 2,244 |
| | £3,497 |

*Shotblasting* is an integral part of low-value spraying and
represents approximately 50 per cent of the sales value of the
process. Some customers require shotblasting work only, and
this produced £780 of sales. Two customers used this service
regularly, eleven used it occasionally and thirty-four once or
twice in the year. The vast proportion came from within Loughborough, but this is inevitable when a process is cheap and

transport costs high in comparison with value of work done.
The trading account (Table 6) for shotblasting shows a loss, but

### Table 6

Shotblasting
Trading Account

|  | £ | £ |
|---|---|---|
| Sales (50% of £3,497 plus £780) |  | 2,529 |
| Electricity | 500 |  |
| Shot | 56 |  |
| Protective clothing | 30 |  |
| Electric extraction | 155 |  |
| Maintenance | 100 |  |
| *Total departmental expenses* |  | 841 |
| Direct labour |  | 1,000 |
| General overhead |  | 1,542 |
| *Total expenses* |  | £3,383 |
| *Net loss* |  | £(854) |

the process is indispensable if metal spraying is to be carried out.
The loss position was the result of inaccurate cost predictions for
the process and capacity under-utilization. In order to justify
continuing with the process in future a substantial price increase
might prove necessary, but in passing the cost on to spraying
difficulties could occur. The shotblasting equipment consists of
two cabinets acquired in 1961 for £480, which cost £500 to
install. Two compressors were obtained in 1961 and 1963 for
£800 plus £400 installation cost, and a third compressor is on
loan.

It is not possible to identify the profitability of low-value metal
spraying because some of the costs, particularly direct labour,
gas and overheads, arise jointly with high-value metal spraying.
The equipment for low-value spraying consists of three wire-
spraying guns purchased in 1965 (£75), 1967 (£350) and 1969

(£350). Labour is the major constraint on expansion; until recently one man only was employed on this activity.

## 2. HIGH-VALUE METAL SPRAYING

The process is employed to reclaim components which could prove expensive to replace. The spray used is expensive, being aluminium oxide, stainless steel or chromium. Many of the components are machined to size after spraying. Sales from spraying amount to £673 and from spraying and machining to £3,432. Of a total of eighty-six customers, seventy-six carried out business less than five times in the year and contributed £1,803 for combined processes. Five companies had dealings six to ten times (£492), a further five more than ten times (£1,136). Only nine companies had accounts exceeding £100. The process is organized on a jobbing basis, and most of the work done must inevitably be for small orders. A distance from factory analysis shows:

| Customer distance | No. of customers | Turnover £ |
|---|---|---|
| Less than 5 miles | 38 | 1,617 |
| 5 miles to 25 miles | 22 | 834 |
| 25 miles to 60 miles | 9 | 668 |
| More than 60 miles | 3 | 313 |
| | | £3,432 |

The combined spraying-machining process may be segregated roughly by value into 50 per cent spray value, 30 per cent finish grinding, and 20 per cent preparatory machining. Therefore sales values are: spray £1,716, grinding £1,029 and machining £687.

Nineteen customers required spraying only (many also required spraying and machining), and three accounted for sales of £100 or more. Eleven customers traded once or twice during the year, and the remainder five or six times. A distance from factory analysis revealed similar results to those for the combined process.

A trading account for metal spraying appears in Table 7. The shotblasting and metal-spraying activities show a combined loss of £1,765 for the year.

### Table 7

#### Metal Spraying
#### Trading Account

|  | £ | £ |
|---|---|---|
| Sales |  | 4,137 |
|  |  |  |
| (50% of £3,497, 50% of £3,432 and £673) |  |  |
| Materials: hard (high value) | 1,427 |  |
|    soft (low value) | 458 |  |
|    gas and oxygen | 320 |  |
| Extraction electricity | 31 |  |
| Masking tape, etc. | 20 |  |
|  |  |  |
| Total departmental expenses |  | 2,256 |
| Direct labour |  | 1,250 |
| General overhead |  | 1,542 |
|  |  |  |
| Total expenses |  | £5,048 |
|  |  |  |
| Net loss |  | £(911) |

Jobs are costed in order that the company will make 25 per cent profit on sales for regular customers and up to 50 per cent from infrequent customers. The pricing of high-value metal spraying is extremely difficult. The process cost is high but is not difficult to calculate. To this cost must be added a profit margin, and, if this is too high, the customer may decide to purchase new components. When quoting for and pricing these jobs Arnold Kopf balances the cost that the customer will bear against an adequate profit margin. A low price might be quoted to encourage high-volume orders.

The factor limiting expansion of high-value spraying is the machining capacity. Ninety-five per cent of the finish machining after spraying is undertaken on a circular grinding machine. Normally this machine is fully employed with a backlog of three or four weeks' work. Customers for spraying require prompt delivery. As regards spraying equipment, the company has a special powder gun purchased in 1965 for £200 and an old lathe acquired in 1961 for £60. It is probable that the equipment will be adequate for the immediate future.

The high- and low-value processes, as well as catering for different needs, cater for different markets. The two processes had a total of 143 customers, but only twelve of these used both processes.

The analysis has highlighted the interrelationship between metal spraying, shotblasting and machining. The loss of £1,765 for the metal-spraying processes may be due to low pricing, but the major factor is under-utilization of capacity. A conservative estimate puts the maximum utilization of resources at 70 per cent. In the case of shotblasting, a 15 per cent increase in turnover coupled with a 15 per cent price rise will make the process profitable. A capacity utilization of 95 per cent would produce a profit of £600 for metal spraying, which would justify expansion of the process on financial grounds, if it can be shown that the machining is profitable and that the grinding loss can be removed through a price rise. Kopf feels there is a market for the process which should be exploited, and the problem is one of making better use of resources. The company has considerable expertise and customer goodwill in this field. There is little capital to be realized if the process was curtailed.

Expansion of low-value spraying would make further use of shotblasting capacity, and the ratio of materials costs to labour costs is lower than for high-value spraying. However, should high-value spraying be maintained at the present level to ensure capacity utilization of grinding facilities? To expand high-value metal spraying an additional grinding machine costing £2,500 plus an additional operator would be required.


## PLASTICS

This section of the company's activities involves the manufacture of products in plastics or perspex. Typical products are tanks, mixing baths and similar items, frequently quite complex. As the products tend to be for a special purpose, they cannot easily be purchased from a manufacturer involved in standard lines of production, and a market for these special products has been created. The work is skilled and frequently carried out to a supplied design. Orders are generally for delivery within two or three months, and it is necessary to carry a range of materials in stock.

Normally orders are for one-off production, but two types of batch work are undertaken on a regular basis. Batches of tanks and panels are manufactured for the special plating plants produced (included in Special Operations). Small electric-plating barrels have been manufactured for one customer for several years. Three types are manufactured in small quantities. It has been apparent for some time that they are unprofitable, and in future Kopf plans to make no effort to encourage production. The original expectations of requirements put forward by the customer have not materialized, and manufacture is not economic. Hand tools are used for most of the work done, but a certain amount is carried out using machine tools. It is not possible to segregate the machining costs, and the sales value of this work has been left in with plastics.

Sixteen customers contributed £7,134 turnover during the year, but three major customers accounted for £5,445. The largest (£2,137) purchases the plating barrels and is situated some forty miles from Loughborough. Sunnyhill Plating Ltd (£1,748) had a combination of three purchases in excess of £400 and a large number of small purchases. The sales to the third largest customer (£1,500), situated fifteen miles away, consisted of small items. A distance analysis of the remaining customers shows:

| Distance from factory | No. of customers | Turnover £ |
|---|---|---|
| Less than 5 miles | 9 | 1,523 |
| 5 miles to 25 miles | 1 | 17 |
| 25 miles to 60 miles | 3 | 149 |
| | | £1,689 |

A large proportion of the customers purchased five or more times during the year. Ninety-one per cent of the turnover is derived from six regular customers. Within a large area there is little, if any, competition.

Plastics work is also undertaken for the special-plant section. The sales value of this work is difficult to assess accurately, but in the year under question it was approximately £800. The company aims to secure 25 per cent profit on sales from plastics work, but the trading account (Table 8) shows a loss of £1,458.

*Table 8*

Plastics
Trading Account

|  | £ | £ |
|---|---|---|
| Sales value (£7,134 + £800) |  | 7,934 |
| Materials | 1,883 |  |
| Adhesives and tools | 100 |  |
| *Total departmental expenses* |  | 1,983 |
| Direct labour |  | 2,820 |
| General overhead |  | 4,589 |
| *Total expenses* |  | £9,392 |
| *Net loss* |  | £(1,458) |

The investment in tools and equipment in this department amounts to £250.

The loss on plastics may in part be attributed to low pricing. A substantial price increase would be necessary before the process breaks even at its present level of activity, but there is little competition. The process is labour intensive, and it would be impossible to increase profitability through higher plant utilization or process economies. Attempts could be made to increase labour productivity. Plastics fabrications are an integral part of the special plating plants, and the manufacture of these would be severely hampered were plastics activities to be curtailed.

If a substantial price increase could be successfully implemented, and if the overhead charge could be reduced, expansion may be considered. Expansion of the market for specialized items made to order from a supplied specification could be on a geographical basis in order to bring economies of selling and distribution. The main difficulty occurring with jobbing work is quoting a price. A considerable amount of supervisory and management time is involved. Some jobs are lost because of late submission of a quotation. In expanding, account should be taken of the capacity requirements for 'special plant' fabrications. Some extra working capital would be required. Three operatives are engaged on plastics work representing 6,000-labour-hours capacity per annum. The cost of labour will increase by steps of approximately £1,000 to £1,200 per man every 2,000 labour hours. Additional raw-materials stocks costing £300 would be required, and a small expenditure would be necessary for additional tools. The manufacture of standard products in batches for stock should be considered; it is technically feasible.

## MACHINING

This activity involves manufacture or processing of components using machine tools, or the fitting of components together. The service is offered in order to use machine tools idle through lack of high-value metal spraying or scarcity of component requirement for special plants. Except in one case, there has been no attempt to move into batch production, which involves heavy expenditure on tools and tends to be very competitive. Regular batch spot-welding work is undertaken for one customer and accounted for £2,253 of turnover, but expenditure on tools was not very high. Other pure machining activities contributed £2,802 to turnover. A customer frequency analysis shows:

| Frequency of customer dealing per annum | No. of customers | Turnover £ |
|---|---|---|
| 1 or 2 times per year | 16 | 902 |
| 3 to 5　,,　　　,, | 4 | 309 |
| 6 to 10　,,　　　,, | 4 | 710 |
| More than 10 times | 2 | 881 |
|  | 26 | £2,802 |

Nine customers also had high-value spraying work done. Sales to one customer amounted to £675, including eleven small electrographic testers at £24·50 each. At this price they appear to be unprofitable unless they can be manufactured and sold in bulk. The work flow is almost totally unpredictable. Little effort has been made to advertise this aspect of the company's activities. Considerable time and effort are involved in costing each job. The service is not run with the objective of making a profit, but simply to cover variable costs and some fixed costs so that, from the point of view of costing, the machining of metal-spraying and special-plant components can be undertaken economically. Also, to keep the plant fully occupied, it is necessary to give competitive quotations which, for the type of plant in use, do not allow a profit margin.

The utilization of plant tends to vary. A circular grinder has a considerable backlog of work at most times, and, if there is to be any expansion of high-value metal spraying, grinding capacity will have to be increased. Other machines are not fully utilized.

In order to obtain an indication of the total sales value of machining work undertaken it is necessary to synthesize from the activities towards which machining contributed:

|  | £ |
|---|---|
| Pure machining | 2,802 |
| Spot welding | 2,253 |
| Machining on high-value metal spraying | 1,716 |
| Machining for special operations * | 4,863 |
| Total† | £11,634 |

\* Includes installation and servicing.
† Excludes considerable non-quantifiable machining on plastics.

The trading account (Table 9 overleaf) shows a loss of £9,306.

The substantial loss on machining is due partly to inadequate pricing but the overhead costs are undoubtedly a contributory factor. Kopf feels that the overhead charge is realistic. The section did not work to capacity during the period and was subjected to an uneven work flow. Spot welding appears to be profitable. One

*Table 9*

Machining
Trading Account

|  | £ | £ |
|---|---|---|
| Sales value |  | 11,634 |
| Tools and consumables | 914 |  |
| Materials: normal | 1,351 |  |
| special | 1,181 |  |
| *Total departmental expenses* |  | 3,446 |
| Direct labour |  | 6,600 |
| General overhead |  | 10,894 |
| *Total expenses* |  | £20,940 |
| *Net loss* |  | £(9,306) |

The plant inventory is:

| Item | Purchase date | Cost £ | |
|---|---|---|---|
| Lathe | 1961 | 1,000 | Secondhand |
| Lathe | 1963 | 450 | ,, |
| Grinder – circular | 1961 | 2,800 | ,, |
| Grinder | 1964 | 350 | ,, |
| Miller | 1966 | 1,300 | New |
| Miller | 1966 | 150 | Secondhand |
| Spot-welding machine | 1966 | 530 | New |

operator, who was also employed on an induction machine, was fully occupied, and the costing allowed for a good margin on profit. This activity is independent of the other machining activities. Machine grinding probably incurs a marginal loss. General machining and fitting are the major loss makers. The costs incurred by these activities were:

|  | £ |
|---|---|
| Materials | 2,600 |
| Wages | 5,000 |
| Overheads | 7,700 |
|  | £15,300 |

The revenue generated amounted to £8,400 approximately. The

low revenue was largely the result of the absence of special-plant manufacture for which these activities are primarily organized. In the current year the increased demand for special plants will give rise to a machining revenue of approximately £25,000. Turning facilities are required both for metal-spraying preparation and for some plastics work. High-value metal spraying is impossible without the turning facilities. The turning of plastics is primarily in the manufacture of plating barrels. If the manufacture of these barrels were abandoned, no machining capacity would be required for plastics work.

If the company were to cease general machining and fitting, overheads would reduce by approximately £800. The draughtsman engaged on designing automatic plants, which could no longer be manufactured, could be dispensed with. His salary, N.H.I., etc. amount to £1,100. A great deal of valuable management time would be saved and devoted to more profitable activities. Disposal of plant would release capital required for purchasing new equipment to expand more profitable activities. Stocks of materials, which are not high, could be disposed of.

## SPECIAL OPERATIONS

These activities are product orientated. Normally the products are electroplating plants and involve machining and plastics work. Two types of plant are produced. Fully automatic plants, incorporating customers' individual requirements, are built to a standard design. In the last five years three plants of this type have been built, but none was constructed during the year under review. Individual plants are also manufactured to specified design, and two were produced during the year. One had a sales value of £2,500 and the other £3,160 including installation. The proportions of work input varied. The first plant was mainly machining with an insignificant amount of plastics work, while the second included approximately £800 of plastics.

The total sales value of £5,663 may be allocated as follows:

| | |
|---|---|
| Machining | £4,628 |
| Plastics | 800 |
| Installation and servicing | 235 |

Normally a profit level is set at 25 per cent of total cost, but it is not possible in the time available to determine the actual profit or loss for the year.

There are some difficulties attached to this activity. A number of specially skilled employees are required, but demand is spasmodic. Arnold Kopf is the only person capable of supervising the design and manufacture of the plants. The components for the machines are required and manufactured in small quantities. A considerable amount of working capital can be tied up in the plants, particularly when the large fully automatic plants are produced. It is difficult to determine the nature of the market for the plants. The special plants are ordered by companies who have a specific type of plating to be carried out in bulk. The larger automatic plants are used when manufacturers have large quantities of small components requiring selective plating. Consequently the larger electronics firms are the only possible purchasers at the present time.

However, the future order position is promising. Orders have been received for a barrel plating machine (£3,500) and an automatic plating plant (£13,800) from Denmark and for an automatic plating plant (£13,500) for the home market. A further order is expected from Holland for an automatic plant, and a number of foreign buyers are interested in these plants. A plant takes six to nine months to build and starts can be made every three months. Present human, physical and financial resources available restrict the spread of manufacture. The building of two or more plants simultaneously would be preferable. Component batch sizes could be increased, and costing paperwork considerably reduced. To increase output, jigs and patterns would have to be purchased. There would also be a substantial increase in work in progress, which is partially alleviated by progress payments. It could increase by £6,000. With the present labour force the length of manufacturing time would increase. The company could expand into the manufacture of other types of complex plant, but would the risks be too high?

After he had examined each activity in isolation, Bernard Quick analysed his findings prior to preparing his report on the profitability of Diversified Engineering's activities and its future prospects. Bearing in mind Diversified Engineering's limited financial resources, he established six criteria against which to measure an activity's growth potential.

1. During the initial stages expansion should be carried out with a minimum capital expenditure.

2. Strain on working capital and cash flows should be minimized.

3. Expansion should first be concentrated on the most profitable activities so that improved return will be achieved quickly.

4. The effects of expansion on overhead costs should be minimized by expanding first those activities with a low overhead to turnover ratio.

5. Activities which make a loss currently should be critically examined for profit potential and, if no potential exists, they should be eliminated.

6. If possible, geographical markets should be developed, and every effort made to obtain customers common to more than one process.

Quick also felt he should comment on and make proposals concerning:

1. The total lack of any cash-flow planning, and strains that this could place on the organization.

2. The problems of pricing items which are transferred from one area of activity to another in the company (i.e. shotblasting to metal spraying), and the effect these prices could have on his profitability analysis.

QUESTIONS

1. What recommendations should Quick make in his report on the profitability of Diversified Engineering's activities and its future prospects? Has he established the correct criteria against which to measure an activity's growth potential?

2. What proposals should Quick make concerning (a) cash-flow planning and (b) transfer prices?

### Table A
#### Trading and Profit and Loss Accounts

| | Year ending 31 October 1968 £ | Year ending 31 October 1967 £ | Year ending 31 October 1966 £ |
|---|---|---|---|
| *Work executed* | 59,421 | 57,702 | 65,248 |
| Cost of work executed | | | |
| Opening stock and work in progress | 5,435 | 2,992 | 5,780 |
| Materials | 9,160 | 11,151 | 8,383 |
| Wages and N.H.I. | 23,997 | 23,658 | 19,165 |
| Sub-contract processes | 10,585 | 8,864 | 7,740 |
| Plant repairs and maintenance | 899 | 964 | 1,408 |
| Tools and consumable stores | 2,851 | 4,263 | 1,864 |
| Fuel and power | 4,233 | 3,104 | 3,325 |
| Depreciation of plant | 1,063 | 1,026 | 1,008 |
| | 58,223 | 56,022 | 48,673 |
| *less* Closing stock and work in progress | 5,466 | 5,435 | 2,992 |
| | 52,757 | 50,587 | 45,681 |
| *Gross profit* | 6,664 | 7,115 | 19,567 |
| Directors' remuneration | 2,304 | 2,202 | 4,000 |
| Executive salaries | 1,600 | 925 | 4,253 |
| Office salaries and N.H.I. | 834 | 771 | 629 |
| Rent | 5,251 | 2,918 | 1,502 |
| General and water rates | 1,265 | 359 | 362 |
| Light and heat | 300 | 260 | 260 |
| Telephone | 392 | 389 | 201 |
| Hire of equipment | 274 | 91 | 95 |
| Insurance | 506 | 154 | 113 |
| Cleaning | 30 | 215 | 225 |
| Decorations and repairs | 1,878 | 84 | 482 |
| Printing and postage | 475 | 222 | 256 |
| Motor transport and carriage | 1,189 | 942 | 1,241 |
| Travel expenses | 275 | 263 | 326 |
| Accounting and audit | 416 | 379 | 358 |
| Professional charges | — | 184 | 175 |
| Advertising | 189 | 83 | 85 |
| Commission | 205 | — | — |
| Bank charges | 358 | 62 | 3 |
| Discounts allowed | — | — | — |
| Hire-purchase charges | — | 12 | 58 |
| Sundry trade expenses | 875 | 370 | 511 |
| Bad debts | — | — | 18 |
| Depreciation | | | |
| Motor vehicles | 314 | 314 | 393 |
| Furniture and fittings | 45 | 31 | 20 |
| | £18,975 | £11,230 | £15,566 |
| *Net profit/(loss)* | £(12,311) | £(4,115) | £4,001 |

## Table B

### Balance Sheets

| | 31 October 1968 | | 31 October 1967 | | 31 October 1966 | |
|---|---|---|---|---|---|---|
| | £ | £ | £ | £ | £ | £ |
| Capital employed | | | | | | |
| 2,500 ordinary shares of £1 each | | 2,500 | | 2,500 | | 2,500 |
| Share premium account | | 2,500 | | 2,500 | | 2,500 |
| Profit and loss account | | (6,154) | | 6,040 | | 9,176 |
| *Total shareholders funds* | | (1,154) | | 11,040 | | 14,176 |
| Current account (Sunnyhill Plating) | | 10,721 | | 10,721 | | 10,721 |
| *Total capital employed* | | £9,567 | | £21,761 | | £24,897 |
| Employment of capital | | | | | | |
| Fixed assets at W.D.V. | | | | | | |
| Plant and machinery | | 9,005 | | 9,227 | | 8,986 |
| Furniture and fittings | | 848 | | 697 | | 380 |
| Motor vehicles | | 943 | | 1,257 | | 1,571 |
| Removal and installation charges | | 6,961 | | 783 | | — |
| Formation expenses | | 60 | | 60 | | 60 |
| | | 17,817 | | 12,024 | | 10,997 |
| Current assets | | | | | | |
| Trade accounts | 16,694 | | 16,928 | | } 32,595 | |
| Prepaid charges, etc. | 206 | | 2,458 | | | |
| Stock and work in progress | 5,866 | | 5,733 | | 4,355 | |
| Cash in hand and at Bank | 81 | | 681 | | 8,758 | |
| | 22,847 | | 25,800 | | 45,708 | |
| Current liabilities | | | | | | |
| Trade creditors | 13,430 | | 8,631 | | 20,086 | |
| Accrued charges | 3,312 | | 2,799 | | 4,661 | |
| Directors' remuneration | 4,000 | | 4,000 | | 4,000 | |
| Bank overdraft | 10,317 | | — | | — | |
| Staff savings | 38 | | 39 | | 61 | |
| Provision for corporation tax | — | | 594 | | 3,000 | |
| | 31,097 | | 16,063 | | 31,808 | |
| *Net current assets* | | (8,250) | | 9,737 | | 13,900 |
| *Net assets employed* | | £9,567 | | £21,761 | | £24,897 |

SUGGESTED BACKGROUND READING

1. *An Insight into Management Accounting*, Chapter 8.
2. G. P. E. Clarkson and B. J. Elliott, *Managing Money and Finance*, Gower Press, 1972, Part I.
3. National Association of Accountants, *Cash Flow Analysis for Managerial Control*, N.A.A. Research Report 38, New York, 1961.
4. Gordon Shillinglaw, *Cost Accounting: Analysis and Control*, Irwin, Homewood, 1972, Chapter 25.

## MORE ABOUT PENGUINS
## AND PELICANS

*Penguinews*, which appears every month, contains details of all the new books issued by Penguins as they are published. From time to time it is supplemented by *Penguins in Print*, which is a complete list of all titles available. (There are some five thousand of these.)

A specimen copy of *Penguinews* will be sent to you free on request. For a year's issues (including the complete lists) please send 50p if you live in the British Isles, or 75p if you live elsewhere. Just write to Dept EP, Penguin Books Ltd, Harmondsworth, Middlesex, enclosing a cheque or postal order, and your name will be added to the mailing list.

*In the U.S.A.:* For a complete list of books available from Penguin in the United States write to Dept CS, Penguin Books Inc., 7110 Ambassador Road, Baltimore, Maryland 21207.

*In Canada:* For a complete list of books available from Penguin in Canada write to Penguin Books Canada Ltd, 41 Steelcase Road West, Markham, Ontario.

# A HISTORY OF MONEY

*E. Victor Morgan*

REVISED EDITION

Adam Smith regarded 'a propensity to truck, barter and exchange one thing for another' as one of the basic ingredients of human nature. Certainly in the growth from the earliest exchanges of rice and honey to the complexities of modern international monetary systems, the invention and development of money ranks with the great dynamics of world civilization, the domestication of animals, the culture of land, and the harnessing of power.

Dealing with money only in its broadest sense, Professor Morgan surveys the ideas, concepts, and institutions associated with it and ranges the whole diversity of this fascinating subject, from money and other means of holding wealth to banking, the money market, the origins of accounting, and the system of 'double entry'. The meaning of 'capital' leads to an impressive analysis of the relationship between government and money, ranging from government finances in Athens to the International Monetary Fund.

Two final chapters survey monetary theory and policy, making clear the relationship between money and fluctuations in business, employment, and prices. Professor Morgan ends a description of the modern British monetary system with a discussion of the highly contemporary problems of full employment and inflation and shows how governments have tried to control money as part of the effort to secure stable economic growth.

# UNDERSTANDING COMPANY
# FINANCIAL STATEMENTS

### *R. H. Parker*

The layman who entrusts his money to a company often has great difficulty in understanding the published financial statements he receives. R. H. Parker, Professor of Accountancy at the University of Dundee, aims to provide that understanding. With the general reader in mind he assumes no previous knowledge of accountancy and emphasizes analysis and interpretation rather than accounting techniques.

How do you find out whether a company is stable; whether its dividends show a fair yield; and whether it is as profitable as might be expected? Referring throughout to the published statements of actual companies, Professor Parker explains many important financial and accounting concepts and deals with taxation, audit, profitability and return on investment, liquidity and cash flows, sources of funds and capital structure and accounting principles. His clear and concise guide to the contents of a company annual report provides all the information necessary to keep track of your money.

'One of the best of its kind for the general reader' – *Scotsman*

'Highly recommended' – *Economist*

# COMPUTERS, MANAGERS
## AND SOCIETY

### *Michael Rose*

*Computers, Managers and Society* is an account, part technical, part sociological and part philosophical, of the computer revolution.

After a general survey of the development of computer-controlled data processing, Michael Rose examines the complex effects of the computer upon the clerical worker – the new opportunities, the dangers of alienation, the threat of technological unemployment. He then focuses upon the fast-developing problems of managers. Many of the standard managerial functions can already be programmed. But should executives delegate qualitative decisions to a machine? And if so, how far can and should these changes go?

'Computerization' presents managers with new opportunities on a structural scale unmatched since the Industrial Revolution. Do they really understand the new situation? Can they, when it is transforming itself so rapidly? And are we enough aware of the effects of the computer upon an even larger social group – society itself – now faced with the need to clarify its whole attitude to technological change?

# MATHEMATICS IN MANAGEMENT

### Albert Battersby

Sophisticated methods of planning, control, and decision-making, together with the advent of the electronic computer, have already brought mathematics well to the fore in modern industry and commerce. At the present rate of advance, mathematics will soon be an indispensable tool of the intelligent manager.

*Mathematics in Management* has been specially written, for managers and others, to provide a sound basis of knowledge about the methods of operational research now being applied in public industries and services, to save resources and prune expenditure. Some such account is urgently needed, since general education has not kept pace with advances in this field, and mathematicians have difficulty in 'talking' to managers.

Among the particular topics covered by Albert Battersby in this new Pelican are network analysis, simple functions, linear programming, simulation, and electronic computers. The author employs a minimum of mathematical notation in his text and, wherever possible, makes his points with the help of drawings. He has also included a set of exercises with full solutions.

### *Also available*
### Sales Forecasting

# THE ECONOMICS OF THE REAL WORLD

*Peter Donaldson*

A sense of economic failure is in the air. The British economy may be working better than ever . . . without booms and slumps, without mass unemployment: yet government after government fails to achieve simultaneously full employment, stable prices, and economic growth.

Explaining why this is so, the author of *A Guide to the British Economy* describes here how a mixed economy is managed and (given the underlying market mechanisms) what can and what cannot be the subject of economic policy. More basically he argues that economics itself is strangely remote from the urgent problems of ordinary people and that policy-makers confuse ends and means. What matters, in his view, is not growth, but growth of what, for whom and at what cost; not full employment, but the nature of work; not just more wealth, but its more equitable distribution.

For *this* is the real world – a world of values and people – neglected by orthodox economics and evaded by policy-makers. Why? Because, suggests Peter Donaldson, if the real issues are to be tackled there has to be a revolution in our whole outlook on economics and society.

# EXPORT MARKETING DECISIONS

*Douglas Tookey*

What is the difference between home and export marketing? How do you select and develop overseas markets?

What is the effect of international trade on the individual company?

By looking at the key process of decision-making, Douglas Tookey sets out to find answers to these questions. In the process he arrives at a new and revisionary position on the problems of export marketing and questions traditional views on the subject.

*Export Marketing Decisions* not only makes an important contribution to the theoretical literature of export management, but will also make useful reading for the practising manager and the student of business management.